D0110601

DISCARDED

DOLLS

WOMAN HOLDING A MALE DOLL
Sessai Tsu Kioka. About 1800

gift

GV
1219
.B62
1972

DOLLS

BY

MAX VON BOEHN

TRANSLATED BY

JOSEPHINE NICOLL

DOVER PUBLICATIONS, INC.

NEW YORK

This Dover edition, first published in 1972, is an unabridged republication of "Part I: Dolls" (including the relevant sections of the Table of Contents, List of Illustrations, Bibliography and Index) of the one-volume English translation *Dolls and Puppets,* originally published by the David McKay Company, Philadelphia, [n.d.]. This material corresponds to the first volume, *Puppen,* of the original two-volume German work *Puppen und Puppenspiele,* published by F. Bruckmann, Munich, in 1929.

The Plates, which were printed in color in the Bruckmann and McKay editions, appear in black and white in the present edition.

International Standard Book Number: 0-486-22847-9
Library of Congress Catalog Card Number: 73-189341

Manufactured in the United States of America
Dover Publications, Inc.
180 Varick Street
New York, N.Y. 10014

ACKNOWLEDGMENT

THE author and the publishers wish to thank those in charge of various public and private collections who have given help in the preparation of this book. They feel that they are specially indebted to the following: the Department of Prints at the Staatliche Kunstbibliothek, the Kunstgewerbe Museum, and the Propyläen-Verlag, Berlin; Herr Georg Zink, the town librarian at Heidelberg; Privatdozent Dr Carl Niessen, of Cologne; the Victoria and Albert Museum and the Bethnal Green Museum, London; the Bayerische National-Museum, the Museum für Völkerkunde, the Theater-Museum (Clara-Ziegler Foundation), and the Armee-Museum, Munich; the Germanische National-Museum, the Bayerische Landesgewerbe Anstalt, Nürnberg; the Staatliche Porzellanmanufaktur, Nymphenburg; M. Henri d'Allemagne, of Paris; the Spielzeug-Museum, Sonneberg; the Kunstgewerbe Museum, Zürich.

Herr Dr Lutz Weltmann, of Berlin, was good enough to allow the use of his literary material for a history of the puppet theatre; for this both the author and the publishers welcome the opportunity of offering him their particular thanks. Dr Weltmann's studies were directed principally toward the literary significance of the puppet theatre, and that subject could not have been introduced into this book without making it inordinately lengthy. It is sincerely to be hoped that Dr Weltmann may have the opportunity of bringing before the public his valuable researches.

Grateful acknowledgment is also due to Herr Direktor Dr Glaser, of Berlin, and Herr Geheimrat Dr Schnorr von Carolsfeld, of Munich, for their courtesy and assistance in providing access to the collections under their care.

YOUNG GIRL WITH DOLL AND DOLL'S CRADLE
Woodcut by the artist using the monogram I.R.
About 1540

CONTENTS

I. Prehistoric Idols   23

II. Ancestor Images   37

III. Fetishes, Amulets, and Talismans   51

IV. Image Magic   57

V. Votive Images   68

VI. Funeral and other Images   76

VII. Waxworks and the Mannequin   93

VIII. Toy Dolls in Ancient Times   103

IX. Early Toy Dolls in Europe   110

X. The Fashion Doll   134

XI. The Toy Doll in the Nineteenth Century   154

XII. The Toy Doll in the Modern Period   171

XIII. Dolls of Exotic Peoples   202

XIV. Dolls used for Decorative Purposes   218

XV. Porcelain Figures   226

XVI. Utensils in Doll Form   235

XVII. The Doll and the Stage   245

XVIII. Edible Dolls   247

XIX. The Doll in Literature   250

Bibliography   253

Index   261

9

ILLUSTRATIONS

PLATES

I.	WOMAN HOLDING A MALE DOLL	*Frontispiece*
II.	DOLLS OF THE TUSAYAN INDIANS	48
III.	GIRL WITH FAN	82
IV.	FROM THE "GALERIE DES MODES," 1780	120
V.	DOLLS OF THE PERIOD OF THE FRENCH REVOLUTION	130
VI.	DOLLS OF THE PERIOD OF THE FRENCH EMPIRE	136
VII.	ENGLISH MANNEQUIN, ABOUT 1800	150
VIII.	ENGLISH DOLL, ABOUT 1830	158
IX.	DOLL, ABOUT 1865	164
X.	ENGLISH DOLL, ABOUT 1875	164
XI.	DOLL	186
XII.	DUTCHMAN. GISELA	186
XIII.	PIERROT WITH LANTERN. ISABELLA	228
XIV.	FIGURE OF A HORSEMAN, AFTER LEONHARDI	228
XV.	NUTCRACKERS, EIGHTEENTH CENTURY	242

ILLUSTRATIONS IN THE TEXT

FIG.		PAGE
1.	MARBLE IDOL FROM TROY (THIRD BURNED CITY)	23
2.	LEAD IDOL FROM TROY	24
3.	FLAT BONE IDOLS FROM TROY	25
4.	AMBER IDOL FROM SCHWARZORT	25
5.	RED CLAY IDOL, ABOUT 3000 B.C.	26
6.	CAKE-FORMED IMAGES IN TERRA-COTTA	27
7.	PHŒNICIAN TERRA-COTTA IDOL	27
8.	FEMALE TERRA-COTTA IDOL FROM NIPPUR, CHALDÆA	27
9.	EARLY TERRA-COTTA IDOL FROM TANAGRA	27
10.	PRE-MYCENÆAN STONE SCULPTURE	28
11.	THE SO-CALLED 'WILLENDORF VENUS'	29
12.	PRIMITIVE BRONZE DOLLS OF PREHISTORIC TIMES	29
13.	CLAY DOLL FROM MYCENÆ	30
14.	MARBLE DOLL FROM DELOS	30
15.	TERRA-COTTA IDOL FROM TIRYNS	31
16.	FEMALE CLAY IDOL FROM KNOSSOS, CRETE	31
17.	CLAY IMAGES, WITH INDICATION OF TATTOOING, FOUND IN CUCUTENI, NEAR JASSY, RUMANIA	31

DOLLS

18. Neolithic 'Island Figures' 32
19. Bronze Dolls from Källeborg and Schonen 32
20. Etruscan Bronze Dolls found in Novilara and Verona 34
21. Etruscan Bronze Figure of a Woman 35
22. Primitive Bronze Doll 35
23. Tub of Ancestors' Skulls of the Ngumba (Cameroons), with Male and Female Ancestor Figures 40
24. Ancestor Figure of the Bangwa (Cameroons) 41
25. Ancestor Figure of the Baluba (Belgian Congo) 41
26. Female Ancestor Image of the Baluba (Belgian Congo) 41
27. Wooden Idols from Sumatra 42
28. Wooden Ancestor Images from Sumatra 43
29. Ancestor Image from the Fiji Islands 43
30. Ancestor Images from the Fiji Islands 43
31. Ancestor Image from the Caroline Islands 44
32. Ancestor Image from the New Hebrides 45
33. Protective Figure from the Nicobar Islands 46
34. Spirit of a Dead Shamanist (in Wood) 47
35. Wooden Idols 47
36. Wood-carved Idols of the Tschuktschi, Siberia 48
37. House Idols of the Ostiaks in Jugan 48
38. Fetish of the Bassonge (Congo) 52
39. Nail Fetish from the Loango Coast (French Equatorial Africa) 52
40. Wooden Nail Fetish of the Bawili, Loango Coast (French Equatorial Africa) 53
41. Wooden Doll "Hampatong" 53
42. Fetish of the Bateka (French Equatorial Africa) 53
43. Leather Dolls from South-west Africa 54
44. Youth and Maiden 58
45. Magic Doll 63
46. The God Sakti Kumulan and the Goddess Dalem Kamenuh 64
47. Male and Female Mandrakes 66
48. Faience Figure of a Priestess of the Snake-goddess in Knossos, Crete 68
49. Clay Doll from a Grave of the Bronze Age near Kličevač, Serbia 69
50–52. Votive Bronzes from Olympia 70
53. Votive Figure, Middle of Seventeenth Century 71
54. The Iron Man of Buttenwiesen 73
55. Sacrificial Iron Man 74
56. Sacrificial Iron Figure of a Woman 74
57. Sacrificial Iron Figure (Lower Bavaria) 74
58. Sacrificial Wooden Figure of a Man 74
59. Ancient Egyptian Grave Dolls 78
60. Egyptian Wooden Doll from a Mummy's Coffin 78

ILLUSTRATIONS

PAGE

61. EGYPTIAN IVORY DOLL 78
62. EGYPTIAN WOODEN STATUETTES—PRIEST AND PRINCESS 79
63. EGYPTIAN "USHABTI" FIGURE OF FAIENCE 80
64. BARBER 81
65. HANDWORKER 81
66. HOUSEMAID 81
67. WALKING GIRL 81
68. GIRL WITH HAT 81
69. GIRL 82
70. STATUETTE OF A CHINESE CONJURER 83
71. SPIRIT CONJURER 84
72. A YOUNG MAN 84
73. CHINESE WOMAN IN FESTIVE CLOTHES 85
74. CHINESE WOMEN WITH LOTUS BLOOMS IN THEIR HANDS 86
75. FUNERAL FIGURE OF KING EDWARD III OF ENGLAND (d. 1377) 90
76. FUNERAL FIGURE OF QUEEN CATHERINE DE VALOIS 90
77. MANNEQUIN OF TUT-ENCH-AMUN 95
78. LIMBED DOLL, FROM THE BEGINNING OF THE SIXTEENTH CENTURY 96
79, 80. GERMAN PROPORTION FIGURES CARVED FROM WOOD 97
81. THE PAINTER IN HIS STUDIO 98
82. THE PAINTER WITH TWO LAY FIGURES 99
83. CHRIST ON THE PALM ASS 101
84. BYZANTINE DOLL'S TUNIC, OF COLOURED WOOL, FROM THE
    CEMETERY OF AKHMIM 103
85. WOODEN DOLL OF IMPERIAL ROME FROM THE CEMETERY OF AKHMIM 104
86. GREEK TERRA-COTTA LIMBED DOLL FOUND IN THE CRIMEA 104
87. APHRODITE 105
88. EARLY GREEK PAINTED CLAY DOLL FROM A BŒOTIAN GRAVE 106
89. GREEK LIMBED DOLLS 106
90. EARLY GREEK LIMBED DOLLS FROM ATHENS, MYRINA, RHODES 107
91. GREEK CLAY DOLL, IN THE SHAPE OF A CHILD, FROM A GRAVE 107
92. GRAVESTONE OF A GREEK GIRL 108
93. GRAVESTONE OF A GREEK GIRL 108
94, 95. ROMAN LIMBED DOLLS FOUND IN ITALY 109
96. NÜRNBERG DOLLS OF BAKED CLAY, FOURTEENTH TO FIFTEENTH
    CENTURIES 110
97. CLAY DOLLS, FOURTEENTH TO FIFTEENTH CENTURIES 111
98. NÜRNBERG DOLL-MAKER AT HIS WORK 112
99. WOODCUT BY JOST AMMAN, 1577 113
100. PRINCESS MARIE OF SAXONY 114
101. CHILD WITH DOLL 115
102. DOLL AS A COSTUME MODEL 116
103. AUGSBURG DOLLS 117
104. BEDROOM IN A DOLL'S HOUSE 118
105. KITCHEN IN A DOLL'S HOUSE 118
106. LARGE NÜRNBERG DOLL'S HOUSE (EXTERIOR) 119

DOLLS

		PAGE
107.	Large Nürnberg Doll's House (Interior)	120
108.	From Weigel's "Hauptstände," 1698	121
109.	From Weigel's "Hauptstände," 1698	122
110.	Dwarf with Peruke	123
111.	Gentleman with Sword	123
112.	Doll in Walking Dress	124
113.	Doll's Sunshade of Red Silk	125
114.	Augsburg Woman: Wooden Doll of the Eighteenth Century	126
115.	Lady of the Eighteenth Century	126
116.	The Children of the Duc d'Orléans	127
117.	Child with Doll representing a Monk	128
118.	Primitive Wooden Doll from Transylvania	129
119.	Twin Dolls of the Haussa Negroes	129
120.	Wooden Limbed Doll from the Grödner Tal	129
121.	Oldest Sonneberg Wooden Toys	130
122.	Egyptian Child's Toy	130
123.	Wooden "Hampelmann," painted in Various Colours	131
124.	Cries of Berlin	132
125.	"Zappelmann": Conductor	133
126.	"Hampelmann": Peasant Girl in Parts	134
127.	"Hampelmann": Ballerina in Parts	134
128.	English Doll's House, about 1760	135
129.	The Breakfast (Detail)	136
130.	Child with Doll (Nun)	137
131.	German Doll	138
132.	Wax Doll: Town Lady, Munich, 1877	139
133.	The Chevalier de Pange	140
134.	Dolls from the Period of the French Empire	141
135.	Bride (Nürnberg), Middle of the Nineteenth Century	142
136.	Dolls in Rococo Dress	143
137.	English Doll of the Reign of Queen Anne	144
138.	English Doll's Shop, about 1850	145
139.	English Wax Doll, about 1780	146
140.	English Doll with Wax Head, about 1800	146
141.	Girl with Doll	147
142.	English Doll, about 1860	148
143.	Male and Female Pedlars (Portsmouth), about 1810	149
144.	Flat Painted Figures	149
145.	English Movable Fashion Dolls, about 1830	150
146.	English Wax Doll, Middle of the Nineteenth Century	151
147.	Trick Dolls of Pressed and Cut-out Cardboard (Metamorphoses)	152
148.	Mannequin	153
149.	Elisa, Princess Radziwill	154
150.	Susanne von Boehn	155
151.	Portrait of the Daughter of Herr Artus	156

ILLUSTRATIONS

PAGE

152. SONNEBERG LEATHER DOLL, 1820   157
153. "PETITE DRÔLESSE! VOUS ME FEREZ MOURIR DIX ANS AVANT MON TERME"   157
154. SPEAKING LIMBED DOLL, NINETEENTH CENTURY   158
155. MA POUPÉE   159
156. "MA SŒUR, REGARDE DONC MA JOLIE POUPÉE"   159
157. SONNEBERG LEATHER DOLLS WITH CHINA HEADS, 1840   160
158. ROCOCO DOLL   161
159. GENTLEMAN WITH STICK. PEASANT WOMAN WITH ROSARY   162
160. OLD MUNICH DOLL   163
161. DOLL'S HEAD OF PAPIER MÂCHÉ   164
162. THURINGIAN EMPIRE DOLL   164
163. ALTENBURG AND WENDISH DOLLS   165
164. NÜRNBERG-FÜRTH TRAIN WITH DOLLS IN COSTUME   165
165. CRIES OF BERLIN   166
166. DOLL OF THE BIEDERMEIER PERIOD   167
167. DOLL OF THE BIEDERMEIER PERIOD   167
168. FRENCH DOLL REPRESENTING A CHILD   168
169. "PUTZENBERCHT"   168
170. "MAMAN DIT QUE VOUS SAVEZ TOUS LES SECRETS DE POLICHINELLE, MOSIEU D'ALBY: QU'EST-CE QUI PEUT DONC LUI AVOIR ABÎMÉ LE NEZ COMME ÇA . . . DITES?"   169
171, 172. DOLLS, ABOUT 1830   169
173. DOLL, ABOUT 1830   170
174. PLAYING WITH DOLLS   171
175. THE YOUNG PHILOSOPHER (DETAIL)   172
176. GIRL WITH DOLL   173
177. NEW YEAR'S PRESENTS AT PARIS   174
178. COPTIC WOODEN DOLL   175
179. ABYSSINIAN CHILDREN'S DOLLS   176
180. SILESIAN BAST DOLLS   176
181. MODERN SWEDISH DOLL MADE ENTIRELY OF WOOD   177
182. ART DOLL   178
183. HUGO AND ADOLAR   179
184. PEASANT AND PEASANT WOMAN   179
185. MR BANKER   180
186. ROCOCO LADY   180
187. ART DOLLS   181
188. CAR MASCOTS   181
189. SPANISH COUPLE   182
190. PEASANT WOMAN WITH BASKET OF EGGS   183
191. AMUSING CLOTH DOLLS FOR THE GRAMOPHONE   184
192. MUNICH ART DOLL   185
193. DOLLS   186
194. MUNICH ART DOLLS   186
195. DOLL: "DU MEIN SCHUFTERLE"   187

15

DOLLS

PAGE

196. DOLL: "MARINA"   188
197, 198. WASHABLE, UNBREAKABLE CLOTH DOLLS   189
199. DOLLS   190
200. DOLL: "THE GERMAN CHILD"   191
201. ITALIAN DOLLS (LENZI DOLLS) MADE OF FELT   192
202. MALAYAN DOLLS   193
203. BRIDEGROOM AND BRIDE FROM JAVA   194
204. COSTUME DOLL: WOMAN PILGRIM (JAVA)   195
205. COSTUME DOLL: HADJI (JAVA)   195
206. PARISIAN COSTUME DOLL: MARQUISE DE POMPADOUR   196
207. PARISIAN COSTUME DOLL: MERVEILLEUSE (DIRECTORY)   196
208. DOLLS IN PARISIAN POPULAR COSTUMES   196
209. FRENCH COSTUME DOLLS AT THE WORLD EXHIBITION AT CHICAGO,
     1893   197
210. DUTCH DOLLS FROM SEELAND   198
211. PARISIAN MODEL MANNEQUINS   199
212. "DER ALTE FRITZ"   200
213. SCHWABING PEASANT WOMAN   200
214. DOLLS IN NATIONAL DRESS   201
215. INDIAN DOLLS   203
216. CLAY DOLLS FROM TIENTSIN, CHINA   204
217. CLAY DOLLS FROM TIENTSIN, CHINA   205
218. JAPANESE DOLL (TOKYO), NINETEENTH CENTURY   206
219. CLAY DOLLS FROM TIENTSIN, CHINA   207
220. ESKIMO DOLLS   208
221. THE DOLL FESTIVAL IN JAPAN   209
222. MODERN RUSSIAN DOLL   210
223. DOLL OF THE APACHE INDIANS   211
224. DOLLS OF THE ZUÑI   212
225. TOY DOLL OF THE PIMA (SOUTH-WEST OF THE UNITED STATES)   213
226. ANCIENT PERUVIAN DOLL, MADE OF GOLD-LEAF AND DRESSED IN
     CLOTH, FOUND NEAR LIMA   214
227. ANCIENT PERUVIAN CLAY DOLLS   215
228. ANCIENT PERUVIAN WOODEN DOLLS   215
229, 230. ANCIENT PERUVIAN CLAY DOLLS   216
231. ANCIENT PERUVIAN CLAY DOLL   217
232. THE SWORD DANCER   219
233. DOLLS   220
234. ORPHEUS   221
235. DOLL   222
236. DOLLS OF WOOL   223
237. PAPER DOLL   224
238. GROTESQUE CLOTH DOLL REPRESENTING MEPHISTO   225
239. CHINESE PRIEST   226
240. DOLL WITH PASSAU CHINA HEAD   227
241. CAVALIER AT A PEDESTAL   228

ILLUSTRATIONS

		PAGE
242.	LEDA	228
243.	SCARAMOUCHE, FROM THE ITALIAN COMEDY	229
244.	LADY IN A HOOPED DRESS	230
245.	CHINAMAN WITH A LUTE	231
246.	WOMAN FROM TEGERNSEE	232
247.	LADY WITH A MUFF	233
248.	EGYPTIAN IVORY PAINT-BOX IN HUMAN SHAPE	235
249.	EGYPTIAN WOODEN PAINT-BOX IN HUMAN SHAPE	235
250.	KOKA-EATER—CLAY VESSEL	236
251.	CLAY VESSELS IN HUMAN SHAPE FOUND IN COLUMBIA	237
252.	CANDLESTICK, ABOUT 1400	238
253, 254.	SKETCHES FOR GOBLETS	239
255.	LARGE VIRGIN GOBLET OF FRIEDRICH HILLEBRAND	240
256.	AQUAMANILE, AFTER 1300	241
257.	AQUAMANILE, FOURTEENTH CENTURY	242
258.	NUTCRACKER	243
259.	BEEHIVE FROM HÖFEL	244
260, 261.	GINGERBREAD FIGURES	248
262.	FIRST LESSONS IN RIDING	251

I
PREHISTORIC IDOLS

THE doll is the three-dimensional representation of a human figure, a plastic creation, which, however, is far removed from the sphere of the fine arts. It has about as much in common with art as the ape has with *homo sapiens*. Both enjoy a complete freedom from dependence on material: in all three realms of nature there is no substance out of which a doll or a work of art cannot be made. In their dimensions also they are so far alike that each may fluctuate in size from a few millimetres to a considerable number of metres. Apart from that it is easier to feel the difference between them than to frame an indisputable definition. This is due to the fact that they proceed from the same source. In the doll we have before us the beginnings of fine art; and to-day, following the precedent of Alois Riegl, these beginnings are recognized to lie in the field of sculpture. Sculpture has the power of reproducing directly corporeal forms. Its subject not only can be appreciated through the eye, like drawing and painting, but, since it can be touched and handled on all sides, appeals to all the senses. Plastic art can be grasped even by primitive man without special training, for it remains within the sphere of all living things familiar with the three dimensions of matter. Painting and drawing presuppose a cultural development which, whether in the creative process or in the appreciation, must abstract from the reality and mentally translate the object on to a flat plane.

FIG. I. MARBLE IDOL FROM TROY (THIRD BURNED CITY)

The first, still tentative, attempt at formative plastic modelling is the doll, but when this plastic modelling develops into art the doll does not disappear; one might say that while the doll was not permitted to enter into art's holy of holies it was allowed to remain in the courtyard of the temple. Art, in rejecting the non-essential and the fortuitous, has striven to present a reflection of the soul; the doll has renounced this psychological motive in order to accentuate and intensify the shallow and the external. The creations of art have to take the spectator's imagination into account; the doll does not allow the slightest scope for the play of the imagination.

The sculptor of the present day works according to the same rules and with the same methods as his predecessor thousands of years ago. He directs his attention to the emotions and reaches the same result as they. The doll, on the contrary, has forced into its service all the refinements of a progressive technique, not striving toward an æsthetic impression, but aiming at ever completer illusion. It can come surprisingly close to nature, but the nearer it approaches its goal the farther is it removed from art; it can create an illusion, but the true essence of artistic enjoyment—the raising of the soul to a higher plane—is denied to it.

Properly speaking, the doll is regarded now only as a child's toy, but, if its historical development be examined, it will be found that the toy doll appears at a comparatively late stage. The doll form, the more or less complete representation of man, existed for thousands of years before the first child took possession of it. For adults it possessed an occult significance with mystical-magical associations which in an inexplicable way united the present and the past and reached deep into the world of the unseen.

FIG. 2. LEAD IDOL FROM TROY

If the genesis of the doll is sought for it will be found, according to the views of Ernst Vatter and of other scholars, in a quality, which is shared alike by primitive races and by children—namely, the ability to discern human and animal forms in all sorts of freaks of nature. Natural and fortuitously developed forms, recognizable in rocks, horns, bones, branches, and roots, must have stimulated the imagination of primitive men, and must have been the point of departure for the shaping, often with but trifling modifications, of figures which were at least something like human beings. In this connexion mention must be made of the so-called *Lösskindel* (loess dolls)—concretions of loam which are occasionally found at Löss and by chance often

PREHISTORIC IDOLS

assume human form. The museum at Strasbourg possesses several examples from Achenheim. Among Palæolithic sculptures it is often to be recognized that the original shape of the material has evidently suggested the object finally represented by the artist. These 'figure stones,' natural fragments of rock in which the more or less striking resemblance to human or animal forms seems to have been still further accentuated by the work of the artist, stand at the very beginning of plastic statuary, and H. Klaatsch would associate them with the otherwise entirely inartistic Neanderthal man. In these he sees the first attempts made to depict natural objects. This tendency to let natural forms which resemble certain objects influence the modelling of figures has remained until the present day peculiar

FIG. 3. FLAT BONE IDOLS FROM TROY

to the spirit of the folk, and forms a striking characteristic in the wood-carving technique of the Alpine pastoral art.

FIG. 4. AMBER IDOL FROM SCHWARZORT

For long the sculpture which was concerned with the representation of human beings remained stationary at this stage of strict dependence on the forms offered directly by nature itself. Hörnes draws attention to the fact that periods of incalculable length, whole thousands of years of primitive culture, are filled with precisely the same sort of art products, and that this runs completely counter to our expectation of finding progress and development everywhere or to our theories cast in terms of decadence and decay.

To the sophisticated modern eye the small plastic figures of prehistoric times will hardly seem like images of men at all. They are block-like, body, head, and limbs of one piece, with the distribution of the limbs indicated by mere scratches. Originally perhaps the features were accentuated by colours which have been obliterated by their long lying in the ground. The art of representation among the prehistoric peoples in this respect runs parallel with that of the nature peoples. There too are figures lacking completely arms and legs; a step forward is marked when two independent legs can be traced; the insertion

25

of arms usually came last. The correspondence between the art of the polar races and that of the Palæolithic is so great that Hildebrand assumes a direct descent of the Arctic peoples from the Palæolithic, regarding the Eskimos as the Aurignac race of to-day. He makes this assertion on the basis of the small statuettes which are by them produced skilfully with the same materials and with the same tools as were at the command of the Palæolithic peoples.

FIG. 5. RED CLAY IDOL
About 3000 B.C.

The discoveries made by Schliemann in the most ancient strata of Troy permit us to follow the development from the formless stone to the human figure. First come the small coniform stones, which only gradually assume human shapes, and do so only if the observer brings with him a lively imagination and a keen desire to recognize this metamorphosis. In the most ancient specimens the head is wanting; a pointed piece of stone to indicate a head marks a higher stage; then a long developed neck appears; and finally small indentations are to be noted as characteristic features, a great advance being made when scratched lines indicate hair, eyes, nose, frontal arches, and necklace. So far as arms are concerned, this type of art does not go beyond the barest suggestion. These sculptures of the Neolithic Age, also called 'board idols,' because of their excessively flat-shaped bodies, give the impression of having originated from plain flat pebbles which could be adapted to human shape by a simple process of cutting and boring.

Closely allied in form to these are the little amber figures, likewise belonging to the Stone Age, which have been dredged up in the Kurisches Haff, East Prussia. For long men adhered to this board-like type. When, however, the artists proved themselves no longer dependent on stones they had found, but had learned to model in clay, there appeared at Cyprus idols of baked clay which just indicated the features, hair, and ornaments by

26

means of white, indented, decorative lines. Only in the upper part of the body can modelling in a true sense be spoken of; the lower part becomes a rectangular 'cake,' which, according to

FIG. 6. CAKE-FORMED IMAGES IN TERRA-COTTA
Cyprus

the highly plausible suggestion of Hörnes, was probably covered with pieces of cloth. Among the bronzes of the Hallstatt and of the first Iron Age these flat idols are again met with; worked in

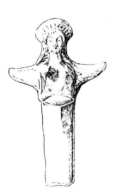

FIG. 7. PHŒNICIAN
TERRA-COTTA IDOL
Sidon

FIG. 8. FEMALE
TERRA-COTTA IDOL
FROM NIPPUR, CHALDÆA

FIG. 9 EARLY
TERRA-COTTA IDOL
FROM TANAGRA

metal, they give the impression of sawed-out or stamped-out tin. A whole depot of such little dolls, which might be regarded as the ancestors of our tin soldiers, was brought to light at Todi, near Perugia.

27

The 'board idols' of Hissarlik are undoubtedly the most primitive examples of prehistoric sculpture, but they are by no means the most ancient. Indeed, the attempts to produce representations of the human form might be traced back to the beginnings of the human race itself, even back to the Ice Age. They begin in the Quaternary period with the Aurignacian civilization in the first half of the fourth Ice Age, and continue through the Solutrian down to the Magdalenian, a period which,

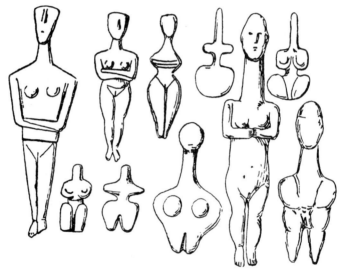

FIG. 10. PRE-MYCENÆAN STONE SCULPTURE
Idols from Amorgos, Naxos

according to Penck, covers about 30,000 to 50,000 years. In the Palæolithic caves of France, at Brassempouy, in the Grimaldi grottoes near Mentone, in Switzerland, and in Moravia figurines have been found which, although they are made of a material—steatite—easy to manipulate, are executed in a very rough and ready manner. The artist's aim has not once gone beyond mere suggestion of features, although, on the other hand, there is a highly abnormal development of breasts and hips. The best-known example of the whole of this group is the so-called 'Willendorf Venus,' which comes from the Aurignacian culture of Willendorf, near Krems, on the Danube. This little figure, only 11 cm. high, is made of limestone and was originally painted red.

Female obesity, which leads to exaggerated development of the lower part of the body, must have dominated men's tastes

28

completely for centuries; it is found spread over the whole of Europe in the relics of primitive statuary, extending to the Mediterranean islands and as far as Egypt. The Hottentots still

FIG. 11. THE SO-CALLED 'WILLENDORF VENUS'
Palæolithic limestone idol

adhere to this ideal, as Schweinfurth discovered during his explorations in Africa. In art it was dominant up to the later Stone Age, with especial persistence in the Balkans. In excavations in Serbia, Rumania, Bulgaria, East Rumelia, and Thessaly,

FIG. 12. PRIMITIVE BRONZE DOLLS OF PREHISTORIC TIMES

alongside others of a stick-like shape, these exaggeratedly obese figurines are frequently met with. Nowadays the original forms are sought for in the sculpture of early African negro art. From such figures with steatopygous bodies the violin-shaped idols,

29

belonging to a culture which extends beyond that of Mycenæ, no doubt originated. During the Copper-Bronze Age these so-called 'violin idols' were disseminated across the Cyclades as far as Troy.

Prehistoric statuettes were at first represented as completely naked, then with diadems, while in the final stage attempts were made to delineate the dress. The artists were conventional, and

FIG. 13. CLAY DOLL FROM
MYCENÆ
1000–800 B.C.

FIG. 14. MARBLE
DOLL FROM DELOS

lost themselves in stylization which, as, for example, in the clay figurines discovered on the Greek mainland in the late Mycen-æan strata, departed far from nature. The 'Rhakmany idols' of Thessaly too belong to the group of statuettes in which only the merest outline of human form is rendered. These are bi-partite, consisting of a cone-formed peg stuck into a wide socket. The peg represents the head, the socket the body, while two wing-like appendages indicate arms; eyes and nose are supplied by painting.

In Europe during the later Stone Age two centres of the so-called idol statuary were established, the common model of which probably derives from the East. One was situated in

Southern Russia, and extended from the Pontine coast across East Galicia and Transylvania as far as Southern Moravia and Silesia. This statuary is traceable through Rumania, Serbia,

FIG. 15
TERRA-COTTA
IDOL FROM
TIRYNS

FIG. 16. FEMALE CLAY
IDOL FROM KNOSSOS,
CRETE
1800–1600 B.C.

Bosnia, and Bulgaria. The figurines, almost always female, are made of clay; they stand naked, in an upright position, with closed legs; the arms are mere stumps. The face is indicated only

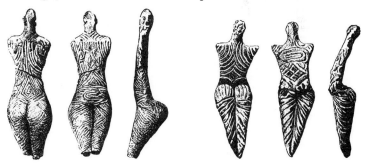

FIG. 17. CLAY IMAGES, WITH INDICATION OF TATTOOING, FOUND IN
CUCUTENI, NEAR JASSY, RUMANIA
Late neolithic

in crude outline; the eyes are represented by points and holes; the nose sticks out from the mass like a beak. Several examples, especially those originating in the Balkans, are ornamented with indented or painted spirals, which, it is conjectured, must represent

31

tattooing. The second group is that of the so-called 'island figures,' little images from 15 to 40 cm. high, carved very

FIG. 18. NEOLITHIC 'ISLAND FIGURES'
Greece

crudely and roughly from limestone and marble. These are found on the Greek islands as far as the coast of Egypt. Hörnes

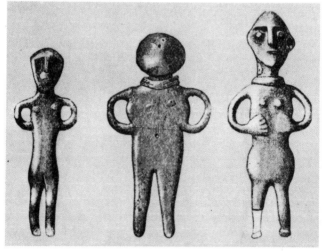

FIG. 19. BRONZE DOLLS FROM KÄLLEBORG AND SCHONEN
About 700 B.C.

is inclined to trace their origin to the Babylonian goddess Istar, while Reinach attributes to them a European origin. The farther north from Egypt are the localities where these pieces have been unearthed the more primitive is the execution, because, as Robert Forrer suggests, of the rustic treatment of the work of the better southern artists.

The productions of prehistoric statuary, thanks to their small size, were disseminated over the whole world of European culture. Late Neolithic Iberian idols of limestone, alabaster, slate, or bone are so similar to the Trojan figures and 'island figures' of the Ægean Sea as easily to be mistaken for these. It is uncertain whether this similarity results from the lack of ability in the primitive modellers or only from a scrupulous retention of early tradition; at any rate, the imaginative quality which they displayed must have been understood by all races.

As we have observed in connexion with the Trojan figurines, all these images pass through diverse stages or planes of perfection. At one end are coarse little blocks of stone or clay difficult of identification, and at the other images which at least resemble natural form. The treatment may be rough or it may be excessively painstaking. Hörnes has proved that the technique and decoration of the clay figures correspond in all details to the then predominating styles in ceramic art, and that these figures have obviously come from the hands of potters. To whichever periods they may belong, however, to whichever region and whichever style, one characteristic is common to the prehistoric figures— their subjects are confined almost exclusively to women. The features may be neglected, the limbs may be treated carelessly, but the sexual features of women are accentuated and brought into undue prominence. The strong preponderance of feminine forms prevails in the doll world even now; in a hundred modern dolls twelve at the most of the masculine gender can be counted. The explanation of these two facts—that the plastic representation of woman precedes by a long time that of man, and that it is to be found so much more abundantly among extant remains —must be sought for in the communal standard of centuries based on the mother-right. Man's prehistoric cultural life comes very close to the cultureless existence of the animal world; the mother occupies the higher *rôle* in the social order; the conception of the father's importance has not yet developed.

Male figurines of the early period are so rare that they can well-nigh be counted separately, and they do not become commoner before the first Iron Age. While the female figurines display only the sexual features, without any recognizable association with the world around them, the figures of men, representing warriors, have a special importance, owing to the accessories assigned to them. Probably the earliest of these are the *schardana*

33

figures, abundantly unearthed in Sardinia and Italy, so called because this (*schardana*) was the name used by the Phœnicians and the Egyptians for the Sardinian mercenaries who, about the year 1000 B.C., were serving in the Egyptian battalions. The little bronze figures, of Phœnician style, bear tall helmets, small shields, and short swords. The Hallstatt and La Tène periods are relatively richer in metal figurines of warriors. Such have been found in Istria bearing Etruscan helmets, with movable rings on the arms and the legs, and with a third ring passing between the legs through the barely suggested clothing. In the

FIG. 20. ETRUSCAN BRONZE DOLLS FOUND IN NOVILARA AND VERONA
Eighth century B.C.

deepest layer of the Altis (the sacred grove of Jove) at Olympia was discovered a similar bronze statuette, an archaic Greek warrior with face-helmet, breastplate, and greaves. To the prehistoric Egyptians belong the 'stake figures,' which consist of sticks at the top of which are faces, generally scratched out in a rough manner, and made lifelike only occasionally, not always, by means of inserted eyes. A thickening represents the body; the arms and legs are not delineated at all. There are also female 'stake figures,' which indicate their sex by a drawing in of the waist, an expansion of the hips, and an arching of the breast. In Africa these figures still hold their ground, for Carl Hagemann, who travelled there for several years, discovered that the Wasseramo tribe, in East Africa, fenced in their dancing place with fantastically arrayed stick images of the same kind.

The prehistoric period provides an immense wealth of

statuettes, which we must call 'dolls,' difficult of classification. No documentary tradition accompanies them. The question naturally arises: What do they represent? A former generation of scholars gave an unhesitating reply; without further consideration they regarded as idols everything that could not be explained. Thus, Schliemann at once thought of the numerous dolls which were found at Troy as representations of the 'owl-headed' Athena. Since then Schuchhardt has discredited "the layman's

FIG. 21. ETRUSCAN BRONZE
FIGURE OF A WOMAN
700–600 B.C.

FIG. 22. PRIMITIVE
BRONZE DOLL

tendency to relate everything unexpected in the relics of prehistoric times to sacrifice and adoration," and consequently other explanations have been sought.

Was it only that the primitive play of imagination was here at work, the creative instinct of man, the endeavour to establish the imaginative pictures which arose in his mind, an instinct in which Conze descries the first motive for the art of sculpture? Must one not suppose that these naïve creations were designed to express fully defined ideas, and that they present not only the first still childish examples of sculpture, but the earliest evidence for the awakening of intellect among the primitive peoples? No animal, not even the most intelligent, can, consciously and voluntarily, create images of itself. Since man had advanced sufficiently to make such images he must have left far behind him that primitive condition when his only cares were for nourishment and reproduction. Without absolute certainty, but with some justifications from analogy, we may draw a parallel between the condition of the nature peoples of to-day (or, at least, of those who were so before they had the misfortune to come into contact with Europeans) and of the primitive races.

The whole of nature is regarded by children and savages as animated; they believe in the power of material objects, in their ability and will to bring benefits or injuries. Hence primitive man feels himself always and everywhere menaced, subject to unknown powers which encircle him at every step, a terrifying emanation of his animistic conception of the world. So the image which he himself had created was regarded by him not as a dead object. We know further, from a very much later time, that classic antiquity did not consider its sculpture as a dead thing, but assumed that it was inspired with divine life. From this belief originated the legends concerning statues which moved of their own accord, raised their hands, and shut their eyes. The myths of the Christian Church took over these conceptions, and had to tell of more than one crucifix which spoke, wept, shed blood, and so forth. In Semitic thought too a demonic element is not to be separated from the representation of man. The Koran has appropriated this notion, for according to its teaching every image made in idle folly will demand a soul from its maker at doomsday. Woe to him! For, since he cannot give it, he will be damned. When some travellers once presented Baghdad women with dolls for their children, these women looked on the gifts as spirits, and retained them in order to keep their children from harm. The doll is put into the sphere of that great mystery which lies in the other world, and is associated with those thoughts which cannot grasp the supernatural, but seek to draw it nearer by means of signs and symbols.

II

ANCESTOR IMAGES

THE mere existence of all these figures testifies to the fact that their makers had arrived at a high stage of knowledge. They must have possessed a religion, and must have been able to formulate conceptions of the unknown powers on which they felt themselves dependent. This feeling expressed itself in awe and terror, a spiritual condition which of itself was bound to lead to the desire of finding protection against inimical influences and of seeking for means of defence. The helplessness of man in face of death must have passed most directly into his consciousness. Not unjustly has Feuerbach called the grave the birthplace of the gods.

To the nature peoples the death of a relation does not signify his complete annihilation, but merely a change in existence. The dead man continues to belong to the family, for it is believed that, although he is invisible, he is near to the living and has the power of returning. Since it is robbed of all pleasures the soul is regarded as full of envy and vindictiveness, and for this reason the Indians of South America consider the dead to be tormenting spirits. From this conviction regarding the insoluble connexion between the present and the past originates that ancestor-worship which is one of the most important elements in primitive culture. The belief in the immortality of the spirit life which is thus manifested truly settled the trend of religious thought among primitive ·races. To this spirit-complex they have given a material being by transferring it to sculpture. The ancestor images represent the dead and form a substitute for the dead, since all the spiritual qualities of the deceased have passed into them. It is the dead man himself who, in sculptured form, continues to participate in the life of the community.

Ancestor-worship has led to still further developments; for, since the image constitutes an object of veneration and adoration, it soon becomes an idol. So long as all the sculptured images of man in the art of the nature peoples were regarded as idols, all the prehistoric figures were designated as idols also. Since it has come to be recognized that the majority of these figures

among the nature peoples are really ancestor images, a change
has taken place in the attitude toward the extant prehistoric
examples. The decision has therefore been reached that the
idol theory must be abandoned and that the majority of these
primitive figures are to be regarded as ancestor images.

However, the assurance is hardly required that in this
mystical sphere, where we move doubtfully on unsure ground in
almost complete darkness, no sharply defined boundaries are
to be determined. Everything is in a state of flux, and no one
can say with certainty at what point the ancestor image becomes
an idol, or when and where it develops into the fetish, the amulet,
the talisman, but it is safe to assume that the ancestor figure
formed the starting-point of all the attempts to gain an influence
over the dominating principle in the unseen and other world.
The living look to the ancestor image for protection from harm:
hence the veneration with which it is regarded—a veneration
which is manifested among the negroes by the smearing of the
image with oil and blood. Among the Golds (or Tunguses)
and Gilyaks of Amur meat and drink are set before the *panja*, a
figure which represents the dead—even pipes for smoking are
provided. During the great fast held after the death of a member
of the Chevsuri tribe, in the Caucasus, an image clothed in the
dress of the dead man is placed on his grave; relatives and
friends make offerings of drink and grain to this figure and hold
a night watch over it. On the death of a distinguished Mongolian
the corpse is burned. Then the ashes are gathered together,
mixed with clay, and formed into a human-shaped figure, which
is set up on the site of the pyre. These figures are held to be
holy. It is but a step to the offering before an idol.

The early stages of the ancestor cult can be traced back to the
middle of the Palæolithic period. Even then men must often
have been afraid of the return of the dead; through this conception alone can be explained the peculiar method of burial
whereby the corpse was set in its grave in a crouching position
with the limbs tightly bound—a practice designed to prevent
the dead from returning. The continued worship of the dead
resulted from the practice of burying bodies first in dwelling caves
and later in houses. "Among our forefathers," writes Servius,
"all the dead were buried in the houses; this is the origin of the
worship of the *lares*." From the coexistence of dead and living,
in one room arose the Roman conception of ancestors as house
gods, which assumed visible form in the *di penates* and the *lar
familiaris*. These ancestor spirits, as patron gods of the Roman
house, were responsible for the family's prosperity. Their little

images, made of wood, polished and shining with wax, were set up on the hearth in the *atrium* and were allowed to participate in the family meals, small dishes of food being placed before them. They were represented in the high-girdled, short-sleeved Doric *chiton*, with a piece of cloth as a belt. On their feet they wore short boots. In their right hands they held drinking-horns and in their left shells for offerings.

The *atrium* of many a better-class house had even a special cupboard in which the *imagines* of the ancestors were kept. At first only the death-mask was taken, and with its help was made a realistically painted and equipped bust, with glass eyes, real hair, and draped in cloth—a custom which was followed up to the fourth century B.C. Later life-size images were produced to represent the entire figure of the dead man. One of these, having the body of wood and the head, hands, and feet of wax, was dressed in the festival garments of the deceased and took his place. At some special obsequies of those related to patrician houses these *imagines* were carried in processions.

The primitive Trojan figurines which Schliemann had regarded as idols are now considered to be similar ancestor images, which were looked upon as the seat of the souls of the departed, and were preserved in the house. At Butmir, in Bosnia, and at Jablanica, in Serbia, so many Neolithic clay figurines have been brought to light that it is impossible to believe that these were not ancestor images. At Butmir seventy-two human figurines were found, the largest 20 cm. high. They were formed like little blocks, the heads on long necks, the features barely indicated. Some were naked, others clothed; among the latter even ornaments and headdress were represented. At Jablanica there were eighty-three figures, exclusively of women. Very similar images have been discovered in Bulgaria; the latter bear a strong resemblance to ordinary chess-men.

The course of development of the ancestor image among the nature peoples of to-day has been clearly sketched out by Eckart von Sydow in his entertaining studies. The mere preservation of the dead man's skull marks the lowest stage. The second stage is reached when this skull is fitted to a wooden frame, whereby the figure is rendered complete. A nose and ears of wood are added, and eyes are supplied from fruit kernels or glass beads. In the New Hebrides a reproduction of the entire body is attempted. On the dead man's skull itself is modelled a face made of coco fibre, clay, and adhesive tissue. Over the surface a resinous stuff is spread and then painted. A stick is added for a nose, round snails' shells for eyes; the deceased's own hair is used, and a plume stuck on the top; the body is built up of bamboo, straw, and bark fibre, and then is covered with resin;

FIG. 23. TUB OF ANCESTORS' SKULLS OF THE NGUMBA (CAMEROONS), WITH MALE AND FEMALE ANCESTOR FIGURES

painting emphasizes details such as navel, nipples, knees, toes, and fingers. The whole figure is then provided with clothing, feathered ornaments, and armlets; in its right hand it is given a shell horn and in the left the jaw-bone of a pig; and at great festivals food is set before it. Such images, however, in tropical climates were liable to swift decay, and the third stage is marked by the making of the entire figure out of carved wood hung round with cloth and rags. A striving toward lifelikeness is often obvious here; among the Maoris even the tattooing of the face is closely imitated.

Africa and Oceania are the chief centres of this ancestor-image

FIG. 24. ANCESTOR FIGURE OF THE BANGWA (CAMEROONS)

FIG. 25. ANCESTOR FIGURE OF THE BALUBA (BELGIAN CONGO)

FIG. 26. FEMALE ANCESTOR IMAGE OF THE BALUBA (BELGIAN CONGO)

cult. In Neu Mecklenburg, Polynesia, the ancestor images are made to commission by hand-workers as an ordinary article of trade. These exceedingly primitive objects, made of chalk, have cylindrical bodies, with arms marked out in relief. They are painted a red-brown and are of two types, male and female, the sexual features being strongly emphasized. On the Solomon Islands and throughout Melanesia are to be found similar wooden figures, 8 to 11 cm. high, on which the marks of tattooing on face and body are duly indicated. Hair and beard are represented by small bristly heads of corn, the eyes by lozenge-shaped pieces of mother-of-pearl. These figures are supposed to symbolize the ancestors. The *korwars* of Papuan negroes of West New Guinea are very similar in form and have the same purpose. They are made of dark wood, and at their manufacture by the medicine-men the relatives of the deceased have to be present. The *korwar*, designed to catch the spirit of the dead man, is carefully preserved. At Sumatra, Celebes, and the neighbouring islands ancestor images, 24 to 27 cm. high, are roughly carved from wood, special prominence being given to the sexual features.

FIG. 27. WOODEN IDOLS FROM SUMATRA

These figures, clothed with small patches of cloth and orna-mented with feathers, represent deceased relatives and are hung up in the houses; it is the custom to give them once a year a sacrificial offering in the shape of an egg, a hen, or a pig. The New Zealand natives also preserve in their houses small carved-wood figures, in each of which dwells an ancestor's spirit. In India small hollow clay figures, in which the souls of Brahmins reside after death, are manufactured by the thousand. The Pangwe, an African tribe, set up male and female figures as tokens on the barrels in which the skulls of their forefathers are collected together. In course of time the images are separated from the receptacle on which they served only as a kind of epitaph, and so become independent.

This interesting tribe both makes use of its ancestor images at those high festivals which are concerned with the worship of the dead and employs them as marionettes, much as the figures in European puppet-shows. The images have feather crests on their heads, and the lower part of their bodies is covered with cloth. They are taken in the hand and made to dance in front of a curtain; they turn and shake, climb up the curtain, and finally, as if tired out by their exertions, hang downward. Whether this play is native to them or influenced by Europeans seemingly cannot now be determined.

Not only among the southern peoples is ancestor-worship common. On the south-western coast of Alaska are to be found monuments to the dead which consist of figures roughly worked out and dressed with cloth. The Cheremis, a Finnish tribe, until a short time ago were in the habit of placing in a corner of their houses ancestor images in the form of roughly carved wooden male figures dressed up in cloth.

Often the ancestor images of the African negroes do not

FIG. 28. WOODEN ANCESTOR IMAGES FROM SUMATRA

exceed the size of small ivory dolls, and are worn by the living on neck or arm; this indicates the passage of the ancestor image into the amulet and talisman. The æsthetic value of these tiny figures is almost negligible. It is to be noted that in these statuettes the head is rendered extraordinarily large in relation to the body and the body in relation to the limbs—a peculiarity which gives the clue to the estimation in which these parts of the body are held, since, by analogy with the living, it is presumed that in the head the soul of the departed establishes itself. When the inhabitants of the New Hebrides desire to converse with the spirits of their forefathers they put their ancestor images in the bushes, sit down near them in the dusk, and entice the souls by playing on bamboo flutes. The spirits proclaim their presence by the rustling of the foliage, and are welcomed with passionate outbursts of joy and grief by their descendants.

From the point of view of technique we are concerned mainly with wooden figures, especially among the negroes. Wood,

43

which is so much easier to handle than the essentially hard stone, answers to the touch of the unskilled hand as well as to that of the skilled, and permits of a freer expression of feeling. Attempts have been made to prove that the hunting tribes in primitive times possessed greater talent than the agricultural peasants for naturalistic sculpturing, due to the cultivation of their powers of observation, but this seems to be an erroneous idea, for the

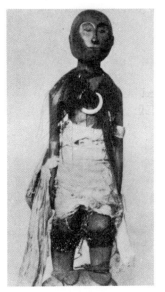

FIG. 29. ANCESTOR IMAGE
FROM THE FIJI ISLANDS
Museum für Völkerkunde, Berlin

FIG. 30
ANCESTOR IMAGES FROM
THE FIJI ISLANDS

agricultural peasant, as a cattle-raiser, has just as much opportunity as the other of observing nature. Apart from that, settled habitation must be regarded as the preliminary condition for the development of artistic skill. The wooden figures made by the nature peoples consist of one model, in which little attention is paid to the arms. The dependence on the material used is again obvious; thus Vatter traces to the shape of the tree-trunk selected by the carvers the decadent, graceful type of ancestor image in Malekula, with arms tightly pressed to the body. Where wood was lacking, as among the Siberian Tschuktschi, little figures, 8 cm. high, were made of the teeth of walruses, while in New Zealand the natives have taken the hard nephrite and, with arduous labour, using only their primitive implements of bone and stone, have shaped from it their small *tiki* images.

ANCESTOR IMAGES

Figures which their makers and possessors held to be inhabited by spirits, and which were supposed to be the embodiment of their dead relatives, necessarily gathered around them a dense atmosphere of superstition. From the ancestor image radiate

FIG. 31. ANCESTOR IMAGE FROM THE CAROLINE ISLANDS

mystical aspirations of the most diverse kinds; thus, when elements of demonic power are regarded as truly bound up with the image of man in doll form, these images entice the soul along strange labyrinths in nature's kingdom of night. In these figures a tendency of man's spirit has taken shape—the tendency which leads him, ever inquisitive and searching for secrets, to

45

desire to subjugate powers which, because they are intangible, can only dimly be felt, but the existence of which has never been doubted. Never has the belief in magic died. Prehistoric man, primitive man of to-day, and civilized European, separated

though they may be by chasms so far as thought and practice are concerned, accept the belief in occult powers—the one openly, the other secretly. The more the modern age departs from faith, the more deeply does it sink into superstitions, and where this tendency is put into practice it cannot—to-day as thousands of years ago—do without images. "They laugh and don't know that they are laughing at themselves."

The change of ancestor image into idol must have come quite automatically. The ancestor images, piously preserved and acquiring a certain cult through the ceremony of anointing with oil, in which were supposed to reside secret powers, from which help and protection were looked for, must soon have come to be regarded as idols, revered for themselves. For that reason Sydow calls the conception on which the art of

FIG. 32
ANCESTOR
IMAGE FROM
THE NEW
HEBRIDES

ancestor imagery is based deification. The ancestor becomes an idol, the symbol of divinity. Thus, the Meso-potamian culture possessed nail-god-desses, which depended on the custom of laying down nails on the foundation stone of a temple as a kind of documentary attestation. These little figures, made of copper, with thick hair on the head and clasped hands, were preserved in brick cases and placed on the foundation stone. It was thought that this attestation, by aid of the divinity, would thus be bound to the earth. The extant pieces belong to the time of Ur-Ninā of Lagash, about the year 3200 B.C.

FIG. 33. PRO-
TECTIVE FIGURE
FROM THE NICO-
BAR ISLANDS

In the New World the Spaniards found idolatry common among the natives, especially those of the West Indies. The small idols of human type were meant to reproduce the forms in which the spirits had manifested themselves. Several of these carvings bore in remembrance the names of deceased relatives—an observance which indicates that even here idol-worship had originated from an ancestor cult.

ANCESTOR IMAGES

Thousands of examples were discovered, and on an island near Haiti, where resided a tribe of idol-makers who confined their activities to making figurines of night spirits, there was a kind of wholesale production of these things. Idolatry must have flourished in Peru also.

Perhaps idol-worship has lost ground in the course of centuries, but it has not completely disappeared, being found among both

FIG. 34. SPIRIT OF A DEAD SHAMANIST (IN WOOD)
Golds and Gilyaks in Amur, Siberia

FIG. 35. WOODEN IDOLS
Golds and Gilyaks in Amur, Siberia

nature peoples and civilized races, even among those who profess Christianity. On the Australian islands prayers are made to the god Tangarva, who is worshipped with human sacrifice. His wooden image is hollow and is filled with smaller wooden images which represent the offerings. At Bali and Lombok, in the Malay Archipelago, there appear the god Sakti Kumulan and the goddess Dalem Kamenuh, the images of which are made of Chinese copper coins gilded at the edges, with faces of coloured sandal-wood. These figures are dressed in white-and-red pieces of cloth, and are borne in procession to the sea temple. In Siberia F. R. Martin came across house idols of pine-wood dressed in costumes of motley cotton material and caps of blue

47

wool. The natives got these made by the Russified Ostiaks in Surgut. Every family possessed at least one such piece, which it kept, carefully hidden, but by no means forgotten, to take on journeys. The Shamanist priests of Amur, whose chief activities

FIG. 36. WOOD-CARVED IDOLS OF THE TSCHUKTSCHI, SIBERIA

are concerned with assisting the souls of the dead in the other world, are aided in their ceremonies by spirits, who are represented by small, roughly carved idols. The Museum für

FIG. 37. HOUSE IDOLS OF THE OSTIAKS IN JUGAN

Völkerkunde in Berlin possesses about twenty such figures, all different from one another.

The cult ceremonies of the Hopi Indians of North America have developed along very peculiar lines. They conduct their worship with dolls, which are set up at altars in subterranean

DOLLS OF THE TUSAYAN INDIANS
Hopi dolls representing Kā-tci-nas (intercessory spirits
between the dead and the gods)

rooms, and which personify the masked dancers who, at the great feasts in July and August, have to represent gods and demons. These motley-coloured wooden dolls, dressed in leather and adorned with feathers, are called *ti'hus*, and create an extraordinarily fantastic impression because of their strange costume, which is said to symbolize storm-clouds. Here are to be found the star-god, the snake-god, the war-god, besides female demons and goddesses. All these figures are modern, and J. Walter Fewkes, who has lived among the Tusayan Indians, is certain that although they may quite probably be images of gods once revered, they are no longer worshipped as idols. They are sprinkled with flour and employed for the ceremonial rites, but when the ceremonies are over they are left to the children to be used as toys: this rapid and surprising transition from idol to playing doll makes us think. It is to be assumed that this is done in order to give the children a living conception of the most important aspects of religion. They are said also to serve as ornaments in the living rooms, and are freely used as articles of commerce. Of these the Museum für Völkerkunde in Berlin possesses a very rich collection. Among the same Indians a serious *rôle* is played by stone house idols, which, although lacking arms and legs, have indications of eyes, and are finished off with feather ornaments round the neck. From time to time they are sprinkled with flour, and, as it seems, are still revered as idols. The holy war-club bundle of the Winnebagos (a tribe of Prairie Indians), in Nebraska, also serves in the practice of a cult. Besides many other objects it includes a richly ornamented cloth warrior-doll with tall leather boots and long plaits.

Among the Chinese, one of the most ancient civilized peoples in the world, no house lacks its little altar, with tutelary deities of divers kinds, to which is rendered a peculiarly personal and intimately coloured worship. The small images are made of steatite and agalmatolite (soapstone or talc), materials which are soft and plastic and so easy to work with. It is the custom to give presents to these luck-bearing figurines, the best examples of which belong to the period from the sixteenth to the eighteenth century, in order to bring blessing to the presenter and to protect him from sickness—a custom showing the transition of the idol into the amulet.

Even among Christian peoples themselves tendencies of a heathen ancestry were retained until late in the nineteenth century, and are possibly to be noticed even to-day, in the shape of a belief in idols. In various peasant farms of Norway worship was devoted to the *fakse* and *hernos*, house idols to which, until a few decades ago, it was customary to offer sacrifice. These were half-life-size human figures carved in wood, with long hair and beard. The feet were only suggested, the figures being finished below in a snake-like form. On Christmas Eve the figure was taken to a high position, and some beer was poured into the hollow of its head; at the time of the winter solstice others were smeared with fat; in summer they were given offerings of whey on the mountain pasturelands. These Norwegian figures find parallels in the Polish and Czech *dziady* ('old men'), likewise intermediate between ancestor images and idols.

The Catholic Church quickly turned to its own advantage the belief in idols which is deeply rooted in the instinct of the folk, skilfully transforming these into figures of mercy. The miracle-working images of Mary and of the saints, arrayed like dolls and covered with rich ornaments, were once to be numbered by the thousand. Several of the famous divine images possessed, and still possess, a rich and costly wardrobe. In the church of the Holy Cross at Augsburg Friedrich Nicolai in 1780 saw a statue of the Blessed Virgin with real hair, powdered and dressed *à la mode* in a silk *adrienne*, with wrist-frills of pointed Brabant. During the same period Gretser saw at the high altar of St Emmeran's in Regensburg a crucifix clad in the full vestments of a priest celebrating Mass. In 1751 in Austria it was forbidden to set wigs on the statues of the saints. A Spanish synod held at Orihuela in 1660 took exception to these fooleries, and decreed that the figures of the Madonna and of the saints should be no longer dressed with real hair, arrayed in silk, and hung with ornaments, but the childishly naïve worship of the folk did not permit of much sympathy for these orders. Many idle nuns, in the seclusion of their cloisters, continued to find a pastime in toying with an infant Christ dressed up as richly as possible.

III

FETISHES, AMULETS, AND TALISMANS

EVEN in ancient times it is to be noted that the smaller images of gods change into fetishes, so that the artistically formed figurines act as substitutes for that which they represent. By the term fetish is understood a natural object or an object of art with which a cult is associated and to which its possessor ascribes supernatural powers. Like the ancestor image and the idol from which it has sprung, it is one of the earliest religious possessions of mankind, and has preserved over thousands of years down to our own day a belief in the power of material objects. This is no mere chance, for it finds its firm basis in the fact that belief in the fetish arouses the power of suggestion which may often bring the desired object to fulfilment. Should the protecting or healing result be long in coming, the fetish or the amulet is not at fault, but want of true belief on the part of its possessor. The fetish to-day is still omnipresent, and does not rely on primitive ideas alone. Its possessor is accustomed to devote to it a wholly personal cult; for the fetish is usually the idol of one man, who, it is true, is wont to abandon it if the protecting or healing power which he attributes to it denies him anything. Any object can become a fetish, but generally human forms are preferred. For this purpose images of gods obviously were eminently suitable. The skald Hallfred was reproached for having taken into his own possession an image of Thor as a fetish.

One of the chief centres of the fetish cult is to be found among the negro tribes of West and Central Africa, where the demand for protective and aiding figures is extraordinarily great. Indeed, there is among these fetishes a regular division of labour. As Pechuel-Loesche records:

> Among these some bring to the merchants good profits, others to travellers comfortable lodgings, others to the fishermen and hunters rich booty, others to childless couples issue. There are others which assist the secreting of mother-milk, the birth and teething of children, the faithfulness of wives and of husbands, the egg-laying of hens, the increase of goats and sheep, the prospering of crops, the

51

good result of a courtship or of a lawsuit, success in war, the recovery of an invalid. Others are expected to loosen fetters, to attract bondsmen, to alleviate the weight of burdens, to strengthen limbs, to make eyes keener, to open up. trade, to give glimpses into the future, to pass judgment on doubtful cases, to divert rain-clouds from the camp, to destroy vermin, to provide food, to prevent external trouble and suffering, especially bodily hurt, to avert witches, ghosts, and wild animals. The timid are not satisfied with

FIG. 38. FETISH OF THE
BASSONGE (CONGO)

FIG. 39. NAIL FETISH
FROM THE LOANGO COAST

a general fetish against the dangers of war—they must have one fetish which protects them against arrows, a second against a blow with a naked weapon, a third against a blow from a club. Maybe they will take still more which preserve them from falling into an ambush, from being caught in a snare, or from being captured, and so forth. A person undertaking a commercial expedition can make use of various fetishes for the purchase of palm-kernels, of palm-oil, or of caoutchouc, for the hiring of reliable porters, for strength in marching, against sand-storms, losing of the way, bad roads, and swollen rivers, against attacks of all sorts, against thieves, and against avaricious landowners. A person about to marry requires a good few fetishes, such as are necessary to keep his wife faithful, to display himself from the very beginning as a strong master, to avert the slipping in of evil spirits on the marriage night.

Most of these fetishes, generally of human shape, are described by Sydow as "frightful phantoms, both repulsive and fascinating," and when we look at them in the museums we realize that he is right. Very important for an understanding of the nature of the fetish are the wooden 'nail fetishes,' which are often stuck all over with nails and bits of glass. This is done in order to entice and incite them to use their power; there are recipes, of a very mechanical sort, for the ceremony. They are

FIG. 40. WOODEN NAIL FETISH OF THE BAWILI, LOANGO COAST (FRENCH EQUATORIAL AFRICA)

FIG. 41. WOODEN DOLL "HAMPATONG" Amulet for head-hunters, Borneo

FIG. 42. FETISH OF THE BATEKA (FRENCH EQUATORIAL AFRICA)

strewn with cola-nut, smeared with blood and oil, caressed, shaken, patted, and warmed. If they delay too long in giving their aid they are beaten, and if the result still fails to appear they are pitched into the fire.

If the fetish is an animated object possessing its own power or an image forming a connecting-link between soul, god, and demon, amulets and talismans are charms which bear no value in themselves, but receive a power imparted to them from without. In contrast to the actively working fetish they are quite passive, merely giving defence, for the most part, against evil spirits. Idols or little images of gods have been from of old chosen for this purpose. In Egypt there has been found a great number of bronze, silver, and lead figurines representing all the

53

gods, some from the New Kingdom, the majority from the later periods and the epoch of the Ptolemies. Apparently even large specimens among them were worn on the neck suspended on chains, thus serving as talismans. Attached to small amulets in the shape of pigs, they proved a protection against the evil eye.

The small dolls which the Eskimos carve out of bone are hung on their kayaks to prevent the capsizing of the boat. Old Japan had its rag dolls, made over a wooden foundation, called *amakatsu* or *otagiboko*, which had an original significance as

FIG. 43. LEATHER DOLLS FROM SOUTH-WEST AFRICA
The first and last are supposed to represent Herero, the other three Hottentots.
Perhaps used for cult purposes
Staatliches Museum für Völkerkunde, Munich

amulets for easy confinement; in later times, however, they descended to the *rôle* of children's playthings. Another kind of painted wooden doll, originating from various Japanese provinces, is shaped very peculiarly, like a cone or a roll, with head often barely suggested and painted face; this represented at first a protective amulet against illness, but later was changed into a fertility charm. In the Batak lands in Sumatra the medicine-men make use of a doll-formed jar with a head made of brown wood covered with tin. This is about 19 cm. high, and is handled so dexterously that the figure seems to be alive. It is called Perminak, and forms a talisman against the bite of poisonous snakes, besides rendering its possessor shot-proof. The Tschuktschi in the Bering Strait carve wooden male and female dolls, with eyes of tin or ivory, some of which serve as protective amulets against ghosts, while to others is assigned the task of enticing seals. The Golds and Gilyaks in Amur carve from bone little human figures which serve them as amulets against the evil spirits who, they think, are the cause of the back-ache, phthisis, consumption, and epilepsy from which they suffer so much. But it is not necessary to roam far afield in order to learn of the customs which depend upon the unshakable basis of superstition. Superstition is to be encountered in the very midst of civilization, on, the asphalt of the great cities. Looking round, one finds the *de luxe* motor-cars of the rich equipped with little dolls which often have the significance of a talisman. These dolls are manufactured out of soft cloth for sportsmen of all kinds; it is said that in Paris the *bébés porte-bonheur* have achieved great popularity since the Armistice and that they are eagerly sought after.

Psychologists and criminologists speak of 'doll fetishism' as a special form of nervous mental disorder. "The love of dolls," says Féré, "can intrude so far as to eliminate entirely any affection for a living issue." Women among whom the love of dolls persists even in advanced age are not rare. Vinchon knew an hysterical French woman who from infancy was so passionately devoted to dolls that she stole silk in order to clothe them smartly; they assumed for her the position of a fetish.

History has to tell of various examples among adults of this love of dolls. According to Indian mythology the goddess Parwati made so lovely a doll for herself that she hid it from her husband Siwa. He saw it, however, and fell so deeply in love with it that he gave it life and made it his mistress. When Cortés met Montezuma he found that emperor and his Court playing with dolls. Queen Catharine de' Medici, when she became a widow, amused herself in the seclusion of her chamber with dolls which had to be clothed, like herself, in mourning. Tallement des Réaux relates that the Duchesse d' Enghien (*née* de Brézé), a niece of Cardinal Richelieu, continued to play with dolls even after her marriage, treating them like children, dressing and undressing them, giving them food and medicine, etc. Henrietta, Duchess of Marlborough, a daughter of the first Duke of Marlborough, was very friendly with the author Congreve, and when he died, in 1729, she caused a life-size image of him to be made; this was so exact that it even showed an open sore on his leg from which he had suffered during his lifetime. She paid a doctor to dress this wound, and went about with the figure as if it were a living being. When a certain Count Harcourt died, in 1769, his grief-stricken widow ordered a large wax image of her husband to be made, got it clad in his dressing-gown, and set it in an easy chair by her bedside. Margravine Sibylle von Baden-Baden caused a hermitage to be built in her favourite park, in the dining-room of which the Holy Family sat at table. The Blessed Virgin, Joseph, and the child Christ were wooden dolls, with heads and hands of wax, dressed in real clothes. Between them stood a little chair for the Margravine when she condescended to eat with the carpenter couple. Countess Augusta Dorothea von Schwarzburg, a princess of the house of Brunswick, consoled herself during her widowhood by playing with dolls. She ordered twenty cupboards to be made in the form of dolls' rooms, in which she herself and her Court were represented naturalistically. Skilled monks of Erfurt modelled the heads of wax, while the Countess herself made the clothes. From 1716 to 1720 this collection was exhibited in Schloss Monplaisir, at Arnstadt, and in 1820 Vulpius saw it at Schloss Augustenburg. Princess Augusta of Saxe-Gotha, the wife of Frederick Prince of Wales (the son of King George II), preferred to pay more attention to her dolls than to her husband. So unceremoniously did she play with these that her sisters-in-law had to beg her to desist in order to prevent the common people from becoming aware of her propensities.

Ancestor image, idol, fetish, talisman, amulet, depend in their general conception upon the idea that the representation of a god or a demon or a man confers upon the person who makes the image and who calls by name the thing represented the power to make use of its strength or to influence it. On these grounds the law of Moses forbade, as idolatry, the making of images. With the image are associated ideas of a magic dwelling within it, a magic powerful enough to make use of the image. Thus it is that the doll, both among ancient and among modern peoples, plays an important part in magical practice. Generally the image is utilized for the purpose of doing harm to some one; seldom does one hear of images employed in order to do a good turn. The active agent undertaking a thing of this nature uses a symbolic magic which is in itself a copy or pantomimic suggestion of the result to be brought about by these means. The belief is that whatever one desires can be carried out in actuality.

IV
IMAGE MAGIC

THIS conviction, that one's desire can be accomplished by proxy, finds expression in the 'fertility magic' of some folk customs. With a certain tenacity superstition associates dolls with the whole sexual life of woman. On the Santa Cruz islands is found the male spirit-doll Menata, the duty of which, in general, is to take care of the women's health. Among the Suaheli a girl during menstruation has always to carry a wooden doll in her hand or on her back. E. von Weber noted that the Fingo girl in the Orange Free State carries about a doll from the time she is marriageable until she has had a child. This doll is then laid aside and a new one provided until the birth of the next child. These dolls are treasured and regarded as sacred. Magic is regularly resorted to in connexion with childlessness among married couples. Some negro tribes of South Africa have dolls which are borne on the back like children, nursed and suckled, and even given names. This use of what scientists call 'imitative magic' is widespread, and is to be found in Africa on the Ivory Coast, in Senegal, and in the Sudan. Among the negroes of the Wapogoro and Wagindo tribes women who desire children get dolls made out of gourds. The sphere of this magic, however, goes far beyond Africa, extending to America, the South Sea Islands, and even to Australia. The last-mentioned fact, according to W. Foy, proves that the magic belongs to a very ancient cultural level, for the Australian natives, both in their physical structure and in their manners and customs, stand at the lowest grade of civilization. The Bataks in Sumatra and the natives of New Zealand often carry about dolls as a protection against sterility. A sterile woman of the Nischinam tribe in California is presented by her friends with a grass doll, which she carries around like a living child. If a pregnancy results other dolls are called into use. In the Torres Strait the expectant mother busies herself with a male doll in the hope of bringing a boy into the world. The Dayak women of Borneo sacrifice a little house filled with their own dolls for the purpose of averting some illness threatening an expectant mother.

When there is fear of an approaching abortion among the tribe of Annamites the magic-man makes two straw dolls for mother and child and carries through his ceremonies with these.

One need not, however, go out of Europe to discover examples of such customs. Russian peasant women who were childless and wished for children used to make a pilgrimage to a famous nunnery at Smolensk which possessed a wonder-working baby doll—apparently an image of the child Christ. This they rocked in their arms, while at their side a nun prayed that they might be freed from their unfortunate sterility. Among the wandering

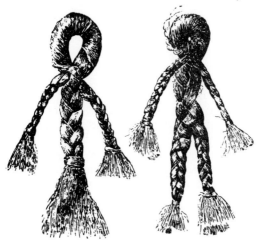

FIG. 44. YOUTH AND MAIDEN
Flax dolls for a bridal spinning-wheel, Brunswick

Perchten of Tal von Gastein it was the custom to fasten a baby doll on to a long cord and to throw it to the young women, who kept it or threw it back according as they desired the blessing of children or not. Not long ago in Brunswick the peasant women kept as a dowry a wedding spinning-wheel finely carved of red wood, especially plum-tree wood, and adorned with ribbons and artificial flowers. This was often hung with six to eight small male and female dolls made of twisted flax, with recognizable head, arms, legs, and dress. These dolls formed a talisman supposed to make the marriage fruitful. Sometimes, too, they were used as a cure for ague, in which case they were burned to ashes and swallowed. The doll could be utilized also for the successful issue of a confinement. At Klingnau, in Switzerland, during Shrovetide a masked fool used to stroll round with a large doll. He visited the houses of the newly married couples and showed the doll to the young wives, for which he was rewarded with a gratuity.

Image magic proper necessitates the making of a figure of the man whose hurt is secretly sought; this figure is pierced with holes, lacerated, and burned, on the assumption that all that is done to it is transferred to the living original. The belief in the efficacy of this magic goes back to dimmest antiquity. Hentze holds that the figurines found in the Magdalenean and Solutrian culture strata are naught but magic images, made in order to gain power over those they represent. On the Chaldean bricks of the time of Assur-nazir-pal II (883–858 B.C.) incantations are spoken of. "They have created effigies conformable with my image and similar to my form." "With an ointment of hurtful herbs have they rubbed me; to my death they have led me." In these texts mention is made, too, of protective measures in which likewise an image has to play its magical part: "Repeat the incantation in a whispering voice and let an image of clay be by." "The incantation of those who have made effigies conformable with my image, similar to my form, who have taken away my breath, pulled out my hair, torn my garments, prevented my feet from moving by means of dust—may the fire-god disperse their charms!" An Egyptian papyrus of the time of Rameses III records the trial of a conspirator who made little wax figures and uttered incantations over them for the purpose of insinuating himself into the Pharaoh's harem. Another man was sentenced for making wax images in order to harm his enemies.

This conception of the possibility and efficacy of image magic was carried to the West from the Orient. Plato is fully cognizant of the practice of wizardry by means of wax figures. In an ode of Anacreon the poet advises the throwing of a wax figure of Amor into the fire that love itself may thereby be consumed. Lucian of Samosata relates that when he was a schoolboy his ears were boxed for his having made some wax figures; this in itself indicates that even such childish play was regarded as dangerous. Among the Greeks and Romans image magic was freely employed in love affairs. In Theocritus's idylls Samaitha puts a charm on her faithless lover:

> The Spirit aids, the mammet melts above;
> And so may he,
> Delphis the Myndian, melt in grids of love,
> As utterly. [1]

Proof of the existence of this love magic in Rome is provided by Horace and Ovid, cloth-dressed dolls being utilized in their day for this purpose. These wooden magic images, representing both sexes, were called *ipsullices*. In the country they were made of bark and hung on the branches of trees.

In the Middle Ages similar love magic is said to have been

---

[1] Translation by Jack Lindsay (*Theocritos*, Fanfrolico Press, 1929).

practised with the use of little images of wax. These were baptized and melted, and thus the person in question was supposed to be inflamed with love. Jakob Grimm records a poem relating to this written by one of the wandering scholars:

> With wondrous magic art
>   I shall teach you how to mould
> Of wax a human counterpart—
>   If its magic you would hold,
> Baptise it in the well; that done,
> Let it stand i' th' heat o' th' sun.

When a girl of the Transylvanian gipsy tribe wants to capture the affections of a lad she makes a doll of dough mixed with his hair, blood, spittle, and nails, and baptizes it in the name of the beloved person. This she then buries at a cross-road under the light of the new moon, defiles it, and says, "N.N., I love you. When your little image is rotted you must, as the dog after the bitch, run after me, your sweetheart." The girls of the Chippeway Indians also employ a love magic, in which they make an image of the loved one and sprinkle it in the region of the heart with a certain powder.

The belief in the power of image magic had a remarkably tenacious life. King Louis X of France ordered Enguerrand de Marigny to be executed for having sought after his life by this means; the Duchess of Gloucester in 1445 was accused of a similar crime against King Henry VI of England; for this she was imprisoned, while her three accomplices were sent to the scaffold. Charles IX of France made de la Mole pay with his head for the same offence. When Urban VIII occupied the papal chair it was prophesied to. Cardinal Ascoli that he would be his successor. Meanwhile, as affairs moved on and the Pope did not die, the Cardinal's nephew lost patience and decided to accelerate Urban's decease. He made a wax image of the Pope, and by melting this slowly to the accompaniment of various incantations he intended to free St Peter's chair for his uncle. Urban VIII did not die from this procedure, which, on the contrary, cost the over-zealous nephew and his accomplices their lives. Even at the beginning of the eighteenth century at Turin there was executed a man against whom no other charge was brought than that he had aimed at the Duke's life by means of image magic.

It is a well-attested fact that to-day, in the East, in America, and in France, there exist coteries devoted to Satanism where these magical practices are still pursued. A little image of the person whose destruction is desired is made of red wax. This is pierced with needles or melted, thus, it is supposed, causing the person in question to become ill or to die.

In China the same ideas prevail. In the year 100 B.C. a certain prince was charged with having injured the Emperor by means of wooden, paper-clad dolls which a wizard had animated with evil spirits. In the year 602 a prince whose father lived too long made a doll in his likeness, pierced it in the heart, and buried it, with the idea of shortening the days of his old lord. When vengeance is desired on an enemy a straw doll is made, with a head of cotton and clad in blood-stained paper. To the accompaniment of divers incantations it is then pierced through with needles. In the Temple of Unfortunate Women at Canton there formerly hung upside down many paper figures of men, made by wives for the reforming of their evil husbands—"so that thereby his heart might be changed." The revenge doll is known also in Japan. A Japanese woman who finds herself betrayed makes a straw doll intended to represent the faithless man, bores it through with nails, and buries it in the place where he sleeps. Whether this is intended to draw him back or is conceived only as a punishment remains uncertain. If one is robbed, a paper doll is made, hung upside down on the wall, and pierced with needles. This doll represents the god of riches, whose business it is to discover the thief, and since he is fastened by the feet he cannot escape before he has fulfilled his duty.

Belief in the revenge image dwells not less strongly in Europe. The Scottish Highlanders are convinced that the death of one they hate may be attained by means of a *corp creadh*—an image of white clay with black glass-bead eyes and teeth made of splinters of wood, which is supposed to represent the person in question. If death only is desired this image is placed in a stream running eastward, and so is washed away. If the enemy is to die slowly and of a painful illness it is pierced with needles, or stuck through with rusty nails, and then placed in slowly flowing water. Formerly similar figures were carried through the villages in election time, the nails with which they were pierced showing contempt for the candidate whose election was not desired. Belief in this revenge image in Britain, however, is by no means confined to the Scottish Highlanders. At a charity bazaar held at London in 1901 there was exhibited an image of the Boer President Kruger which visitors were allowed to pierce thrice on payment of sixpence.

Among the Walachians a revenge image is employed which shows love magic used in the interests of a betrayed girl. The figure has to be made by a witch, who must carry out a tripartite

61

magical ceremony, consisting of baptism, incantation, and curse. The girl sticks a needle into the heart of the figure, spits on it, defiles it, and finally buries it under an elder-bush in the name of all the evil spirits. In India, too, wooden figures pierced with nails are made use of to bring injury to enemies. The Aymara Indians of Bolivia make small clay images of their enemies and stick thorns into them; so long as these thorns are allowed to remain in position the adversary is supposed to suffer. The Chippeway Indians of North America make wooden images of those to whom they desire harm; these they pierce in the head and breast so as to cause their enemies pain, or bury them when they desire to take their opponents' lives.

Among the Parivara, a Hindu tribe, a faithless wife was in the past punished by death; nowadays this punishment is carried out symbolically, a clay doll of the adultress being made, pierced with thorns in the eyes, and cast aside.

Opposed to these are the healing dolls, which to a certain extent have to act as an antidote to black magic. In the Middle Ages when it was thought that an illness had been caused by witchcraft, a little doll was made of wax and a priest bidden to read three Masses over it on a fast day. The figure was then pricked in the place where the invalid felt pain, the witch thus being forced to retract the spell. In China, under similar circumstances, a paper image of the sick man is cut out, and this has to be burned with some accompanying ceremonies in order to remove the disease. In Amoy, indeed, paper images of this kind are made for all the inmates of a house, loaded (as images) with every illness which could afflict the living persons, and then cast into the fire. Similar customs are known in Japan. Twice during the year, at the symbolic purification festivals in the Shinto temples, paper dolls representing the faithful are laid before the altar of *kami* in order to act as a protection against all possible evil. When a member of the Orang tribe, in the Malay Archipelago, falls ill a wooden image is made into which the evil spirits are driven by means of incantations; afterward this is thrown from the shore into the sea, which carries it away along with the illness. At Celebes in such cases male figures are worked out of fibre bound round with strips of bast; as soon as the priest has charmed the disease into them these substitutes for the patients are removed, sometimes being placed on coco-nuts filled with rice, and cast, along with their evil spirits, into the sea. A similar magic is practised in the Balkans and in the Caucasus for the purpose of calling down rain as necessity arises. The maidens of the village make a female doll, carry it round on an ass, and eventually place it on a raft made of straw and branches which is set alight and thrust into the current of the river.

In Borneo there are luck images manufactured from wood gathered in certain peculiar circumstances—*e.g.*, in moonlight on some lonely and hardly accessible spot. These bring all possible benefits to their possessors and are hung up over the hearth. At each festival season they are consecrated anew, being smeared with the blood of sacrifice — often enough that of a man. In the islands near Sumatra are dolls which guard the owners from being devoured by evil spirits. These dolls are hung up over the money chest to increase its contents, or are employed to bring success on head-hunting expeditions, and so on.

Dolls are used for many other matters connected with magical rites; these have always to be images of men, for to such is ascribed the greatest efficacy. The Baluba tribe of the Southern Belgian

FIG. 45. MAGIC DOLL
Celebes

Congo maintain that the great spirit Nkulu gave a thumb-sized model to one of their medicine-men so that the necessary magical figures could be made from it. In Africa are to be found magical figures, such as the *nomori* of Sierra Leone, the meaning of which the negroes themselves no longer know, and which they do not even manufacture any more; these, however, they regard as possessing magical powers, and when they find them they bury them in their fields. The number of African magical figures is exceptionally large, since each has only one possible application. Their power is bound up with magical matters with which they are, so to say, laden. They are employed even in legal affairs, use being made of them in order to reveal the unknown perpetrator of a crime, usually a theft, by the thrusting of a red-hot iron nail into a wooden figure. Through this the guilty one is made ill, and can become well again only when he has made restitution and the nail is removed. Although plastic images are rare among the Akikuyu of East Africa, that tribe possesses a kind of magical clay doll which serves in the celebration of dances at the maize-harvesting. These figures may be of either sex and are carefully preserved. The Luiseño Indians of Southern California make life-size

FIG. 46. THE GOD SAKTI KUMULAN AND THE GODDESS DALEM KAMENUH
Made of gilded Chinese copper coins. Bali

figures of elder-wood, with fringed coats, which are used for the image dances performed at their puberty festival. These are carried about, symbolically presented with gifts, and burned at the close of the ceremony.

A special magic seems to rule over the birth and growth of children. Greek mothers, after the birth of their first child, were wont to consecrate a little image in the temple of Eileithyia, and similar customs are to be found among the nature peoples. Catlin relates that when a child of the Odschibbewa Indians (of Lake Superior) dies, the mother makes a feather doll as a substitute, and carries this about with her tied up in a bundle along with the clothes and toys of the dead child. The Indians call the whole thing a 'doll of misfortune.' According to Richard Andree, an animistic idea lies at the root of this custom: since the child is still too small to be able to fend for itself in the other world, the mother must support it until its spirit has sufficiently developed.

The doll is employed too for the purpose of getting in touch with the other world. When a Chinaman wishes to learn something from the dead he makes a doll into which a witch, the doll's 'aunt,' has charmed the soul of a child, and which is then burned so that the information sought may be gathered on the other side of the grave. At Bali and Lombok when a special supplication is to be made to the gods, female wooden figures with painted white face, black hair, and yellow breast and arms, and having an inscription on their backs telling of the desires which the gods are bidden to fulfil, are sacrificed on the altars of the temple. Very common is the use of dolls possessing magical power in order to obtain rich harvests. On the Santa Cruz islands bottle-shaped dolls with real hair and decorated with ornaments are carried by the women on their backs like children, and borne with them to the plantations in the expectation that they will secure a good harvest. There, too, the *tapa* doll—husband and wife represented in intimate embrace—is employed as a kind of fertility magic in the cocoa plantations. Up to a short time ago the primitive tribes in Central India indulged in human sacrifice during their fertility rites; now they make use of monkeys or, more commonly, dolls of wood or straw. It was the custom formerly in India, in order to increase the harvest, to stick an iron hook into the back of a living man, to draw him upward and swing him round; nowadays this magical practice is carried out only symbolically, by means of a doll, *sidi viranna*.

Image magic has maintained itself most strongly among the wandering gipsies of Hungary—the so-called tent gipsies. For this purpose they make use of anything which has to do with the dead. From gum removed from the trees in a churchyard, from the hair and nails, burned to powder, of a dead child or virgin girl, and from the ashes of the burned clothes of a dead man they make little figures—the so-called 'dead men' (*manush mulengré*). These are human images supposed to bring to the possessor the favour of demons. They are also ground down to powder and mixed with forage as a protection against witchcraft; for this paste the rotten wood of old coffins and grave crosses is also used. Those gipsies who work as broom-makers or tree-fellers make the image of an earth spirit, *phuwusch* or *maschurdalo*, which they cast into the bushes; fishermen and seamen make a similar figure, called *nivaschi*, which they throw into the water; both serve as a protection against devils. In these images the features are rendered in a very rough and ready manner.

The belief in the animation of the doll reaches a culmination, vital yet half devilish, in the mandrake, or 'gallowsman.' The mandrake, which is mentioned even in the Bible, bears a name which itself signifies a living idol. It is in reality the root of the white bryony, which closely resembles the human form, or of the mandragora (called also *Allermannskraut*), which grows in the Southern Alps. Pliny knows of it and speaks of its peculiarities. In the Middle Ages it was believed that it originated from the last seminal effusion of a man hanged on the gallows, and that when uprooted it uttered a moaning cry. Since he who digs it up must die, it is tied to the tail of a black dog, which is then made to drag it from the earth. It must be washed with wine, bathed, nursed, and suitably clothed. Its demonic character is revealed by the fact that it will not leave its possessor; of itself, if it is carried away, it returns to him. Should anyone desire to get rid of the root he must sell it more cheaply than he has

FIG. 47. MALE AND FEMALE MANDRAKES
From the *Hortus Sanitatis*, Mainz, 1491

bought it, and the last purchaser has to keep it. It brings luck to its possessor, makes him rich, opens up secrets to him, and many professional thieves to-day still hold to the conviction that with its help the doors of any castle can be unlocked. The former Court library in Vienna possesses the mandrakes, of both sexes, which belonged to Emperor Rudolph II, each wrapped in a little dark velvet mantle. Perger tells a story of how a peasant, whom a gipsy girl initiated into the secret, pulled up a bryony root on a Monday morning under the favourable conjunction of the moon with Venus and Jupiter. He planted it in the grave of a man, and for a whole month watered it each evening before sunset with whey in which he had drowned three bats. Then he pulled it up; by this time it looked much more like a man in shape than before. After heating his oven with verbena he dried the root and covered it with a little bag made of a piece of linen. So long as the peasant possessed this root he was lucky in whatsoever he did—he won at play, he found various objects of value, and daily increased in wealth.

Throughout the entire Orient the mandrake is regarded as a valuable talisman, for it is believed that it makes its possessor proof against cut, thrust, and bullet; it is esteemed as an aphrodisiac; since, too, the conviction is held that it can cure its possessor's illnesses and transfer them to others, it is a highly coveted article. Luschan records that at Mersina and Antioch skilful artisans are employed in the trade of working these mandrakes into human shape. By wrapping up the root of the growing plant, and so training it to assume the desired form, surprising results, it is said, are produced, the mandrakes thus grown revealing a most naturalistic resemblance to men. In Mariazell mandrakes were used by the priests at high festivals and sold to pilgrims as 'lucky mannequins.'

A similar image appears in the Habsburg art collection in the Vienna museum: a little black glass figure inserted in a prism of imitation topaz. It was regarded as a "*spiritus familiaris*, which was cast out of one possessed and imprisoned in this glass." Visitors to the imperial treasury at the beginning of the eighteenth century always found this curiosity "touching to look upon." As the greatest rarities could be produced so easily clever forgers devoted themselves to providing examples of the Baphomet for a sensation-seeking public. In the eighteenth century, when secret societies flourished and Freemasonry sprang into fame, historic interest in the Knights Templars awoke, and artists readily seized their opportunity by manufacturing forged antiquities, offering to the public the Baphomet, which was said to have been the idol of the unfortunate Knights and to have been used by them in ceremonies both mysterious and obscene. They made coarse, grotesque figures, fantastic abortions of an imagination rioting in misunderstood symbols. The result was, as always, advantageous to the impudent swindlers. Scholars and laymen alike fell victims to the importunity of active dealers, and an Orientalist such as Joseph von Hammer-Purgstall, widely versed in Eastern studies, was actually persuaded to occupy himself with these alleged idols and their meaning.

V
VOTIVE IMAGES

THE mystery inherent in the primitive belief regarding man's image has produced also the votive image, or *ex voto*. The man who strives to catch in idol, fetish, amulet, or talisman something

of divine power, in order to make use of it for his own protection, has likewise endeavoured at all times to persuade the divinity he worships to be gracious and propitious to him. For this purpose sacrifices serve—especially sacrifices of highly esteemed objects (with Richard Andree we recall here the ring of Polykrates!) and, in an ideal sense, images of the persons making sacrifice, who thereby symbolically present themselves as offerings to the god. This use of the *ex voto* figure is extremely old. In Samuel v and vi a description is given of how the Philistines carried off the Jewish Ark of the Covenant, and of how they were punished therefore by

FIG. 48. FAIENCE FIGURE OF A PRIESTESS OF THE SNAKE-GODDESS IN KNOSSOS, CRETE
About 1800–1600 B.C.

"emerods in their secret parts." They were forced not only to restore the ark, but to provide golden replicas of the affected parts of their bodies—which Luther euphemistically calls "thumbs." Hörnes is inclined to regard as votive in origin the many figures preserved from the Hallstatt and La Tène periods; among them, certainly, there is no lack of unquestionable votive figures. In the sanctuary of the snake-goddess at Knossos, in

68

Crete, great numbers of plastic female votive images of glazed clay were unearthed. They belong to a time which lies some two thousand years before the Christian era, and show the women in a very peculiar national dress which anticipated the hoop petticoat of the rococo period by some four thousand years.

A female figure found at Kličevač, in Serbia, wears a curious dress so similar to that worn by the Knossos dolls that Hörnes suspects that there is a connexion between the two. Dress and ornament on this image of the Bronze Age are carefully indicated by engraving; possibly it also was a votive figure. A whole depot of votive dolls, belonging to the early Mycenæan period, was unearthed in 1913 on the road between Mycenæ and Nemea; among these female board-shaped figures with long dress and the *stephane*, or high headdress, predominated. Bell-shaped figures too have frequently been discovered in Bœotia. In the deepest strata of the Altis of Olympia primitive images of bronze and terra-cotta have been unearthed by the hundred; these are regarded by Furtwängler as *ex voto* figures, since they were found on the altars of Zeus and Hera. Identical figures, childishly clumsy in form, have been discovered in the

FIG. 49. CLAY DOLL FROM A GRAVE OF THE BRONZE AGE NEAR KLIČEVAČ, SERBIA

sanctuary of Asklepios in Epidaurus, in the Temple of Isis at Pompeii, at Vulci, Calvi, Cervetri, and elsewhere. In 1836 the Alpine lake at Monte Falcone yielded nearly seven hundred small bronze votive figures, all male images, with arms outstretched in the ancient gesture of prayer.

Only those votive figures made of clay or metal have been preserved, but the characteristic material for this purpose was wax. According to Macrobius, the gift of a wax image formed a symbolic substitute for the expiatory sacrifice of the whole man, but such images are no longer extant. In earliest times the living man was sacrificed, and this offering was later replaced by the little *ex voto* doll. At the close of the ancient Roman festival of the Saturnalia the citizens were accustomed to give each other presents of these wax and clay figures. Such *sigilla*, at any rate those of clay, have been plentifully preserved; the Louvre and

69

other archæological collections have got dozens of examples. The Roman legend ran that Hercules it was who, after his victory over Geryon, abolished human sacrifice, substituting for it the *argei*, small dolls which, as substitutes for the living persons,

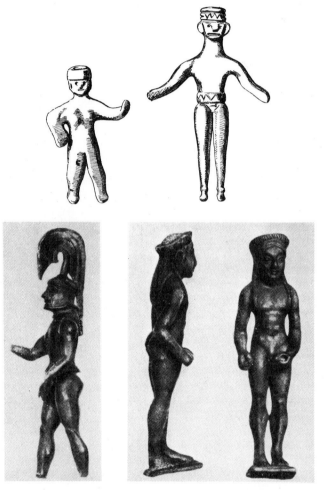

FIGS. 50–52. VOTIVE BRONZES FROM OLYMPIA

were thrown, during the month of May, at full moon, into the Tiber from the Pons Sublicius by the vestals.

The wax offering subsisted throughout the whole of the Middle Ages; so far as Germany is concerned there is documentary proof of it as early as the eleventh century. Just as in the saint-

70

worship of the Christian Church ancient polytheistic images lingered on, the heathen gods merely assuming new masks, so also the tendencies toward sacrifice and self-offering remained alive. The faithful Christian made an image in some precious material of his own body weight, wax, too, because of its costliness, being used for this purpose. The idea repeatedly alluded to of image-power, of the superstitions associated with the human figure, led also, by the material sacrifice, to the preservation of the gift as an efficacious thing since it had taken the form of the human body. To this connexion of ideas the votive doll owed its origin, and the desire to make the image as true and lifelike as possible imparted a naturalistic style to wax sculpture. Portraiture in wax, as I. von Schlosser has emphasized, moved in a peculiar *milieu*, conditioned by its association with the Church, in which ancient demonic conceptions are strangely bound up with ecclesiastical and secular pomp. Superstition, seizing its opportunity, here clad itself in its richest raiment.

FIG. 53. VOTIVE FIGURE, MIDDLE OF SEVENTEENTH CENTURY

Upper Bavarian. Modern wax casting from the original mould

Photo Delia

The miracle books mention wax offerings taking the form of human figures—men, women, and children —some as heavy as twelve pounds. Commonplace gifts of pure wax were remelted and made into candles, but the presentations of princes, in their armour or rich dress, were often carefully preserved. When in 1398 the son of Philip the Bold, Duke of Burgundy, was bitten by a mad dog the distracted father, in order to avert ill consequences, set up an image of his son's weight in the church at Vienne. At Paris in 1389 King Charles VI of France ordered Dino Raspondi to make a life-size wax image in his likeness to be placed on the grave of the blessed Petrus of Luxembourg at Avignon. The artist received 360 gold francs for his work, a sum that would represent a small fortune in our times. In 1466 Queen Anne caused wax figures of herself and her daughter to be set up before the gracious image of the Lady of Cléry. When in 1478

71

Lorenzo de' Medici luckily escaped a conspirator's dagger he got life-size wax images of himself, each different from the other, but all magnificently dressed, placed in three separate Florentine churches.

The erecting of magnificent votive figures became literally a mania in the later Middle Ages—not only Popes, emperors, and kings, but ordinary citizens and peasants set up their life-size plastic replicas in those churches and chapels with which they were connected. In 1518 Ottheinrich, Count Palatine of the Rhine, presented a life-size wax figure of himself to the church of St Wolfgang on the Obersee. The church, however, which won greatest fame in this regard was the church of the Servites— SS. Annunziata—in Florence. The churches of Orsanmichele and the Madonna delle Grazie also possessed numerous *boti*, as these figures were called in the Florentine dialect, but they could not vie with SS. Annunziata. The oldest examples there went back to the thirteenth century; even in the fourteenth century the church was so overstocked that further additions had to be prohibited. The cloth-clad figures, some of them on horseback, hung on cords attached to the roof or stood on pedestals and consoles. Covered with dust and decayed, eaten by moths and mice, they must have presented a miserable spectacle.

The flourishing of this art came in the fifteenth and sixteenth centuries, when the figures were made of canes over a wooden frame, with wax face and hands. These were dressed in cloth and painted. Orsino de Benintendi, whom Vasari praises as a modeller in wax, received for each one of his figures twenty-five gold ducats. The sculptor Montorsoli, a pupil of Michelangelo, and Benvenuto Cellini, who made a wax figure for the Cardinal of Ravenna in 1548, gained great fame in this style. Pietro Tacca made an image of the Grand Duke Cosimo II, who died in 1621, in so lifelike a manner, with crystal eyes, real hair, beard, and eyebrows, that his mother could not bear to look on it.

At the beginning of the seventeenth century the Florentine church of the Servites possessed 600 life-size *boti* and countless smaller ones. Since these seriously impaired the appearance of the church and formed a menace to visitors, for the rotting cords could no longer bear the weight of the figures, which came crashing down and caused much damage, they were then removed, but the custom did not disappear. The church of S. Maria delle Grazie in Mantua still possesses a similar collection, but its figures are of *papier mâché* and make no claim to artistic perfection.

Life-size clothed wax figures were still being offered a short time ago at the church of the Fourteen Saints at Lichtenfels. Special attention there is devoted to lifelikeness in appearance, the illusion being increased by the dress. These figures are preserved in glass cases. The offering of smaller votive figures has not yet ceased, but they are no longer moulded solidly as before, but are hollow, and the material used contains more tallow than wax. Some moulds for such wax figures are very ancient; in spite of their antiquated modes, they have outlived the centuries. Richard Andree and his wife discovered in the stock of the Court waxmoulder Ebenböck, in Munich, moulds which belonged to the seventeenth century and were still in general use. While wax was certainly the commonest material employed for the making of these votive figures it was not the only substance used; pious souls have also utilized gold and silver for this purpose. The Elector Charles Albert of Bavaria—who later became Emperor Charles VII—set up in 1736 a silver statue of his first-born prince at Alt-Ötting. Its weight corresponded to that of the body of the boy, who was then eight years old. Children are often to be found among these votive figures, either because children were desired or because it was thought that living children would be protected by means of this 'betrothal' to a sacred spot. In earliest times these children were always represented as babies in swaddling clothes, or, as they are called in Southern Germany, *Falschkind*. Except for the head every vestige of human shape

FIG. 54. THE IRON MAN OF BUTTEN-WIESEN
Augsburg Museum

has vanished; the poor little creature is done up in a parcel, body, arms, and legs strapped tightly and condemned to complete immobility. An ancient votive figure of this kind is the famous *Santissimo Bambino* of the church of Ara Cœli in Rome, an object greatly reverenced by Catholics and possessing its own little cart on which it is borne to invalids who desire its aid.

Costly *ex voto* figures were, of course, unobtainable by less opulent folk, who had to make use of simpler materials. In Bavarian villages iron, which was itself of greater value than it is now, was much used for this purpose. These votive figures, of both men and animals, are, with a few exceptions, always forged; sometimes they are cut from sheet-iron, but are hardly ever moulded. When the village blacksmith was called on to prepare them they were worked out pretty roughly, with the lineaments of the body barely suggested. Men are naked, women are recognizable by their long clothes, and sometimes the sexual features are heavily accentuated, no doubt because it was believed that the *ex voto* figures could alleviate 'secret' pain. So far as the models are concerned the tradition has remained stationary, the more so because the primitive technique

FIG. 55 SACRIFICIAL IRON MAN
Found near St Leonhard, in Lavanttale, Austria

FIG. 56. SACRIFICIAL IRON FIGURE OF A WOMAN
Found near St Leonhard, in Lavanttale, Austria

FIG. 57 SACRIFICIAL IRON FIGURE (LOWER BAVARIA)
'Captive of St Leonard'

FIG. 58. SACRIFICIAL WOODEN FIGURE OF A MAN
Drei Ähren

permits hardly any thought of progress. Thus a number of the extant examples appear certainly to be antiques, and there are coarsely fashioned specimens, such as the great iron man of Buttenwiesen, in Augsburg, which have been accepted by anti-quarians as prehistoric house gods. As a matter of fact, as Richard Andree has shown, the oldest of these iron figures belong to the later Middle Ages. In no respect, as their appear-ance leads us to conjecture, do they reach back to the beginnings of art; it is only that the creative process, which remains the same over long centuries, has produced identical results. A decline is first marked when the figures are no longer forged, but are cut, silhouette-fashion, out of sheet-iron. To-day it often happens that such an image is borrowed at a price for the ordination, and then is returned to the sexton after the festival.

The most interesting pieces of this kind are the so-called 'Captives of St Leonard,' male figures with forged rings and chains, representing a peculiarly close fettering to that saint who had been revered since the twelfth century. The average size is from 10 to 12 cm., but there existed larger ones of 40 to 50 cm. high. These large and coarse *ex voto* figures became in time connected with all kinds of superstitions. They are called 'Leonard's louts' or else *Würdinger*, after an Aigen family of that name who possessed a remarkable example, a knight in armour and helmet, 145 kg. in weight and 78 cm. high. When Richard Andree wrote his book in 1904 there were still at Aigen six such 'Leonard's louts,' rough-bodied figures, 40 to 50 cm. high and 30 to 50 kg. in weight. They served then as tests of strength and conscience for the country lads. He who desired to be protected from illness during the following year had, at St Leonard's festival, to lift one such 'lout' up to his shoulders and then throw it backward to the ground. For this there was required not only a great muscular strength, but also an innocence of all the deadly sins, for only the pure could pass the test.

VI

FUNERAL AND OTHER IMAGES

THE ancestor image, as we saw, is rightly to be regarded as the oldest doll form; this leads logically to the idol, and from that on to the fetish, the amulet, the talisman, and the votive figure. It all started at the grave regarded as a guide to the unknown world beyond. The grave, however, has produced still another creation likewise connected with death—the grave image. The idea of dualism of body and soul developed late among primitive peoples, who refused to see in death merely the final cessation of life. Primitive man was unable to rise to the conception that after death all is done with; instead, in face of his helplessness, he set up an ideal philosophy which granted to the soul a wandering and a future life. He considered those who had passed away as still living, and as a result the earliest cult of the dead is nothing but a continuation of social duties across the great barrier. The beginnings of the ritualistic cult of the dead reach back in Europe to the Palæolithic Age; in the East it is a later development. Up to the present day this cult has been maintained in some districts in its original form of the sacrifice, which was determined by wholly concrete, earthly ideas. The soul of the departed in its wanderings through the other world, it was thought, could not do without that which in the widest sense was necessary for its nourishment and existence here. Because of this there was presented to it clothing, weapons, and ornament—and not only these, but women, servants, slaves, and horses, which followed the corpse to the grave. In the Assyria of pre-Babylonian times we know that at the burial of kings rich sacrifices of men and animals were offered up. In prehistoric Germany slaves were killed at the obsequies of nobles and rich men so that they might serve their masters in the other world; thus many of his servants were burned with Sigurd's body. The dying Brunhild commanded five girls and eight noble boys, their foster-brothers, to escort her to the other world. In 1314, at the funeral rites of a Lithuanian grand duke, his horse, his favourite servant, and three captive German knights were burned alive on the pyre which consumed his corpse. The same custom was known in the Greek heroic period. Homer describes how at the burial of Patroclus twelve Trojans were slain so that they might accompany the hero's soul in the other world as attendant spirits. The Vikings, too, set their dead sea-kings in burning ships, together with followers, horses, and hounds. Herodotus, writing about 450 B.C., declares that even the Scythians beyond the Pontus followed this custom. At the burial of one of their princes the dead man's concubines, his cup-bearer, his equerry, and fifty of his best servants together with their horses were strangled and appointed as a retinue for the dead man.

This gruesome custom ruled throughout the whole world. Wives and servants in crowds followed the Peruvian Incas to their death; it is alleged that about a thousand dependents of his family and house were slain on the demise of Huayna Capac. In many provinces of Peru not only were weapons and treasures buried with prominent persons, but their wives were buried alive or else hanged themselves by their own hair. At the death of Atahuallpa his wives and servants refused to allow the privilege of following their lord voluntarily to the other world to be taken from them. In the Congo, according to Kund, no man of importance could die without the slaughter of wives and slaves to serve him in the other world. Often enough the number of these unfortunate persons is said to have reached a hundred or more.

In China the voluntary or, if that could not be secured, the enforced death offering of living persons endured till late in historic times. Probably introduced by the Tartars, it was practised first, according to Chinese records, about the year 768 B.C. in the Tsin district. Prince Ts'in Ou-Kong, who died in 678 B.C., ordered sixty-six of his household to follow him to the other world. At the death of his son and successor Mou-Kong the number of sacrificed persons amounted to 174 of the retinue, besides three heroes of noble birth chosen by lot. The songs in which the folk bewailed the cruel fate of these victims still survive. Emperor Chin Shih Huang Ti, who reigned from 246 to 210 B.C., commanded all who belonged to his Court to be killed after his death and laid in his grave. People of high rank ordered at least their favourite concubines to be buried alive with them. It is reported that at the death of very prominent persons hundreds to thousands of living people had to share their fate. The two travellers Huc and Gabet in their wanderings through Mongolia noted that at the burial of princes or chieftains a great crowd of their relations had to be ready to serve them in the other world. The prettiest children were selected and made to swallow quicksilver until they died, preference being given to this kind of death because the miserable human sacrifice retained

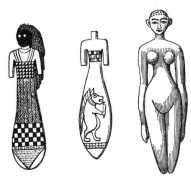

FIG. 59. ANCIENT EGYPTIAN GRAVE DOLLS

thus its fresh colours. Their bodies, equipped with fans, pipes, and other articles of their service, were placed round the body of the dead prince.

Without going further it is evident that suchlike customs must be fatal to all social life. When on each occasion of death a large part of the movable possessions of the deceased was rendered useless by being placed in the grave, and so many servants were killed outright (in such low estimation was held the value of human life), the very existence of civilization was imperilled. Very soon, therefore, a means was sought of substituting a symbolic for a real death sacrifice. No longer was genuine money placed in the grave, but in its stead coins of pressed tin, such as are still to be found in Greek graves. In place of the massive offerings of gold, such as Schliemann, for example, dug up in Mycenæ, recourse was had to gilded paper or clay, and in place of slaughtered women, slaves, or even free-born persons the graves were filled with dolls.

The soil of ancient Egypt, being dry enough to preserve such objects unimpaired through centuries, has yielded the richest treasure-trove of these grave images. From the Vth Dynasty images of servants, generally in considerable numbers, are to be found in the Egyptian graves. During the period of the New Kingdom

FIG. 60. EGYPTIAN WOODEN DOLL FROM A MUMMY'S COFFIN

FIG. 61 EGYPTIAN IVORY DOLL

(1600 to 1100 B.C.) these figures were produced in the mass. They are stamped in clay, carved in wood, covered with stucco and painted, made of limestone and alabaster, often inlaid with pieces of coloured glass, embossed in copper, produced in diverse materials and of every quality. The shape is cursorily defined, the resemblance to human forms being just suggested; indeed it seems that no real attempt is made to imitate it. The little female figures, supposed to represent the concubines of the deceased, are made generally of flat wooden

FIG. 62. EGYPTIAN WOODEN STATUETTES—PRIEST AND PRINCESS
End of XVIIIth Dynasty
Cairo Museum

boards painted conventionally with wood beads for hair and no legs, "so as not to be able to run away." In the grave, unearthed in 1919 at Thebes, of Mehenkwetre, a landed proprietor and chancellor of Pharaoh, belonging to the XIth Dynasty, about 2000 B.C., were found many dozens of these dolls. There were small ships with crews for fishing, passenger boats, a carpenter's workshop, a stall for cattle, a slaughter-house, shepherds, and other representations of what had been the dead man's property on earth, and which now accompanied him to the kingdom of the dead as substitutes for the riches left behind—all giving the illusory impression of toys, yet not created for that purpose.

79

DOLLS

The *ushabti* figure served as a substitute for the soul of the dead. In the Middle Kingdom this is usually a portrait image of the deceased, taking the form of the enshrouded mummy. Only the head and hands, which hold whip and staff, are free. The *ushabti* figure may be of gold or bronze, but usually it is made of glazed clay. These images have a magical significance. In the other world they were supposed to undertake any work demanded of the dead man. In *The Book of the Dead* the deceased, speaking to his *ushabti*, is thus introduced:

> O Image, if I be summoned and appointed to do any work whatsoever of the labours which are done in the underworld, and if at any time I be appointed to sow the fields, to fill the watercourses with water, to bring the sands from the East to the West, then do you say: "Here am I."

The custom of providing *ushabti* figures for the dead was so deeply rooted that even those Egyptians who embraced Christianity, instead of renouncing it, preserved it in slightly altered form. In the graves of Akhmim Panopolis, belonging to the period from the fourth to the seventh century, are to be found tin figures $4\frac{1}{2}$ cm. high, representing Lazarus shrouded in bands. He serves as a funeral symbol of the Resurrection.

FIG. 63. EGYPTIAN "USHABTI" FIGURE IN FAIENCE

No other land, even distantly, can be compared with Egypt in respect to riches of this kind, but it is probable that this is due to the nature of the soil, especially adapted for the preservation of perishable objects; other ground of a less favourable condition would not protect them in the same way. The Greeks certainly knew the use of the grave image, for graves of the archaic period have yielded little figures, similar to those of the Egyptians, engaged in all kinds of useful work—stamping corn, kneading dough, and baking bread. Among them are female mourners, others with pitchers, and still others making music with flute or tympanon, and so on. Archæologists believe that these terracottas formed a substitute for the retinue which the deceased had in life, serving instead of the human sacrifice customary in the heroic period. Some classical scholars, such as Adolf Furtwängler and Robert Schmidt, treat even the Tanagra

FIG. 64. BARBER
Terra-cotta grave figure
from Tanagra

FIG. 65. HANDWORKER
Terra-cotta grave figure
from Tanagra

FIG. 66. HOUSEMAID
Grave doll from Eretria

figures, which have so rapidly and so justly become famous, as genuine grave images.

FIG. 67. WALKING GIRL
Terra-cotta from Tanagra
Sabouroff Collection

FIG. 68. GIRL WITH HAT
Terra-cotta from Tanagra
Sabouroff Collection

Greek clay sculpture flourished in Corinth, Thisbe, Megara, and Myrina; it was a considerable article of export to the Crimea, Crete, and other neighbouring localities. Since the seventies of the last century Tanagra, in Bœotia, has been added to the already known centres of manufacture, and, because of the high artistic quality of its ware, it has cast all the others into the shade, since 1873–74 the necropolis on the Kokkali hill near that city having yielded many of those little figures which in refinement of form, in easy grace, and in elegance of appearance have not been surpassed even by the porcelain art of the eighteenth century. In

FIG. 69. GIRL
Terra-cotta from Tanagra
Sabouroff Collection

the first enthusiasm for this newly discovered source of antique beauty it was believed that we had here to do with products of the age of Praxiteles, but a critical examination of style and technique has served to remove the Tanagra figures from these by a century. They could hardly have existed before the first half of the third century B.C., and so belong to the period of Hellenism; although Furtwängler is perfectly right in saying that they are the finest extant specimens of Greek art after the time of Alexander the Great.

Like other Greek terra-cottas, they were shaped in moulds, with freely modelled heads and limbs joined on separately. The lines of these Tanagra figures are particularly fresh and sharp; one can see how the clothing has been worked over with the modelling stick. The cold colours are carefully and tastefully conceived. The subjects are generally beautiful girls in the bloom of youth; boys and young men appear but rarely. All move on the border-line between the ideal and reality, borrowing their motives from contemporary pictorial art. The usual subject is a young woman endued with an undeniable charm, sitting or standing, holding in her hand a distaff, a ball, a fan, a mirror, an apple, a letter-board, a bunch of grapes, a mask, a lyre, or some similar object. Within their own limits the modulation and beauty could not be surpassed. The terra-cottas from Myrina, in Asia Minor (second and third centuries B.C.), vie with those of Tanagra. Here special attention was devoted to figures in movement: figures of Eros, goddesses of victory, dancing youths of effeminate appearance, hermaphrodites, satyrs, alongside of many caricatures. Of these Greek

82

GIRL WITH FAN
Terra-cotta from Tanagra
Sabouroff Collection

terra-cottas only a small fraction have been discovered in private houses; the majority were found in graves, so that we are justified in concluding that all of them were grave images.

The Romans shared with the Greeks the custom of making offerings at the grave; among them, indeed, it is authenticated even at the beginning of the imperial period. Most of the extant Roman clay figurines too have been found in graves, some of which contained as many as thirteen pieces. They were manufactured in the mass by hand; in Pompeii shops have been unearthed in which images of this kind were exposed for sale —gods, porters, gladiators, toga-clad citizens, and so on. The custom of the homeland was, of course, carried over to the distant provinces. On the Rhine, especially in the neighbourhood of Mainz, numerous figures of Mars and Mercury, some about 6 to 13 cm. high, made of bronze and silver, and others in a cheaper quality, of white clay, have been unearthed. The workshop of Servandus, which flourished in the second half of the second century at the barley market in Cologne, produced figurines of Bacchus, Venus, Diana, and Mercury which were so popular that

FIG. 70. STATUETTE OF A CHINESE CONJURER
Earthenware. Han Dynasty

they were copied in other districts. The habit of making grave offerings endured into the early Middle Ages, being first condemned as a heathen practice in the Carolingian epoch.

In China, where the death sacrifice was widely practised, the offering of living persons was abolished, then reintroduced, and eventually disappeared completely after the time of Confucius (551–478 B.C.), its place being taken by images. It seems that even before the time when living persons were sacrificed straw or paper images were burned at the funeral and then placed in the grave—a practice that endured up to recent times. The reform instituted by Confucius consisted in the substitution for the human offering of a wooden doll with movable limbs, which was placed in the grave of the deceased. Whereas, too, in the past part of the actual possessions of the dead man was sent to

83

the flames, now men were satisfied with representations in paper of the objects of value. Marco Polo, who visited China about 1280, records this, and speaks too of the male and female paper figures which were burned with the corpse. These once real, but now fictional, offerings spring from fear inspired by the dead man's spirit. Men were convinced that the soul looked around

FIG. 71. SPIRIT CONJURER
Earthenware. Han Dynasty

FIG. 72. A YOUNG MAN
Earthenware. Han Dynasty

for means of subsistence, and that if these were refused it proceeded forcibly to procure them by tormenting the survivors. Consequently, for the sake of their own quiet, men provided the dead man's soul with whatever it might require. On his part, the deceased received a kind of guarantee that his descendants continued to care for him and to make sacrifice to him.

Out of this conception has arisen an artistic activity of high æsthetic value. Beginning under the Han Dynasty (206 B.C. to A.D. 220), and continuing during the Tang period (A.D. 608 to 922), it was barely extinguished before the fourteenth century. These long centuries, of course, have provided a vast quantity of such images; the extant examples number thousands, and presumably only a few of the actual graves have been opened. As in all human affairs, here too vanity entered in. Owing to the custom of exhibiting the grave offerings before the funeral, rivalry among the rich and aristocratic soon made itself evident, until eventually the authorities decided that action must be taken to control these funeral luxuries. In 741 the Tang Emperor Kao Tsung issued an edict prohibiting the use of offerings made of gold, silver, copper, tin, or even wood, only clay objects being permitted. Even the number of offerings was specified : those who stood above the fourth class might be given ninety pieces, those over the sixth class sixty pieces, those over the tenth class forty pieces, while the common people were allowed only fifteen objects. These decrees had the result which comes of all unenforcable laws—they were circumvented, until an edict of 1372 allowed of only one object as a grave offering.

FIG. 73. CHINESE WOMAN IN FESTIVE CLOTHES
Probably Tang Dynasty

While grave sculpture during the period immediately following the Tang era was mostly carried out in wood the Tang figures themselves are of clay, and in the early Ming period the terra-cottas again form an exception. The better-class ware was made of a finely granulated, baked, and glazed clay, executed in various shades. The humbler ware was only roughly baked and left unglazed; this was painted when cold, and sometimes with many colours. Hollow moulds were used for the making of the figures; after the moulding the seams were covered over, but remain visible, the figures being hollow within. Owing to the great demand, there must have been a genuine mass production of these grave images, but there were among the modellers some outstanding artists who introduced an individual style into their work. The wealth of models, so far as forms represented is concerned, is extraordinarily great. All branches of Chinese

85

culture over a period of 1500 years appeared here in countless variations. Among the male figures are horsemen who act as bodyguards in front of and behind the coffin, detachments of

FIG 74. CHINESE WOMEN WITH LOTUS BLOOMS IN THEIR HANDS
Earthenware. Later than Han Dynasty

soldiers in full armour, civilians in respectful attitude, bands of musicians, wrestlers, boxers, clowns, and actors. The forms are naturalistically conceived, and the figures are often shown with dramatically seized attitudes. The love—indeed, we may say the passion—of the artists is, however, for the women, who not only are represented much more frequently than the men (in some graves have been found hundreds of female figures), but are characterized in greater variety. Harem women, dancing girls, servants with fan or spittoon, are here in diverse forms. Often they wear highly fantastic costumes and headdresses, and they are conceived in every possible attitude; but never are they represented as naked. The artists have brilliantly delineated the peculiarly charming and rich dresses and gestures of these women. *Così fan tutte* beyond death and the grave. The gleam of the varnish preserves their coquettish laughter and the unfathomable glance of their hollow eyes—a strange escort on the way to eternity. Another class is consecrated to divinities whose duty it is to protect the grave from demons and the corpse from the defilement of evil spirits. These so-called guardian gods for the most part are fashioned in grotesque, and occasionally in bizarrely contorted, forms. In Japan too, the culture of which is closely allied to that of China, it was the custom on the death of an emperor to bury alive with him his entire retinue. Shikune, under the Emperor Suimin, is said to have been the first, in 24 B.C., to prohibit this practice, substituting for the sacrifice of living persons the offering of clay images.

So far we have been engaged in a sphere where the doll has a magical significance. The *rôle* which fell to its lot as a magical figure was no small one; but it had other important tasks to fulfil in the ordinary life of the citizens—above all in religious cult. Throughout the whole of antiquity the employment of images in divine service was common. As a supreme example of this Schlosser adduces the presentation of the body of Adonis, an originally Oriental divinity, whose worship was celebrated by Greek women in processions where figures of the lovely youth were borne around. At the Roman *lectisternium* the gods were solemnly entertained, figures with wax heads and real clothes taking the place of the divinities. Images, too, were sometimes used for the purpose of executing justice or wreaking vengeance. Thus Trebellius Pollio relates that on one occasion a figure of the usurper Celsus, whose body had been thrown to the dogs, was strung up on the gallows, as a visible symbol to all of the ignominy with which his memory should be regarded. Many centuries later Pope Pius II took a similar revenge on one of his political opponents, Sigismondo Malatesta, of Rimini; failing to capture this man, he got a speaking likeness of him burned with due solemnity in front of St Peter's, Rome.

The symbolic expression of scorn and vengeance by means of the image, when the guilty person is not at hand, has remained alive up to the present day. Gersau was once the smallest Swiss republic and, as a sign of its sovereignty of justice, had a gallows in front of its gate. To annoy their neighbours the Lucerners, on one occasion in the eighteenth century, hanged a straw image on this gallows, but the people of Gersau got the laugh on their side by dressing up the figure as a Lucerner in his official costume. Not long before the outbreak of the War a Russian monk Iliodor, a close rival of Rasputin in sanctity, got a great image dressed in a Jewish caftan to be carried round in processions he organized at Zarytsin. Ulrich von Wilamowitz-Möllendorf in his reminiscences relates that when he visited Schulpforta, about 1860, a straw figure dressed like a scarecrow was made by the third-form boys at the conclusion of the autumn examinations and then was carried round the building on a pole as the 'examiner.' In January 1929 the English League against Imperialism held a meeting in London at which Saklatvala, the Communist member in the House of Commons, "protested" against the "activities of British Imperialism in Afghanistan" and against the part played there by Colonel Lawrence under the guise of Aircraftsman Shaw. Amid the acclamations of the audience a life-size image representing Colonel Lawrence was burned.

The trade in clay images at Rome was very large; whole streets were occupied by their manufacturers, and there were special markets where they were sold. Because of the great demand they were usually made in moulds over a wood base or left hollow; when, as was rare, they were formed by hand the figures were made solid. During the excavations at Pompeii, according to Kekule, it was noticed that these small clay images were not to be found in the more opulent houses; the palaces in the Strada di Mercurio and the Strada di Nola contained hardly an example worth speaking of. The nearer an approach is made to the excavations in the Strada Stabiana, which was the centre of the industrial and commercial life of the city, the richer become the discoveries. A mass of heterogeneous cheap ware was unearthed in the dwellings of the slaves, many more in the barracks of the gladiators and in the poorer houses. It is rather touching to note that in the confusion of the city's ruin the people in their flight sometimes snatched up nothing but their clay dolls; among the bodies found in the Foro Triangolare were unearthed clay figures which they had taken with them in preference to all their other goods.

Aristocrats and rich people were not content with the cheap clay figures; they got great wax images made, clad in real garments. According to the statement left by Kallixenus concerning the *pompa* of Ptolemy Philadelphus, there were in the King's pavilion groups of such figures, representing ancient actors, placed in separate niches. These images seem to have been indispensable, especially at the obsequies of distinguished people. The custom originated from the practice of exhibiting the corpse to the public gaze for some time (in Rome, for example, seven days) before the burial or cremation—a practice which, in warm climates, necessitated special precautions. Thus, just as the Egyptian mummies were furnished with portrait-masks, death-masks were put on the faces of corpses in Nineveh, Phœnicia, Carthage, Greece, and Italy. These were made of bronze, iron, or clay—in Mycenæ even of gold. In Cumæ a grave of the Diocletian period was unearthed containing two skeletons which, in place of the heads belonging to them, had wax heads fitted with glass eyes. A remarkable parallel is provided by the mummies from the New Hebrides preserved in the Berlin Völker-Museum. The bodies of bamboo, moss, and bark, painted in naturalistic colours, bear real human heads. On the island of Bali, even at the present time, it is customary to burn corpses, but as this is expensive they are often allowed to remain lying for a considerable time; in the tropic climate, however, they rapidly decompose, and a palm-leaf image is burned in their stead. This custom is in use also for those who die far from their homes. Great solemn funerals, especially of kings and princes, demanded long preparations and such a lapse of time as often led to the decomposition of the body. Wherefore from the merely masked corpse a step was taken toward the image representing the dead man and magnificently arrayed. On the great Diplyon vase found at Athens, belonging to a period between 1000 and 800 B.C., it is clear that the artist has depicted a funeral procession bearing a corpse wrapped in cloths on a hearse, while the dead man is represented once more as an image lying on his death-bed.

This custom the Romans inherited from the Greeks. At Cæsar's funeral, according to Appian, the statue of the murdered man was made of wax; it showed the twenty-three bleeding wounds inflicted by the conspirators, and was so contrived as to turn to all sides during the processional march. At the funeral rites of Germanicus the body was unobtainable, and accordingly a clothed wooden image with a wax head was substituted for it. At the entombment of Pertinax there were two images of the Emperor, representing him respectively as awake and asleep; pages warded off the flies from these just as if he had been living.

DOLLS

Ammianus Marcellinus, in describing the obsequies for the son of the Chionite king, Grumbates, who had fallen in the year A.D. 359 before Amida, tells how the prince lay on a high catafalque, surrounded by ten biers with figures representing his retainers.

Imperial Rome bequeathed this 'funeral sculpture,' as a prerogative of the high aristocracy, to the Middle Ages; during the feudal period it survived even the most violent political turmoils. England and France are the two countries where these peculiar funeral ceremonials, when for the corpse is substituted an image, were raised to a fine art. To these rites belong, too, those connected with the *chambre de parade*, in which the image was put on a bier, the table set, and the food served daily before the burial. Since the lord was treated as though he were still alive, every attempt was made to render the image as naturalistic and lifelike as possible. The figures were life-size, the bodies made of wickerwork, hard-boiled leather, oak, and, in order to reduce the weight, left hollow, with straw over a wooden base and the whole covered with stucco.

FIG. 75. FUNERAL FIGURE OF KING EDWARD III OF ENGLAND (*d.* 1377)
Westminster Abbey

FIG. 76. FUNERAL FIGURE OF QUEEN CATHERINE DE VALOIS
Westminster Abbey

Head and hands were of coloured wax; arms were generally movable. Hair and beard were provided, and the figures were dressed in garments from the dead man's wardrobe. There is documentary evidence for the use of these figures from the first half of the fourteenth century, but the earliest extant example is that of King Edward III of England, who died in 1377. A large collection of such figures, so far, at any rate, as England is concerned, is preserved in the Islip Chapel at Westminster Abbey, where their tattered appearance has given them the nickname of 'the ragged regiment.' Clad in their State robes, they stand in glass cases—kings and queens and other historical celebrities such as Cromwell, Pitt, and

90

Lord Nelson in the uniform he wore at Trafalgar. They would have been of great value for the history of costume had they not been restored, but when James I visited Westminster Abbey in 1606 along with his brother-in-law, King Christian of Denmark, the dean got all the existent figures newly clad, a procedure that was repeated in the eighteenth century. Queen Elizabeth, for example, whose costume must have been exceedingly interesting, was entirely redressed in 1760.

In France there is documentary evidence for the use of the funeral image from the death of King Charles VI in 1422. At the obsequies of Henry II, who died from a wound received in a tournament, the King's image, set on a throne, was carried round in a procession lasting several days. These figures came from the hands of artists: Jean Perréal made those of Louis XII and Queen Anne, François Clouet those of Francis I and Henry II. When Henry IV was murdered three sculptors immediately set to work. Malherbe saw one of the examples, and described it as similar to "the bodies made like dolls in the Palais"—that is to say, like a mannequin of the fashion shop then established in the Palais de Justice. The head and hands were of wax, realistically formed: the dress a red silk vest and a royal mantle of purple velvet embroidered with golden lilies; crown, sceptre, and *main de justice* were also provided. This image lay in state for eleven days. Twice daily meals were brought to it by officers of the Crown, these being subsequently given to the poor. Louis XIII was the last monarch to have his death solemnized with this great funeral pomp in the olden style. The custom was revived when the dissolute Marat was stabbed on July 13, 1793, by the dagger of Charlotte Corday. On that occasion there was exhibited, not the hideous corpse of the incurable leper, but an image made by the famous painter David.

The images of the English kings were preserved in Westminster Abbey; those of the French monarchs were kept in Saint-Denis. There the German travel-writer Johann Jakob Volkmann saw the whole series of funeral images from Charles VIII to Louis XIII, clad in ermine mantles, crowns on their heads and sceptres in their hands, sitting large as life, on chairs in glass cases. During the Revolution the iconoclastic rage of the mob destroyed these remarkable relics, the head of Henry IV alone surviving the ruin; this is now preserved as a bust in the Musée Condé at Chantilly. The high aristocracy and the clergy followed the example of the Court. When, for instance, the obsequies of the two Guise brothers, murdered in the Château de Blois by command of Henry III, were solemnized at Toulouse in 1588, three different images of the Duke and of the Cardinal respectively were exhibited to the public. One represented them as they were being murdered; in another they knelt in prayer; and in the third they lay on the catafalque. These images are said to have been on show at Toulouse for a long time.

Other countries too followed this custom. The doges of Venice down to the last, who died in 1797, were honoured in the same way. When the celebrated painter Elisabetta Sirani died at Bologna in 1665—of poison, as it was believed—a full figure of the artist sitting at her easel was shown at her funeral in the church of S. Domenico. Frederick William I of Prussia himself, who hated all foreign things, and in particular detested the French from the bottom of his heart, did not escape this foreign ritual. When he was buried at Potsdam in 1740, there was exhibited in the *chambre de parade* an easy chair on which was placed "the likeness in wax of the highest-souled king." The last known example seems to have been that of King Victor Emmanuel of Italy. In January 1878 a life-size wax image of the dead monarch, leaning against a wall in a room of the Quirinal, was exhibited at his funeral.

VII

WAXWORKS AND THE MANNEQUIN

FROM these exhibitions developed the waxworks, for it was but a step from this spectacular art of the aristocracy to the booth art at the annual fairs of the people. This descent, if so it be called, carried to extremity that desire for naturalistic representation which has been associated with the wax image from the very start. Those engaged in this work did not seek merely for a reflection of reality; their object was complete illusion. The votive figures had this quality; it was emphasized too in the funeral image; and the waxworks simply carry this almost painful tendency toward naturalism, to use Schlosser's happy phrase, "to the verge of indiscretion." The lineaments are represented in such detail (down even to the small hairs of the beard), and such a startling lifelikeness is aimed at, that there can be no possibility of any æsthetic appreciation. The oldest panopticons were the churches, with their naturalistically reproduced votive figures. The first genuine secular collection of life-size wax figures was that shown at the Doolhof in Amsterdam, apparently as early as the sixteenth century. There there were groups and single figures, among them William the Silent, Henry IV of France, Gustavus Adolphus (and, later, Queen Christina and Cromwell), who were gazed at in astonishment by travellers as great spectacles.

Works of art so well calculated to suit the popular taste appeared as profitable business propositions to the promoters themselves. Among the itinerants in Germany were many who travelled about with wax figures which they exhibited for money. In 1605 a certain Ambrosius Müller, of Erfurt, wished to show at Nürnberg the figures, "made in wax," of John Huss, Luther, and Melanchthon, but the magistrates packed him off, "since there have been idols enow here already." In the following year Christoph Gagler, of Klagenfurt, fared no better with his "idol work." At Paris in 1611 François de Bechefer got up a similar show, in which was to be seen the lately murdered King Henry IV. Here we come on that element of the horrible which seems to have formed so great an attraction of these waxworks from that time onward. This interest in the waxworks went along with a fashion in Society circles for portraiture in wax. In the seventeenth and eighteenth centuries those who could pay for it liked not only to be painted, but to be moulded in wax; the life-size figures dressed in real clothes exercised apparently an extraordinary fascination. Antoine Benoist, wax-embosser to Louis XIV, became famous for his life-size portrait in wax of Queen Anne of Austria with her Court ladies. They were represented as standing, richly clad, "for all persons of rank deemed it an honour to honour the artist with their finest clothes for this purpose." Considerable numbers of images of this kind have been preserved in various art-historical collections; thus Peter the Great is shown in the Hermitage at Leningrad, and the great Prince Elector King Frederick I in Schloss Monbijou, where, too, may be found some children's toys belonging to a Hohenzollern prince who died in infancy. From the end of the seventeenth century comes the wax figure of Luther, still to be seen, clad in the dress of a Protestant minister, in the Marienkirche at Halle. He sits before a table, his clenched hand placed on a Bible; formerly he wore a peruke, but this has now been replaced by a cap. On the death of Frederick the Great Johann Eckstein made two wax figures of that monarch, although these were no longer used for a funeral parade. One of them went to the Hohenzollern Museum; the other, clad in the uniform worn by the King in the Seven Years War, went to Brunswick.

In Paris during the second half of the seventeenth century there must have been several waxwork collections open, on payment, to the public, for the aforesaid Antoine Benoist in 1668 succeeded in securing from the king a special privilege for his waxworks, a privilege which was renewed from time to time and in 1718 continued in favour of his son for a period of twenty years. Unless there had been competition such a privilege would not have been required. A wax-sculptor of uncommon talents was Johann C. Creutz, who, since he lived in Paris, called himself Curtius. He was specially renowned for the marvellous anatomical models in wax which he executed with a master's hand. In 1783 he opened his waxworks, in which the Caverne des Grands Voleurs provided a special attraction for a novelty-seeking public. On July 12, 1789, his exhibition was stormed by the mob, and the busts of Necker and the Duc d'Orléans were carried off to be borne in triumph through Paris. The artist got his niece, Marie Grosholtz, to come to Paris, where he instructed her in his art; she modelled many heads

WAXWORKS AND THE MANNEQUIN

after the life, and gave lessons to Mme Élizabeth, the sister of Louis XVI. In the year 1794 she married a certain M. Tussaud, from whom she was separated six years later. In 1802 she moved to London, taking with her the whole of her uncle's vast collection. Tussaud's waxworks, carried on by the son, grandson, and great-grandson of the foundress, has remained one of the chief spectacles in London for well over a century, the Chamber of Horrors in especial forming a centre of attraction, the interest of which is augmented with every new murder. The original collection was destroyed by a great fire in 1925. After reconstruction the exhibition was reopened in 1928.

At the same period that Curtius opened his panopticon in Paris the Hofstatuarius Müller, who was in actuality a Count Deym of Stritež, founded his show in Vienna at the Stock im Eisen. It included all the celebrities of the time—the entire royal family, the potentates of Christendom—Frederick II, Catherine of Russia, Louis XVI, Marie-Antoinette, the Dauphin, and others. It gained additional brilliance from a number of *galant* automata in such settings as the bedroom of the Graces. The artist died in 1804, but his collection survived him. The Musée Grévin, in Paris, and Castan's panopticon, in Berlin, have retained their popularity right down to the present time. Up

FIG. 77. MANNEQUIN OF TUT-ENCH-AMUN

End of XVIIIth Dynasty (about 1350 B.C.). From *Tut-ench-Amun*, by Carter and Mace

Photo Harry Burton

to about 1880 wax sculpture was practised as a free art in Mexico, where *mestizos* at the annual fairs improvised wax figures. These were painted and clothed and sold at moderate prices. In 1878 A. Montanari brought a selection to the Paris exhibition, where they were much admired on account of the peculiar vigour of their style.

These wax figures always move "on the threshold of art"—one step more and we arrive at the mannequin. The invention of the dress-doll used by tailors to aid them in trying on dresses, and serving as an excellent advertisement in fashion shops because of the exact fit of the clothes, has been ascribed, but wrongly so, to Poppæa, the beloved of Nero. She was not needed

95

to invent it, for this useful article was in existence long before her time. In the grave of Tut-ench-Amun, dating from about the year 1350 B.C., there was discovered, alongside the great carved, gilded, and painted death image of the King, his dress-figure sharply cut off at the middle and above the elbows. This is life-size and is painted white, obviously to suggest a shirt; unquestionably it was used to try on Pharaoh's garments. Near by in the grave was found the dress-chest. When the tyranny of Galeazzo Maria Sforza, Duke of Milan, became at last too terrible to be endured a conspiracy was formed among the aristocracy, as a result of which he was murdered in 1476 in the church of S. Gottardo. So as to be absolutely certain of success, these conspirators practised on the Duke's dress-figure. The popularity of these mannequins has not waned. Edmond de Goncourt knew a French duke who possessed twenty-five mannequins, on which all his wardrobe was set out so that his suits should not take on false forms or creases. The masters of the *grande couture*, whether they are settled in Paris, in London, or in Berlin, keep mannequins of their foreign customers on which they can execute their orders.

FIG. 78. LIMBED DOLL, FROM THE BEGINNING OF THE SIXTEENTH CENTURY

Erroneously ascribed to Dürer

Closest akin to the mannequin is the lay figure, the aid of the prentice painter and sculptor. It is difficult to determine its age, but it is first mentioned in Filarete's work on architecture, written about 1460. In Germany it does not appear before Dürer's time. These lay figures were of various sizes. Vasari relates that Fra Bartolommeo got a life-size wooden figure made in order to study the folds of drapery; this interesting object is still preserved in the Accademia delle Belle Arti at Florence. G. B. Armenino, of Faenza, and Bernardino Campi, of Cremona, both of whom wrote in the second half of the sixteenth century, give plentiful instructions concerning the manufacture and use of these modelling figures. The smallest kinds were employed by painters engaged in sketching out compositions containing many figures, so that they might get an impression of the physical reality, carry through difficult foreshortenings in the building up of groups, and regulate the positions of single figures so as to give a clear idea of distance. Such things could not be studied so easily on the living model—at any rate when a view

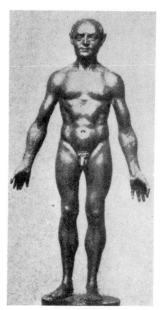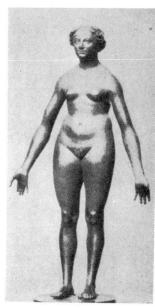

FIGS. 79, 80. GERMAN PROPORTION FIGURES CARVED FROM WOOD
Frankish work, about 1530
Hofmuseum, Vienna

from below was desired. Paolo Uccello, in the first half of the fifteenth century, was said to have employed little horses of this kind for his battle scenes. These figures were usually modelled in clay and then cast in wax from a mould; by kneading and bending they could be put into any attitude desired. Drapery was represented by wet paper or pieces of cloth. Perugino was said to have ordered the figures he required from Sansovino, who also made the models for those of Andrea del Sarto. Antonio Begarelli, a celebrated clay-modeller, was credited with having made the little figures required by Correggio when he was engaged in painting the cathedral dome at Parma. Michelangelo himself, it is said, employed such figures when engaged on *The Last Judgment* in the Sistine Chapel. Tintoretto

97

carried out his studies in light by aid of small clay and wax figures made and dressed by himself. From him his talented pupil El Greco acquired the habit of working with figures; Pacheco recounts that he saw in the master's *atelier* in Toledo a whole cupboard of figures which had been made by the artist himself.

FIG. 81. THE PAINTER IN HIS STUDIO
Ostade
Dresden Art Gallery

Since these painters' lay figures were made of clay or wax they must have been immovable, but the extant modelling figures of the sixteenth century are of wood and have movable limbs. The German examples have been ascribed to Albrecht Dürer, but wrongly so. It is certainly true that Dürer, on his journey to the Netherlands in 1520, presented "a carved little child" to the Portuguese agent at Antwerp, but this was not necessarily of his own workmanship. The Nürnberg master, as several of his drawings and woodcuts prove, worked much with ball-limbed lay figures, but assuredly he did not make any of these. In the collection of Count Valencia de Don Juan is preserved a small modelling figure, very carefully fashioned of beech-wood, 23 cm. high. Neck, body, arms, and legs, even fingers, toes, and jaws, are movable. An old inscription ascribes it to Dürer. The female counterpart, likewise of beech-wood and likewise movable, in 1864 belonged to Alexander Posonyi in Vienna. This came from the Nürnberg art collection of Paul Praun and was also ascribed to Dürer, but the fact that the proportions do not accord with Dürer's militates against this assumption. Emil Michel suggests Conrad Meyt as

FIG. 82. THE PAINTER WITH TWO LAY FIGURES
D. Chodowiecki
From Basedow's *Elementarbuch*

the maker of the male figure. Another female figure of this kind was preserved in the Leipzig collection of Hans Felix; it was modelled with delicacy of feeling, but its face, with its rigid features, was quite unlike Dürer's. The Kunsthistorische Hof-museum in Vienna possesses three wooden proportion figures, representing man, woman, and child, which Schlosser conjec-tures must have originated in Franconia about 1530. Two wooden modelling figures, 25 cm. high, belonging to the begin-ning of the sixteenth century are also preserved in the Ferdin-andeum at Innsbruck. The most beautiful and masterly of all extant examples are, in the opinion of E. F. Bange, the two beech-wood figures in the possession of the Akademie der bildenden Künste in Berlin. These are 19 cm. high, with ball-joints which render even the fingers and toes movable. Bange suggests that

99

the carver was one of the Regensburg-Salzburg school connected with the master J.P.—possibly even that master himself. The Kaiser-Friedrich-Museum, too, possesses a female wooden specimen of this type in addition to an anatomical male lay figure carved from wood, with movable limbs; the latter probably belongs to the second half of the sixteenth century and is derived from the anatomical figure made by Prospero Bresciano. These objects must have been very common in the Renaissance period; several examples are included in the inventory of Margaret of Austria in 1524. Since they mostly appear in pairs, is it possible that they were amorous toys?

The lay figures have not yet disappeared from the painters' and sculptors' studios. As time passed by they were gradually improved. At Paris in the eighteenth century Anciaume was especially famed for their manufacture. On April 18, 1774, the widow of the copper-plate engraver Gravelot advertised that she had for sale three English lay figures, each $2\frac{1}{2}$ ft high, with copper joints and various coloured costumes.

In spite of the fact that the naturalistically treated wax figure will always remain a difficult problem for the student of æsthetics, it yet has some connexions with fine art. A group of ·Spanish sculptors carried this naturalism to extremes in their plastic work. Endeavouring to secure absolute truth to reality, they aimed not at any artistic impression, but solely at the illusion of immediate realism. The *imagenes de vestir* of the Spanish churches, figures set up at certain ecclesiastical festivals, have this end in view. The sculptor supplied only the head, hands, and feet; the costumes, for the most part over-rich and costly, were made of real cloth and gold embroidery. To secure the realistic impression real hair as well as glass eyes and glass tears were utilized, while the colouring went to extremes in its naturalistic representation of blood and wounds. All the large and many of the smaller Spanish churches possessed sets of such dressed-up images representing the persons connected with or suffering in the Passion; these, arranged in groups, were carried around in the processions of Easter week. They were called a *paso*. The greatest Spanish artists occupied themselves on work of this kind. The *Paso del gran poder* of Montañes and Zarcillo's *paso* in the Ermita de Jesús, Murcia, are works widely famed and reverenced, more closely associated with Spanish feeling than the white marble alone admitted by the æsthetics of the academicians. "This was the last time in Europe," says Sobotka in reference to these works, "that fine art was also a popular art." The highly renowned *Cristo de Burgos* is distinguished by naturalism of the crudest sort; in this cathedral Crucifixion the realistic representation of bleeding and festering wounds is carried to such a disgusting extreme that a legend has arisen to the effect that the figure had a human skin. It is, however, really covered with cured and painted leather—which, to be sure, is bad enough!

FIG. 83. CHRIST ON THE PALM ASS
Carved wood. Lower Bavaria
Kaiser-Friedrich-Museum, Berlin

The contemporary art of sculpture on this side of the Pyrenees did not go to such extremes of naturalism. The figures of the Sacro Monte of Varallo, the Crucifixion of which was executed by Guido Mazzoni under the direction of Gaudenzio Ferrari, are much more tasteful in form and colour. German sculptors too avoided these excesses of the Spaniards. The chief image in the Palm Sunday processions has always been the 'palm ass'—Christ sitting on an ass run on rollers. This group appeared at Augsburg as early as the time of St Ulrich, who died in 973, but all the extant examples in public collections belong to the fourteenth and sixteenth centuries. In some specimens (for instance, that in the Georgianum at Munich) the figure of Christ is carved naked, and is wrapped in a cloth mantle. They were so richly decorated at the festival that an Austrian proverb speaks of being "dressed up like a palm ass." At the Nonnberg in Salzburg there was an especially famous palm ass which was so decked out at the processions with rose-wreaths of coral, garnets, etc., that it was rumoured to be worth a whole kingdom. In 1782 Archbishop Count Colloredo ordered it to be broken up for firewood. In 1780 the custom of bearing round the palm ass in procession was denounced "because it offends against good taste." This anathema reached even to the palm ass of the church of St Peter in Munich. The people there clung to it with such tenacity that, in spite of all decrees, it was not abolished until a functionary of the church, on March 17, 1806, solemnly ordered it to be sawn in pieces. Small palm asses were given as toys to those children who, sitting behind and in front of the figure of Christ, took part in the procession. A palm ass was, according to Strele, still in use in his time at the convent of the Dominican nuns at Lienz; the figure of Christ there was clad in silk.

VIII

TOY DOLLS IN ANCIENT TIMES

It is certain, then, that the image is of boundless antiquity, but it is doubtful whether the toy doll is as old. For there is this to be borne in mind—that no dolls have been discovered in childrens' graves of the prehistoric period. Of course, there might have been such made of perishable material; in defence of this view may be adduced the striking fact that, while no dolls have been discovered in neolithic settlements or in the Swiss lake-dwellings, there has been found a number of dolls' utensils. The arguments put forward by Walter Hough must here be taken into account. He draws attention to the fact that the oldest dolls known to us—the ancestor image and the idol—were objects having a religious and magical significance, and were handled only by priests and medicine-men. Everything militates against the supposition that, at a time when men believed in the magical properties of the artificial human figure, children would have been permitted to play with objects so enwrapped in dangerous mysteries. The possibility, however, remains that the little figures, as belief faded and they lost their place in the rite, were handed over as toys to children. The play doll might easily have developed from the idol in the course of time, one and the same piece perhaps serving different purposes in ages of differing beliefs.

FIG. 84. BYZANTINE DOLL'S TUNIC, OF COLOURED WOOL, FROM THE CEMETERY OF AKHMIM

A progress of this kind is to be noted among the Hopi Indians, who, at the conclusion of their ceremonies, give their cult images to children to play with. Similar examples, too, have been recorded in the history of modern civilization. Roger Edgeworth, Canon of Bristol Cathedral, complained in 1544 that Catholic churches were being plundered, the figures of the

Madonna and of the saints being handed over as dolls to the children. In any case, the toy doll is the youngest sister of the

image. As such, however, it does not belong to the primitive possessions of human culture; it is not spread throughout the entire world, but is confined to civilized peoples. There are savage races (or were, at least) which do not possess toy dolls; Richard Schomburgk in British Guiana and Forbes in the Malay Archipelago came across tribes whose children do not know how to play. American ethnologists have demonstrated that the Indians first adopted the toy doll from emigrants in the time of Queen Elizabeth. In most of the Indian tongues there is no word for 'doll'; in

others it is identical with the word 'baby.' It is evident at the first glance that the objects made for their children by some of the nature peoples of to-day betray European influences.

FIG. 85
WOODEN DOLL
OF IMPERIAL
ROME FROM THE
CEMETERY OF
AKHMIM
Height, 40 cm.

Toy dolls, then, exist only where there is civilization, but, while it is almost certain that they were not known among primitive peoples,

they are to be met with fairly freely among the various civilized races of antiquity. The Vorderasiastische Museum in Berlin possesses a little alabaster doll which certainly does not belong to a religious cult; its arms are missing, but from the holes in the shoulders it is evident that these were movable. Apparently, too, it was designed to be dressed. Among the extraordinarily rich array of figures left by the ancient Egyptians there are many which were obviously used as toys. These are made of wood or linen stuffed with papyrus strips, the facial features being embroidered and the hair represented by threads. Some specimens are

FIG. 86. GREEK TERRA-
COTTA LIMBED DOLL
FOUND IN THE CRIMEA

clad in woollen dresses or loin-cloths, and the arms and legs are often movable. Occasionally these dolls have portions added in wax; neckcloths, armlets, and rings on the feet are frequently supplied. The least shapely in appearance are the drollest—Wilkinson thinks for the purpose of catching the attention of small children. Indeed, they are sometimes so rough that only a child's fancy is capable of recognizing in them a human form. There are also dolls made movable in the style of puppets, representing women slaves at their washing or harvesting, etc.

FIG. 87. APHRODITE
Terra-cotta dolls from Myrina

The Agyptische Museum in Berlin has a little limbed doll of this kind dating from about the year 1900 B.C. In the necropolis of Akhmim Panopolis, belonging to the sixth and seventh centuries A.D., Robert Forrer unearthed many large toy dolls made of cloth and wood; their hair was fixed by means of asphalt, their faces were painted, and they were clothed with woollen costumes. There, too, were found single articles of dolls' dress and dolls' utensils.

The oldest example of a Greek toy doll is a clay rattle box made in female shape, but of which the head is missing. This was found by Schliemann in one of the lower strata at Troy. In children's graves too of the Mycenæan and of other archaic periods are to be found small female dolls, often representing women with children in their arms. It is to be observed that most Greek dolls represent women. The wax doll was called *dagynon* in Ionic, *dagys* in Doric; *plaggon* was the designation for

FIG. 88. EARLY GREEK PAINTED CLAY DOLL FROM A BŒOTIAN GRAVE
Louvre, Paris

'doll' in general. The manufacture of these objects was a widely disseminated trade; doll-makers were called *koroplastoi*. Most were made of clay, but plaster and wax were also employed, the

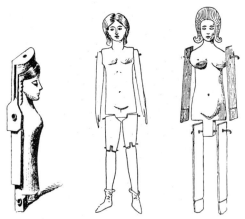

FIG. 89. GREEK LIMBED DOLLS

latter being spread on a wooden base and then worked over by hand. The arms and legs of the figures were frequently movable. Throughout classical antiquity Sardis, the capital of Lydia, was renowned for its manufacture of such toys. In Athens the

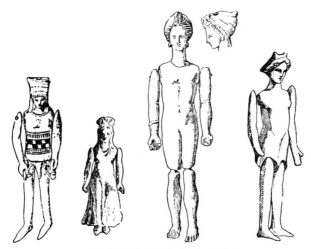

FIG. 90. EARLY GREEK LIMBED DOLLS FROM ATHENS, MYRINA, RHODES
Children's toys. Terra-cotta

merchants had their stalls in the *agora*, where they sold their articles to the children. Better-class examples were often executed with pains-taking care—these were of fine light-brown clay, only lightly baked and painted when cold. While heads and breasts were generally modelled in careful detail, the body was left rough, since it was intended to be covered with garments. Demosthenes, Lucian, Dio Chrysostom, and Suidas—all have left us some information about the Greek doll. Plutarch tells a pretty story of how his two-year-old daughter Timoxena begged her nurse to give milk to her doll as well as to herself. The little girls found pleasure in making clothes for their dolls, and the young Greek maidens, who were wont to be married at twelve or thirteen years of age, played with them up to the time of their betrothal, when they dedicated the dolls and all their wardrobe to Artemis or the nymphs. There are still extant gravestones of Greek girls who had died young on which this dedication of dolls is recorded. Sappho, according to Athenæus, dedicated her doll to Aphrodite: "O Aphrodite, despise not my doll's little purple

FIG. 91. GREEK CLAY DOLL, IN THE SHAPE OF A CHILD, FROM A GRAVE
Biardot Collection

107

neckerchief. I, Sappho, dedicate this precious gift to you!"
The *Anthologia Palatina* has preserved an epigram in which
Timarete consecrates her doll with its accessories to Artemis
Limnatis.

> Timarete before her marriage has offered up to Diana her
> tambourine, and her valued ball, and her cap, the defender of her

FIG. 92. GRAVESTONE OF A
GREEK GIRL
Avignon

FIG. 93. GRAVESTONE OF A
GREEK GIRL
Athens

> locks, and her dolls, O Limnatis, as is fitting for a virgin to a virgin,
> and her doll's dresses. And do thou, daughter of Latona, place thy
> hand over the girl Timarete, and preserve holily her who is holy. [1]

The Latin for the newborn child before it has been given a
name is *pupus* or *pupa*; from these words *Puppe* is derived, and
this has been adopted as a loan word in several languages to
signify the plastic representation of a little child. The Roman
toy dolls were for the most part made of clay; their manufacture
was widespread, and the products were a staple article of commerce. More carefully worked figures were made for the rich.
In the grave of a little girl in the Prati di Castello at Rome was
found a carved wooden doll, 30 cm. high, with movable limbs.
The hands were carefully executed, but the arms and legs were

[1] Translation from *The Greek Anthology*, by George Burges (Bohn's Classical
Library), pp. 412-413.

represented only by smooth strips of wood. In the sarcophagus of the Empress Maria, a daughter of Stilicho and wife of the Emperor Honorius (384–423), which was opened in 1594, there was discovered a beautifully ornamented little ivory doll. The Roman girls, like their Greek predecessors, were wont to dedicate their dolls to a goddess on the eve of their marriage. According to Persius they made an offering of these dolls to Venus or to the *lares*. Dolls were at that time no less dear to the hearts of Christian children than they were to the little pagans; several examples have been found in childrens' graves in the catacombs.

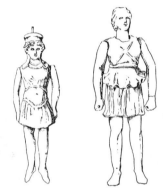

FIGS. 94, 95. ROMAN LIMBED DOLLS
FOUND IN ITALY
Children's toys

IX
EARLY TOY DOLLS IN EUROPE

THE toy doll did not disappear in the medieval child world. Although no extant examples exist from the earlier centuries, literary records testify to their importance. In the *Indiculus Superstitionum*, belonging to the eighth or ninth century, rag dolls (*simulacra de pannis*) were mentioned. The word for a doll in

FIG. 96. NÜRNBERG DOLLS OF BAKED CLAY,
FOURTEENTH TO FIFTEENTH CENTURIES
Germanisches National-Museum, Nürnberg

Old High German was *Tocha*, in Middle High German *Tocke*. From the fifteenth century the word *Docke* was adopted, while Geiler von Kaiserberg had already used the word *Puppe*, which rapidly won popularity. *Tocke* apparently at first meant a little block of wood, which makes us believe that the oldest German dolls were rather primitive things. In its acquired sense the word was widely used. Wilhelm von Oestreich, Oswald von Wolkenstein, and *Der jüngere Titurel* loved to compare beautiful young girls with lovely *Tocken*, naming them *Sommertocken*. Neidhardt von Reuenthal called his Vriderun a *Tocke*; Hugo von Langenstein called St Martina a heavenly *Tocke*; and when

EARLY TOY DOLLS IN EUROPE

Clara Hatzlerin wishes to give expression to her ill-humour at decked-up peasant girls she calls them village *Tocken.* Luther, in rebuking female vanity, speaks of woman as a pretty *Tocke.* The toy doll as such is a familiar subject among writers. *Mai und Beaflor,* Hadamar von Laber, and *Virginal* refer to the children's *Tocken.* Wolfram von Eschenbach refers to them

FIG. 97. CLAY DOLLS, FOURTEENTH TO FIFTEENTH CENTURIES
Germanisches National-Museum, Nürnberg

oftener than other poets, since in his little daughter, with whom he loved to play, he had, of course, a real child before his eyes. In the *Titurel* he makes the young Sigune beg that her dolls be not forgotten when she is going on a journey, and in conversation with Schionatulander she asks whether she may still keep on loving her doll. In the *Willehalm* he is describing the beauty of coats of mail: "Here came the sun's gleam on many coats of mail; my daughter's *Tocke* is hardly so lovely." This shows that these dolls were dressed up as richly as possible for their little owner. Geiler von Kaiserberg, the Strasbourg preacher, alludes to this when he accuses parents of teaching their young daughters "to be proud of their dolls." A century later Fischart complains that women decked themselves up as girls decked up their dolls, and Simplizissimus says of himself, "she decked me up like a French doll." Guote, the daughter of Rudolf von Habsburg, married in her teens to Wenzel von Böhmen, had nothing of greater interest to tell her husband than how she had dressed her doll.

The extant examples, however, in no wise give an impression of special magnificence. The oldest of all, belonging to the

FIG. 98. NÜRNBERG DOLL-MAKER AT HIS WORK
From the *Hortus Sanitatis*, Mainz, 1491

thirteenth century, is made on the model of the Trojan dolls, mentioned above—a rattle box of baked clay in the shape of a wreathed and smiling woman. Similar specimens originating in the thirteenth century have been discovered in the soil of old Strasbourg. In Nürnberg too some clay dolls, dating back to the fourteenth century, were brought to light in 1859 under the pavements—children in swaddling clothes, monks, little men, and lovely women dressed in the fashion of the time with large hoops. Some of them have a remarkable circular hollow on the breast about the size of a florin, apparently designed to hold a christening gift. Hefner-Alteneck found numbers of such figures in the course of excavations at the city of Tannenberg. These little clay dolls are, however, of the simplest pattern, not necessitating the use of clothes. This must have taken from the children a great part of the charm of these dolls when regarded as toys. Such dolls found in the cities were apparently not single articles, but seem to have been shop stock—a fact proving that the manufacture of dolls must, even at that time, have been a rising industry. In 1413 at Nürnberg, which has remained a principal centre of this industry up to the present day, a doll-maker of the name of Ott is recorded, and another, named H. Mess, is mentioned in the year 1465. Amusing and instructive are the illustrations in the various editions of the *Hortus Sanitatis*, a favourite fifteenth-century work dealing popularly with medical subjects. These show the doll-maker at his trade and,

XLVII.

Ein Handwerckßfraw in der Schlesien.
Hesichstu augenscheinlich klar/   Drinnen in der Schlesien/
Jn was klaidung vnd gebahrt.   Die Handwerckßframen einher gehn.
M iij

FIG. 99. WOODCUT BY JOST AMMAN, 1577

although they have no pretensions to photographic exactitude, indicate that dolls with movable arms are intended.

In the sixteenth century the iconographic records increase. Jost Amman, Tobias Stimmer, the artist using the monogram J.R., and other illustrators of civic life have immortalized in many of their sketches little girls playing with their dolls. The doll must then have been a popular article, for Fischart ironically ejaculates: "What marvel is it that wives manage to get round their husbands so easily? From their childhood they are used to play with dolls; they merely continue their game with their husbands after marriage!" These pictures reveal the fact that all the little girls played with dolls which impersonated women, invariably dressed in the contemporary fashion; dolls representing children had not yet made their appearance.

In 1584 Margarethe Schleicher, a little girl of Nürnberg

113

received a present of a doll dressed like a real Nürnberg bride, with her large peculiar head-gear. At Christmas 1619 Frau

FIG. 100. PRINCESS MARIE OF SAXONY
Painting by L. Cranach. About 1540

Löffenholtz presented her seven-year-old daughter Barbara with a large doll and a *hennsla buben* (a male doll, the word *hennsla* being connected with *Hänschen*); her five-year-old and three-year-old children also received dolls.

The wax doll appeared in Germany during the seventeenth

FIG. 101. CHILD WITH DOLL
Historical Exhibition of Ancient Art, Paris, 1879
Albert Goupil Collection

century. Joachim von Sandrart praised the products of **Daniel Neuberger** in Augsburg: as hard as stone were these, and so marvellously coloured that they seemed to be alive. In 1632 the town of Augsburg presented King Gustavus Adolphus with a sumptuous art cabinet costing 6500 reichsthalers. The designer,

115

the well-known Philipp Hainhofer, inserted in it a pair of
dolls which to-day are to be found preserved in Upsala—a
cavalier and his lady, $9\frac{1}{2}$ and $11\frac{1}{2}$ cm. high, holding each

FIG. 102. DOLL AS A COSTUME MODEL
Height, 75 cm. Beginning of the seventeenth century. French
Figdor Collection, Vienna

other's hands in readiness to dance by means of a mechanism no
longer operative. The gentleman has movable head and arms;
he wears a tunic and silken breeches trimmed with silver braid,
a pointed lace collar, a grey broad-brimmed hat, high boots of
brown leather, and a sword. Around his waist he has a yellow

116

silk sash with silver fringe; over his right shoulder a blue cloak with silver lapels. The lady's head unfortunately is missing, but her dress, consisting of a yellow silk damask costume ornamented with silver braid and a sash of rose-coloured silk with silver fringes encircling the waist, has been carefully preserved. Since this was a gift to a king it certainly represents the

FIG. 103. AUGSBURG DOLLS
From the art cabinet of Gustavus Adolphus in Upsala. About 1630

best in the doll line which could then be obtained in Germany. Hainhofer, who was active as a connoisseur, an art-collector, and an art-dealer, supplied also a large set of toy dolls with another of his art cabinets which he sold to Duke Philip II of Pomerania in August 1617, and which is now to be found in the Schlossmuseum at Berlin. This represented a farmyard full of dolls, including soldiers, girls, farm servants, carriers, cavaliers, and peasants of both sexes. One woman was seated milking a cow, and even a "closet," "in which a girl is sitting doing the needful," was included. There were many animals, and the various kinds of poultry were even covered with real birds' feathers. The model, 210 cm. long, 165 cm. wide, and 120 cm. high, was made by Mathias Kager, the animals modelled by Johann Schwegler. Among ladies of quality these farmyards were popular toys—and also expensive, for they cost from 500 to 800 gulden. Duke William of Bavaria gave several of them as

FIG. 104. BEDROOM IN A DOLL'S HOUSE
Seventeenth century
Bayerische Landesgewerbe-Anstalt, Nürnberg

FIG. 105. KITCHEN IN A DOLL'S HOUSE
Seventeenth century
Bayerische Landesgewerbe-Anstalt, Nürnberg

presents; he sent various specimens to the Queens of France and Spain, some archduchesses, and other princesses, but these have all now disappeared. Only a few scattered examples of

seventeenth-century dolls' houses have been preserved, all certainly the property of adults, for their well-preserved condition

FIG. 106. LARGE NÜRNBERG DOLL'S HOUSE (EXTERIOR)
Eighteenth century
Germanisches National-Museum, Nürnberg

testifies to the fact that they have never fallen into children's
destructive hands. Duke Albert V of Bavaria got a sumptuous
doll's house made for him; this was placed in the art gallery of

119

the Residenz in Munich, but unhappily is not now extant. In 1631 at Nürnberg Anna Käferlin set up a complete doll's house,

FIG. 107. LARGE NÜRNBERG DOLL'S HOUSE (INTERIOR)
Eighteenth century
Germanisches National-Museum, Nürnberg

including even a library, an armoury, and a music room, which she exhibited on payment. Paul von Stetten records in 1765

FROM THE "GALLERIE DES MODES," 1780

that at Augsburg there were dolls' houses which had cost 1000 gulden and more. Doll-making remained a free, unincorporated trade, in which all kinds of hand-workers participated. In

FIG. 108. FROM WEIGEL'S "HAUPTSTÄNDE," 1698

Nürnberg alone there were seventeen workshops devoted to the manufacture of dolls. The council of that city on November 17, 1600, gave permission to Barbara Beuchin, daughter of Georg Breitner, of Bamberg, to display for sale the dolls of her own making in the market-place near the Schönen Brunnen. In the year 1700 there were six master doll-makers in Nürnberg.

The toy doll in France, one need hardly remark, was an

Dockenmacher von Trachant.
Liebt und begehrt, was ewig währt:

Mein Schat; und meiner Freude Ziel
ist Gott, soll meine Seele sprechen.
Des Reichtums buntes Docken-Spiel
kan leicht ein Unglücks-Stoß zerbrechen,
Vergnügung fehlt ihm die es weist,
wie den Trachant-Bild Menschen-Geist.

FIG. 109. FROM WEIGEL'S "HAUPTSTÄNDE," 1698

esteemed object. A traveller who visited Paris in the middle of the fifteenth century saw some exhibited for sale:

> Non desunt puppæ gratissima dona tenellis
> Virginibus miro culta formaque decora.

Antoine Astérau, who wrote a description of Paris in the same century, saw on the stalls of the Palais de Justice, where various articles of luxury were regularly set out for sale, "charming and attractively dressed dolls." In the year 1455 Raoulin de la Rue supplied Princess Madeleine, daughter of King Charles VII,

FIG. 110. DWARF WITH
PERUKE
Eighteenth century
*Bayerisches National-Museum,
Munich*

FIG. 111. GENTLEMAN
WITH SWORD
Wooden doll. Seventeenth century
*Bayerisches National-Museum,
Munich*

with a doll representing a woman on horseback attended by her foot servants. In the sixteenth century Paris played an important part in the doll trade. Emperor Charles V, in spite of his hatred of France, ordered dolls to be sent from Paris for his little daughter. In 1530 he paid Jean Beauvalet, chaplain of St Gudule's in Brussels, ten francs—then a large sum—for this purpose. King Henry II got six dolls sent from Paris to his daughters; these cost him nine francs. In 1571 Duchess Claudia of Lorraine instructed P. Holman to get for her in Paris four to six of the most beautifully dressed dolls he could find. They had not to be too large, however, since they were destined for her newly born granddaughter, the Duchess of Bavaria.

FIG. 112. DOLL IN WALKING DRESS
First half of the eighteenth century
Germanisches National-Museum, Nürnberg

No definitely authentic example of French workmanship of this period has been preserved. That particular doll which has become well known through its appearance at various exhibitions and in prints, and which was shown first in the Albert Goupil Collection at the world exhibition of 1878, is not an original, but is an ingenious patchwork made up of various old parts. The dress is a sixteenth-century child's dress of silk (originally white) with embroidered underclothing, which had belonged to the wardrobe of a statue of the Madonna in a Venetian convent. There Bardini, the dealer in antiques, procured it. In the Vanutelli Collection in Florence he found the

FIG. 113. DOLL'S SUNSHADE OF RED SILK
Eighteenth century
Germanisches National-Museum, Nürnberg

marble head of a child doll which had been made in the fifteenth century, perhaps in Donatello's studio itself, or, at any rate, somewhere near. This he bought and provided a fine head for the costume by making a smaller painted replica of the marble. The body, arms, and legs of the figure were made of new material, the collar and cap to fit it being supplied out of the lining of the dress. The small doll is thus a Neapolitan crib-figure of the eighteenth century for which a dress in the style of the sixteenth century has been made out of old cloth. In this way, out of antique material which came from Venice, Florence, and Naples—all, without exception, of Italian origin—was created a 'French' doll. A pretty game, which, however, didn't succeed in deluding the experts.

In 1604 Sully sent the young Dauphin, later Louis XIII, a state coach filled with dolls. In 1605 the Prince received a male doll, and in 1606 a very beautifully dressed little noble;

DOLLS

in 1608 he was presented with a Capuchin monk of earthenware. In certain rhymes put into the mouth of the clown Gros-Guillaume in 1619 reference is made to a plaster doll which he promises to Dame Perrine. Dolls of this material must have been the finest quality; the better class went in for luxuries in dolls as in other things. Richelieu gave the Duchesse

FIG. 114. AUGSBURG WOMAN:
WOODEN DOLL OF THE
EIGHTEENTH CENTURY
Bayerisches National-Museum, Munich

FIG. 115. LADY OF THE
EIGHTEENTH CENTURY
*Bayerisches National-Museum,
Munich*

d'Enghien a doll's room with six dolls, all of which could be dressed and undressed—grandmother, mother, child, midwife, nurse, and lady's maid. Cardinal la Valette d'Épernon presented Mlle de Bourbon, later Duchesse de Longueville, with a magnificent doll together with a rich wardrobe. It cost him 2000 thalers, a sum which in the first half of the seventeenth century represented a small fortune. When a little Spanish Infanta came to France in 1722, to be brought up with the young

126

EARLY TOY DOLLS IN EUROPE

Louis XV and later to be married to him, the Duchesse d'Orléans presented her with a doll which had many changes of clothes; this cost her 22,000 francs. In 1779 Mme de Montholon paid twenty-five louis d'or for a doll. Esther Singleton believes that

FIG. 116. THE CHILDREN OF THE DUC D'ORLÉANS
Engraving by Joullain after the painting by Coypel. About 1760

we must conclude from the evidence of the fairy-tales of the Baronne d'Aulnoy that the French dolls of this time had movable heads and even movable eyes. This development, however, was not reached till a century later; in the year 1700 it can have existed only in the imagination of the authoress.

We must picture for ourselves the dolls of past centuries— whether they be German or French or English—as simple and fairly primitive objects. The body often consisted of a bundle of rags, to which arms and feet were attached by tape; sometimes it consisted of a leather bag filled with bran or sawdust. A step forward was marked when the arms and legs were jointed, and so made movable. Occasionally, however, the legs were left out altogether, the whole doll resting on a hoop petticoat.

FIG. 117. CHILD WITH DOLL REPRESENTING A MONK
Engraving by Ingouf after the painting by Greuze. About 1760

The old Nürnberg toy dolls were made entirely of wood covered with cloth, the heads being always carved and painted. The English dolls were characterized by disproportionately large heads.

Alongside of these dolls designed for the children of the higher class there were others of a wholly inartistic sort which came from the hands of the folk. These contented themselves with a simple reproduction of bodily and facial forms, providing for the childish imagination merely the barest indication of the

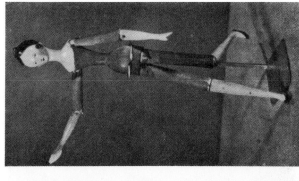

FIG. 118. PRIMITIVE
WOODEN DOLL FROM
TRANSYLVANIA
Spielzeug-Museum, Sonneberg

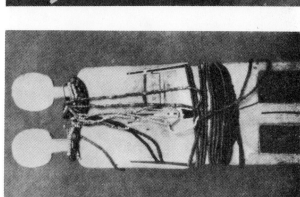

FIG. 119. TWIN DOLLS OF THE
HAUSSA NEGROES
Spielzeug-Museum, Sonneberg

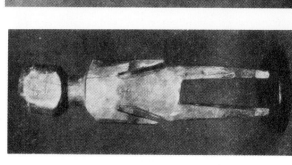

FIG. 120. WOODEN LIMBED DOLL
FROM THE GRÖDNER TAL
Spielzeug-Museum, Sonneberg

human image. This is thoroughly characteristic of pastoral art, which for the most part makes use of wood as a medium of expression, no matter whether its home is in the Alps, Thuringia, the Erzgebirge, or the Carpathians. Even the actual specimens

FIG. 121. OLDEST SONNEBERG WOODEN TOYS

produced in different districts resemble each other in an extra-ordinary manner. Bohemian wood-carved or turned dolls are so similar to those from the Grödner Tal that the one could be taken for the other, and the Christmas angels from the Saxon

FIG. 122. EGYPTIAN CHILD'S TOY
Leiden Museum

Erzgebirge might be their sisters. Typical of all of these is the cone shape, and the same taste, with its passion for bold colours, is to be traced in the painting of the figures. The famous toy industry of Sonneberg, the beginnings of which are to be found in the fourteenth century, originates from the work of the hunters, charcoal-burners, and woodmen of the district.

About the middle of the eighteenth century arose in Paris the vogue of that type of doll named, after the place of its origin,

130

DOLLS OF THE PERIOD OF THE FRENCH REVOLUTION
From a catalogue of toys. Reproduced in Henri René d'Allemagne's
History of Toys

pantin. The diarist Barbier mentions that these were first seen in children's hands in 1746, but that it was not long before adults took delight in the toy. In 1747 they were to be found in all the best houses. D'Alembert writes concerning them:

> Posterity will find difficulty in believing that there were in France people of mature judgment capable of spending time, in a fit of

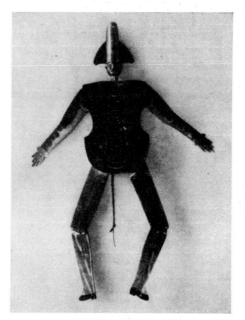

FIG. 123. WOODEN "HAMPELMANN," PAINTED IN
VARIOUS COLOURS
Eighteenth century. Height, 89 cm.
Germanisches National-Museum, Nürnberg

weakmindedness, with this ridiculous toy, and that with an ardour which in other countries would hardly be pardoned in tenderest youth.

Artists devoted themselves to it; the famous Boucher made a painting of a *pantin* for the Duchesse de Chartres, for which he was paid 1500 francs. The popularity of the toy endured until 1756. At last the police interfered and prohibited it, ostensibly "because the women, under the lively influence of this continual jumping, were in danger of bringing children into the world with twisted limbs like the *pantins*."

It is not surprising that French authors have assumed that the *pantin* was an invention of Paris, "the city of light," and there is really no need to deny it to them; but the French were not required to invent this puppet. It was known in classical antiquity; the principle of moving a figure by means of a thread attached to the loose limbs was practised by the Egyptians for their toy dolls. Plato, Herodotus, Horace, and Apuleius—all

Koff koff allerang,--wolfeil Spielwerg vor Kinde .

FIG. 124. CRIES OF BERLIN
Etching by Rosenberg. About 1786

refer to them, and literary records testify to their early existence in Germany. In the sixteenth and seventeenth centuries they were called *Hampelmann*, and in Thuringia also *Zappelmann*. In an account drawn up for the Saxon Court at Torgau in 1572 these puppets are mentioned—"stuffed dolls which are pulled with strings." Schwieger says in the *Geharnischte Venus*: "common *Hempelmänner*, these little toy dolls are often more sought after than things brought from both the Indies." In 1710 Amaranthes writes of "how one can decoy good money out of people's pockets just as one can decoy children with the *Hampelmann*." The word *Hampelmann* was often applied to simpletons, while "giggling like a *Hampelmann*" was said of silly laughter. This toy was a favourite object of comparison in a derogatory sense. Thus Heinrich Heine speaks of Wellington as a *Hampelmann* whose strings were pulled by the aristocracy. In 1848 was published at Frankfort a very witty satire on parliamentary rhetoricians:

EARLY TOY DOLLS IN EUROPE

Michel's March Acquisitions, Toys of Right and Left for Old and Young. Published by Eduard Gustav May. In this the orators of that gathering which had been greeted with such extravagant hopes, and which had ended so dismally, were represented as puppets—Beckerath as a bag of money, Mittermaier in Court dress, Heckscher as a lackey, Dahlmann as a toad, Robert Mohl in a dressing-gown, M. Mohl as a groom, Radowitz as a monk, Jahn with a very long beard, Rösler as a canary, and so on.

FIG. 125. " ZAPPELMANN ": CONDUCTOR
Richard Gräff
Werkstätte für den Hausrat, Theophil Müller, Dresden

X

THE FASHION DOLL

MORE skilfully than any other nation the French utilized dolls as a profitable means of propaganda, employing them freely in the service of their trade in ladies' fashions. French fashions,

FIG. 126. "HAMPELMANN": PEASANT
GIRL IN PARTS
French engraving. About 1750

FIG. 127. "HAMPELMANN": BALLERINA
IN PARTS
French engraving. About 1750

and not by chance, are highly favoured by women of all the five continents. Yet only rarely are these fashions real inventions of Paris; usually they come from other sources; but there they are executed with so much taste, and the French women know how to wear their clothes with such a peculiar charm, that Paris fashions capture all eyes and are eagerly imitated. The French never spare themselves self-praise, and just as some-

FIG. 128. ENGLISH DOLL'S HOUSE, ABOUT 1760
Lent to the Bethnal Green Museum, London, by Mrs Walter Tate
By permission of the Victoria and Albert Museum

thing always remains in the mind when we hear slander of others, so this general and constantly repeated self-praise never misses its mark, the hearer always having it impressed on his memory. At a time when as yet the press was non-existent, long before the invention of such mechanical means of reproduction as the woodcut and the copperplate, to the doll was given the

FIG. 129. THE BREAKFAST (DETAIL)
Engraving by Lépicié after the painting by Boucher. About 1740

task of popularizing French fashions abroad. The fashion doll first makes its appearance in the account books of the French Court. Queen Isabeau of Bavaria got dolls sent to the Queen of England to give that youthful monarch an idea of the fashions of the French Court. In 1396 Robert de Varennes, the Court tailor of Charles VI, received 459 francs for a doll's wardrobe executed by him. As this was a considerable sum, it is to be concluded that the dolls were life-size, made to the measure of the English Queen. The next record dates from a century later. In 1496 Anne of Brittany, the then reigning queen, ordered a great doll to be made and dressed for the Spanish Queen,

136

DOLLS OF THE PERIOD OF THE FRENCH EMPIRE

About 1800-10

THE FASHION DOLL

Isabella the Catholic. Isabella was then forty-three years old, an age which in a period when girls were wont to marry at fourteen years seemed to be on the threshold of senility, but was very smart and particular about her dress, never giving audience to foreign ambassadors twice in the same costume. This fact

FIG. 130. CHILD WITH DOLL (NUN)
J. B. S. Chardin

must have been well enough known in the French Court; the actual dress put on this doll was deemed to be wanting in perfection, and it was decided to re-equip it with a much costlier *ensemble*.

Marie de' Medici, when Henry IV, no longer in his first youth, took her as his second wife, was full of eagerness to learn all about the prevailing French fashions. "Frontenac tells me," writes the King to her, "that you wish to have samples of our fashions: I am therefore sending you several model dolls." In the seventeenth century this export of dolls, hitherto left to chance, was systematized and organized. Furetière in his *Roman Bourgeois* informs us that in the *salon* of Mlle de Scudéry, the well-known novelist, there used to stand two dressed dolls— the one a large *pandora* in full costume, the other a small *pandora* in *négligé*. Fashion dolls of this kind were first sent to England and then to other countries. As early as 1642 the Strasbourg

FIG. 131. GERMAN DOLL
Stuffed body with a china head (1850–60), dress, and *coiffure* (1878).
Height, 68 cm.
Germanisches National-Museum, Nürnberg

satirist Moscherosch ridiculed the German women of his time for getting dolls sent to them from Paris in order that they might copy costume and *coiffure*. Still more sharp expressions appeared in the anonymous lampoon of 1689 called *Der deutsch-französische Modegeist* (*The Spirit of Franco-German Fashion*). "And the worst of it is," we read there, "that not only do our women-folk themselves travel to France, but they pay as many thalers for their models, these dressed-up dolls, to be sent to them, as would serve them to emulate the very frippery of the devil." Such satire, however, did not trouble the German ladies. A certain A. Leo, who from 1671 to 1673 accompanied a Herr von Lüttichau on the Grand Tour, in

1673 sent from Paris to his pupil's aunt, Frau von Schleinitz, a doll "which he had got made in the latest fashion, especially in so far as the head and hair were concerned."

FIG. 132. WAX DOLL: TOWN LADY, MUNICH, 1877
Spielzeug-Museum, Sonneberg

The fashion doll penetrated as far as Venice. At the Sensa, the fourteen-day fair in the Piazza S. Marco, was annually exhibited a doll clad in the latest Parisian fashion, and for a whole twelve months this remained the dressmakers' model.

The chief destination for these exported fashion dolls was England, and even war could not hinder their passage. Writing in 1704, the Abbé Prévost observes:

> By an act of gallantry which is worthy of being noted in the chronicles of history for the benefit of the ladies the ministers of both Courts granted a special pass to the mannequin; that pass was

FIG. 133. THE CHEVALIER DE PANGE
Painting by Drouais. About 1760

> always respected, and during the times of greatest enmity experienced on both sides the mannequin was the one object which remained unmolested.

Such announcements appeared in the English papers as "Last Saturday the French doll for the year 1712 arrived at my house in King Street, Covent Garden." During the Regency the French Ambassador in London was Dubois, who later became Cardinal, and, in order to win favour with the English ladies, he wrote to the dressmaker Mlle Fillon in Paris, ordering her to send a large mannequin designed to show how the French women were dressed and coiffeured and how they wore their underclothing. His nephew, however, in reply to his order stated that this was not such a simple matter, that it would cost at least 300 francs, and that neither Mme Law nor Mlle Fillon

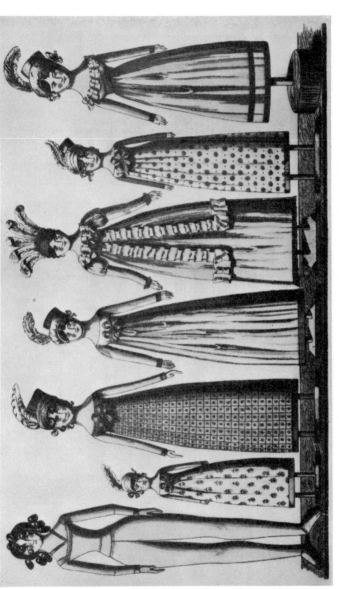

FIG. 134. DOLLS FROM THE PERIOD OF THE FRENCH EMPIRE

About 1800–10

From *Histoire des Jouets*, by Henri d'Allemagne

would risk the expense unless they were sure of being reimbursed. In 1727 Lady Lansdowne sent to Queen Caroline's ladies-in-waiting a mannequin in Court dress with the request that, after

FIG. 135. BRIDE (NÜRNBERG), MIDDLE OF THE NINETEENTH CENTURY
Bayerisches National-Museum, Munich. Photo Kester and Co.

it had circulated among them, they should dispatch it to Mrs Tempest the dressmaker.

In his trade lexicon of 1723 Savary mentions the beautiful dolls, elaborately coiffeured and richly dressed, which were sent to foreign Courts. No longer were they called, as formerly,

FIG. 136. DOLLS IN ROCOCO DRESS
Bayerische Landesgewerbe-Anstalt, Nürnberg

by the name of *pandoras*, being styled now 'dolls of the Rue Saint-Honoré,' a street which in the eighteenth century was the centre of the Parisian tailors, just as the Rue de la Paix is to-day. They were also called the *grands courriers de la mode*, under which title they were invoiced as having arrived at Dover in 1764. These fashion dolls were made life-size in order that the clothes with

FIG. 137. ENGLISH DOLL OF THE REIGN OF QUEEN ANNE
Victoria and Albert Museum

which they were dressed might be immediately worn. "The *chic* imparted to fashion by French hands," writes Mercier in his *Tableau de Paris*, "is imitated by all nations, who obediently submit to the taste of the Rue Saint-Honoré." Mercier, a good journalist, once took a stranger who doubted the existence of the fashion doll to Rose Bertin in order to convince him that it was a reality. Rose Bertin was the dressmaker of the elegant world; she worked for the Queen, and neither she nor the other Court dressmaker, Mme Éloffe, neglected the dressed-up mannequins. In 1777 Bertin clothed for Prince Rohan-Guéménée a large, beautifully coiffeured doll in a ball dress of white-and-rose silk

144

over the hoop petticoat. It was to have cost 300 francs, but that sum was never received by the dressmaker, for the Rohan family went bankrupt in millions. Mme Éloffe supplied the Comtesse Bombelles on August 18, 1788, with a life-size mannequin in Court dress for 409 francs, 12 centimes. Marie-Antoinette took pleasure, through the good offices of the furniture-designer

FIG. 138. ENGLISH DOLL'S SHOP, ABOUT 1850
Presented to the Bethnal Green Museum, London, by Miss Lester Garland
By permission of the Victoria and Albert Museum

David Röntgen, of Neuwied, in sending to her mother and sisters dolls dressed in the latest Parisian styles. Risbeck too, who visited Vienna in the last decade of the century, mentions them: "French fashion rules here despotically. Periodically mannequins are sent here [Vienna] from Paris and serve the ladies as models for their dresses and head-gear."

Not only dressmakers, but hairdressers made use of dolls. Thus on one occasion Mme de Sévigné promised her daughter a doll coiffeured according to the latest mode, while Melchior Grimm described in his well-known correspondence how the hairdresser Legros, who was the most popular Parisian 'hair-artist' in the time of the Pompadour, had many enemies, and how these had been silenced by the exhibition of thirty coiffeured dolls at the annual fair of Saint-Ovide in 1763. These beautiful dolls, to which was entrusted so important a cultural mission in the spreading of French fashion, have even found poets to sing their praises. Algarotti, in his Italian epistle to Phyllis, celebrated in song the

FIG. 139. ENGLISH WAX DOLL, ABOUT 1780
Presented to the Victoria and Albert Museum by Miss Ethel Diton

FIG. 140. ENGLISH DOLL WITH WAX HEAD, ABOUT 1800
Presented to the Bethnal Green Museum, London, by Mrs Greg
By permission of the Victoria and Albert Museum

charm of the French mannequin, and Delille, a fashionable French poet of the day, in 1786 praised Rose Bertin's dolls:

Et jusqu'au fond du Nord portant nos goûts divers,
Le mannequin despote asservit l'univers.

The French example did not remain unimitated. *The Gentleman's Magazine* contained a note in 1751 to the effect that several mannequins with different styles of dress had been made in St James's Street in order to give the Tsarina (Elizabeth) an idea of the manner of dressing which at the moment was in fashion among the English ladies. Catharine II designed articles of an absolutely unique cut for the young grand dukes, and in order to show King Gustavus III of Sweden how she clothed her

146

grandchildren she got dolls made and dressed according to her directions. In the end the Parisian fashion mannequins succeeded in reaching North America. In *The New England*

FIG. 141. GIRL WITH DOLL
Sir Joshua Reynolds. About 1785

Weekly Journal of July 2, 1733, appeared the following advertisement:

At Mrs Hannah Teatt's, dressmaker at the top of Summer Street, Boston, is to be seen a mannequin, in the latest fashion, with articles of dress, night dresses, and everything appertaining to women's attire. It has been brought from London by Captain White. Ladies who choose to see it may come or send for it. It is always ready to serve you. If you come, it will cost you two shillings, but if you send for it, seven shillings.

In similar manner, only in a less flowery style, two dressmakers of Irish nationality in New York advertised in 1757 to the effect that the latest mannequins had arrived from London. In 1796 a certain Sally MacKean wrote to her friend Dolly Madison, "Yesterday I went to see a mannequin which has just come from England to give us an idea of the latest fashions."

FIG. 142. ENGLISH DOLL, ABOUT 1860
Presented to the Bethnal Green Museum, London, by Mrs Greg
By permission of the Victoria and Albert Museum

It need not, however, be concealed that very soon the suspicion developed abroad that the Parisian tailors and dressmakers were making use of these mannequins merely for the purpose of getting rid of their old stock. Horace Walpole wrote from Paris on September 22, 1765, to George Montague: "The French have become very plain in their dress. We English still pray to their old idols." Even Prince Henry of Prussia, who in 1769 asked Darget to get him some cloth from Paris, thought it necessary to add a warning that he did not wish for such as had been made for German princes and barons, but the sort which the Prince

148

FIG. 143. MALE AND FEMALE PEDLARS (PORTSMOUTH), ABOUT 1810
Presented to the Bethnal Green Museum, London, by Mrs Greg
By permission of the Victoria and Albert Museum

FIG. 144. FLAT PAINTED FIGURES
Lady with fan, man smoking, man with a muff. Eighteenth century
Bayerisches National-Museum, Munich

de Conti and the Marshals Contades and d'Estrées were then wearing. The wars of the French Republic and of Napoleon I put an end to the free passage of the mannequins, nor were these so necessary now that the fashion journals provided a complete substitute. Their use, however, has not wholly ceased. French fashion mannequins cost eighty francs before the War, and many

FIG. 145. ENGLISH MOVABLE FASHION DOLLS, ABOUT 1830

such figures, about a metre high, along with complete *trousseaux*, were supplied for the harems of some Oriental grandees.

England was responsible for the invention of one particular kind of figure used for the purpose of displaying new fashions in dress. Up to comparatively recent times the English tradition in regard to the toy doll is remarkably meagre; indeed, it seems that originally English dolls had no special name allotted to them. They were simply called 'little ladies' or 'babies,' and it is only in the eighteenth century that the expression 'doll' begins to be used. The English themselves are in doubt con-

ENGLISH MANNEQUIN, ABOUT 1800

cerning the etymology of this word. Some consider that the
term 'doll' is connected with the diminutive of endearment

FIG. 146. ENGLISH WAX DOLL, MIDDLE OF THE NINETEENTH CENTURY
Presented to the Victoria and Albert Museum by Frank Green

'Dolly' (for Dorothy); others think it is a derivative from 'idol';
still others turn to the Norse *daul*, which signifies a female domestic servant. Even though we know almost nothing about the
older periods, it must be presumed that the little English girls

151

had their dolls. The portrait painted about the year 1600 of Lady Arabella Stuart as a child shows her with her doll dressed exactly like a grown-up woman, just as were the German and

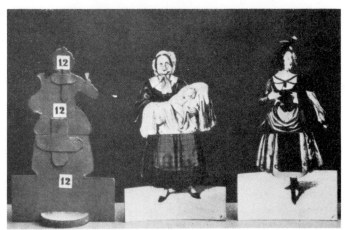

FIG. 147. TRICK DOLLS OF PRESSED AND CUT-OUT CARDBOARD
(METAMORPHOSES)
Germanisches National-Museum, Nürnberg

French toy dolls of that time. Only toward the end of the eighteenth century did England enrich the doll world with new inventions. Silhouettes cut out of paper had been known for a long time in Germany; in the Germanische National-Museum, in Nürnberg, is a picture-sheet of the seventeenth century with fashion-plates intended to be cut out; but the English made out of this something entirely new. They invented the one-sided figures to be cut out of paper, for which many different garments were provided, the costumes thus being rendered changeable. These paper figures, 8 in. high and supplied with six sets of clothes, were put on the market in 1790 by English firms. In the *Journal des Luxus und der Moden* of 1791 they are called attention to, and Bertuch, who was always on the look-out for novelties, at once proceeded to imitate them. Such a figure, with its wardrobe of six changes, cost then three shillings. The French adopted this invention as a means of cheap advertisement for their fashions; Gavarni, for example, lithographed a whole series of such fashion-plates intended to be cut out.

FIG. 148. MANNEQUIN

XI

THE TOY DOLL IN THE NINETEENTH CENTURY

ONLY in the nineteenth century does a real improvement in technique become apparent. Greater demands from the public led to greater efforts on the part of the producers; pleasing devices came to improve the doll, and eventually factory pro-

FIG. 149. ELISA, PRINCESS RADZIWILL
Etching by Haller. About 1810

duction, because of a careful specialization of labour, reached an accurate elaboration of even the tiniest details, and evolved something of perfection in its own kind. The leather bags were better stuffed, being now filled, not with bran, liable to pour out when the least injury was done to the cover, but with animal hair or seaweed and finally with fine wood shavings. The coarse leather used in past times was replaced by thin sheepskin to which were affixed arms and feet of porcelain. *Papier mâché*, the invention of which is by some ascribed to Italy and by others to France, was used in Sonneberg in 1810, and by its means, with the use of casts from sulphur moulds, dolls were made, although it is true that these were still somewhat clumsy in shape. In

154

THE TOY DOLL IN THE LAST CENTURY

1850 gutta-percha took the place of the leather bag. The flexibility of the limbs, which until then was somewhat fettered, was improved by the introduction of ball-joints; Jumeau and Son in Paris invented the movable neck, and after that innovation greatest attention was paid to the head. The wooden head with hair indicated only by paint was replaced by the China head, and the hair marked only by modelling was replaced by as

FIG. 150. SUSANNE VON BOEHN
Sketch by Ulrich von Sulpius. 1858

realistic substitutes as were possible—flax, untwisted silk, and mohair of the Angora goat, sometimes even real human hair. An unmistakable revolution ensued from the introduction of the wax head with glass or enamelled eyes. By 1826 eyes that could close had been invented. For long England enjoyed the fame of producing the best and prettiest wax dolls. At the Parisian world exhibition of 1855 the English dolls modelled by Napoleon Montanari aroused great enthusiasm. To-day we have our dolls' heads with real hair, eyelashes, and eyebrows, fitted with teeth and movable eyes. To the inventor of the metronome, Mälzel, we owe the first speaking doll. In 1827 he took out a patent in Paris for a doll which could say "Papa" and "Mamma" when it was squeezed. The first doll which could walk by itself appeared in 1826. These early experiments, of course, have long been superseded, for now we have dolls which can speak, sing, and cry at will.

Up to the nineteenth century all dolls were made to represent grown women. About 1850 the limbed baby doll, or *Gelenktäufling*, was introduced from England into Germany. This term signifies

FIG. 151. PORTRAIT OF THE DAUGHTER OF HERR ARTÚS
Painting by Chaplin. 1878

a baby doll of flesh-coloured *papier mâché* dipped in a wax solution to give an impression of the human skin. The limbs are movable, and the dress is only a little chemise. In 1855 at the Parisian world exhibition these baby dolls were for the first time introduced to a large public. Since then they have won great popularity, and have almost entirely ousted the dolls representing women.

The specialization of work has greatly facilitated and improved the manufacture of dolls. In the Parisian workshops of the forties of the last century a doll was reckoned to consist of ten

FIG. 152. SONNEBERG LEATHER DOLL, 1820

separate pieces, but to-day we have gone far beyond that. In the doll industry there are indeed more separate branches than

FIG. 153. "PETITE DRÔLESSE! VOUS ME FEREZ MOURIR DIX ANS AVANT MON TERME"
Lithograph by Randon. 1860

157

in any other trade. There are eye-cutters, eye-setters, arm- and leg-moulders; such advertisements as "A moulder of small hands wanted" serve to indicate the wide scope of this specialization of labour. Much toil and care is demanded for the assembling of the parts, for the painting, where various problems involved by the conjunction of different kinds of materials have

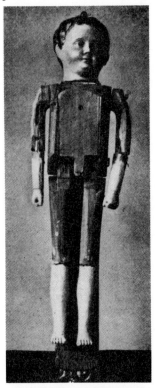

FIG. 154. SPEAKING LIMBED DOLL, NINETEENTH CENTURY
Bayerisches National-Museum, Munich

to be surmounted, and finally for the costuming. Formerly the purchaser of the doll's body had to attend to the clothing herself, or the little girl to whom it came as a present had to take that business into her own hands.

A good example of this is provided by Queen Victoria; until she was fourteen years old she used to play with her dolls, and found amusement in associating herself in the dressing of the otherwise very simple figures. Of the one hundred and thirty-two specimens she possessed she clothed thirty-two herself. Only

ENGLISH DOLL, ABOUT 1830
Presented by Miss M. A. Rooth to the Victoria and Albert
Museum, London

FIG. 156. "MA SŒUR, REGARDE DONC MA JOLIE POUPÉE"
Engraving by Noël. 1806

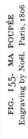

FIG. 155. MA POUPÉE
Engraving by Noël. Paris, 1806

about seven or eight were dressed as men; for the rest the young owner found her models in her ladies-in-waiting and in the famous singers, dancers, and actresses of the time, these including such persons as Marie Taglioni, the Duchess of Clarendon, and

FIG 157. SONNEBERG LEATHER DOLLS WITH CHINA HEADS, 1840
Spielzeug-Museum, Sonneberg

Lady Bedford. The late Queen was truly a little pedant, for when she was a child she kept a catalogue of her dolls, with careful enumeration of their names and dresses.

Apparently at that time only the French dolls were put on the market all ready dressed; about 1850 there were in Paris several workshops engaged solely in supplying articles for the doll's wardrobe. Natalis Rondot, who prepared a report on the

French exhibition of 1849, speaks in laudatory terms of the work of the French artists engaged in this branch of the doll industry. He writes:

> So far as dolls' costumes are concerned, the Parisian dressmakers have no equal. With great dispatch and wonderful skill they are able to make use of the smallest pieces of cloth, producing from these elegant attires. The doll's cloak and dress are correct

FIG. 158. ROCOCO DOLL
About 1750. Height, 50 cm.
Germanisches National-Museum, Nürnberg

replicas of the latest fashions; the doll dressmakers are not only skilled in the cut, the preparation of underclothing, and general outfit; they show taste in the selection of materials and colours. Thus these dolls are not only dispatched into the provinces and abroad as samples of fashion; they have become indispensable for the general export of fashionable novelties, for it has been realized that without the aid of the doll the tradespeople do not know how to sell their goods. The first little cloaks sold in India, for example, were there worn on the head until the fashion doll arrived at Calcutta to show the ladies their mistake.

Paris here indulged in great luxuries. At the world exhibition of 1867 dolls were exhibited with real cashmere shawls costing over six hundred francs. The dolls which thirty years later were presented in Paris to the daughters of the Tsar cost several thousand francs.

FIG. 159. GENTLEMAN WITH STICK. PEASANT WOMAN WITH ROSARY
Wooden dolls. Eighteenth century
Germanisches National-Museum, Nürnberg

In 1870 Germany introduced the wholesale factory method in the production of dressed dolls, and through this innovation the German firms took a leading position in the doll market. Even in the Middle Ages there had been a considerable exportation of dolls from Germany: "Toys from Nürnberg hand go to

FIG. 160. OLD MUNICH DOLL
Bayerisches National-Museum, Munich. Photo Kester and Co.

every land " was a proverb of the time. The Sonneberg industry, which had already shown good promise in the fifteenth century, reached fruition in the sixteenth century, but was for a long time disorganized because of the Thirty Years War. Augsburg and Nürnberg, however, recovered quickly, and by the eighteenth century these towns were producing toys wholesale. In the nineteenth century this dominating position of Germany was

FIG. 161. DOLL'S HEAD OF PAPIER MÂCHÉ
Bayerische Landesgewerbe-Anstalt, Nürnberg

FIG. 162. THURINGIAN EMPIRE DOLL
About 1810. Height, 56 cm.
Germanisches National-Museum, Nürnberg

strengthened, so that, according to the impartial view of Jeanne Doin, "before the War the German doll reigned everywhere." This was a result which Germany, again according to the testimony of this French lady, "owed to a methodical and patiently conducted effort." "The irresistible activity of inventive Germany," she continues, "was equal to the requirements of the moment." She goes on to say that:

All countries drew thence their supply of china heads, for Saxony supplied these post paid at ten centimes a piece, while in France they cost forty centimes on the spot. The material was

DOLL, ABOUT 1865
Sketch by Walter Trier

ENGLISH DOLL, ABOUT 1875
Presented by Mrs Galloway to the Victoria and Albert
Museum, London

perfect, the work careful, the dispatch prompt and regular. This competition, added to facilitation in the payment of accounts, was irresistible, and ruined the French doll industry.

The French industry otherwise had been very active since 1862. The total value of the toys produced in Germany was

FIG. 163. ALTENBURG AND WENDISH DOLLS

raised from thirty-six million marks in 1894 to one hundred and forty million in 1913. A third of these amounts came from the

FIG. 164. NÜRNBERG-FÜRTH TRAIN WITH DOLLS IN COSTUME
Spielzeug-Museum, Sonneberg

sale of dolls alone. In present-day Germany the most important centres of the doll industry are Sonneberg, Nürnberg-Fürth, Ruhla, Waltershausen, Ohrdruf, Giengen, on the Brenz, and the Saxon Erzgebirge—the headquarters being in Bavaria, Thuringia, and Saxony. Some of these factories have been in

165

DOLLS

existence since about 1880. It will be understood that the making of dolls at home by hand labour, with only very little mechanical assistance, has almost completely disappeared. In the year 1910 in the Meininger Oberland alone twenty-five thousand persons were engaged in the manufacturing of dolls. At that period Germany's dolls dominated the world market; of the total

FIG. 165. CRIES OF BERLIN
Etching by Rosenberg. About 1786

European products more than two-thirds were supplied by Germany, and even of all the dolls annually made throughout the entire world Germany contributed more than half. As Privy Councillor Crämer has pointed out, this industry was the more important for Germany in that its profits for the major part were represented in wages, which was of deeper significance for the national economy than if the manufactured articles had been themselves of greater intrinsic value. The actual amount of wages may be estimated at from 70 per cent. to 75 per cent. of the total value of the goods.

The War temporarily interrupted this development, and led to the manufacture of these goods in other countries; non-German firms then flourished, since the strongest competitor had been put out of action. The Japanese factories in Kioto and Osaka stepped forward, and in August 1914 France had begun to

166

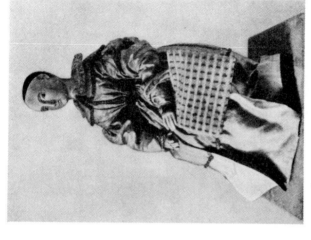

FIG. 166. DOLL OF THE BIEDERMEIER PERIOD
About 1840. Height, 76 cm.
Germanisches National-Museum, Nürnberg

FIG. 167. DOLL OF THE BIEDERMEIER PERIOD
About 1835. Height, 60 cm. The wig is missing.
Germanisches National-Museum, Nürnberg

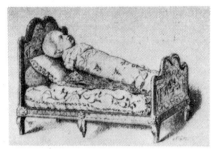

FIG. 168. FRENCH DOLL REPRESENTING A CHILD
About 1760

FIG. 169. "PUTZENBERCHT"
Etching by Göz, 1784

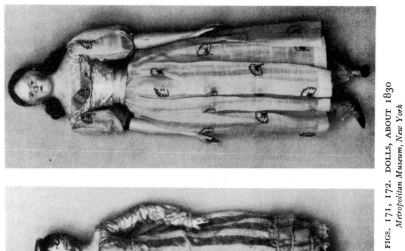

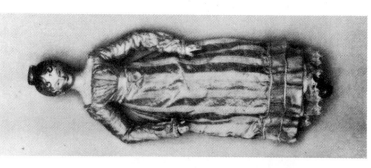

FIGS. 171, 172. DOLLS, ABOUT 1830

Metropolitan Museum, New York

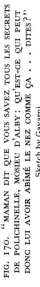

FIG. 170. "MAMAN DIT QUE VOUS SAVEZ TOUS LES SECRETS DE POLICHINELLE, MOSIEU D'ALBY: QU'EST-CE QUI PEUT DONC LUI AVOIR ABÎMÉ LE NEZ COMME ÇA . . . DITES?"

Sketch by Gavarni

think of the "Renaissance of the French Doll." The manufacturers began by imitating the cloth dolls of Margarethe Steiff, of Giengen, which resulted in the abandoning of paths hitherto trodden in France and in transference of attention from the elegant fashionable lady to the simple child. Whether these efforts will have a success remains to be seen.

FIG. 173. DOLL, ABOUT 1830
Bayerisches National-Museum, Munich

XII

THE TOY DOLL IN THE MODERN PERIOD

ALTHOUGH the toy doll has been in existence for several centuries, it was discovered by science and art only about the year 1900. It was at that time that the educationists began to get interested in it, and hand in hand with them came the artists,

FIG. 174. PLAYING WITH DOLLS
After the sketch by Chodowiecki. From Basedow's *Elementarwerk*

who believed that it was their duty to reform the doll. This was the period when, with a great flow of rich rhetoric, attempts were made to raise domestic furniture to artistic levels, when fashions themselves had to submit to reformation on the part of architects and painters; and clearly the doll had no claim to special indulgence. For the high educational significance with which it is invested the doll has to thank the fact that it is a representation of the human form. Because of this it satisfies the awakening instincts of the child, and develops these into lasting

171

emotions. Touching and seeing, the growing soul comes to an understanding with the world around it, and then with that which exercises the greatest influence upon it—with man. For this reason the doll takes the highest place in the imaginative play world of the child. The child who does not possess a doll

FIG. 175. THE YOUNG PHILOSOPHER (DETAIL)
After the painting of L. Boilly. 1790

will very soon make a substitute out of rags, a broom, sticks, bottles, pillows, which the realizing power of its imagination will endow with life. The moment of illusion, the autosuggestion, the self-deception—whatever it may be called—is so powerful that the child looks upon the doll of its choice as a living part of itself, and takes it to its heart with a passion which is but the greater the uglier the actual object is in reality. When she was a child Carmen Sylva played with her mother's footstool as if it had been a doll, and when Queen Elizabeth of Prussia, on a visit to the palace, made use of this footstool, the little Princess pushed her away, tore the stool from under her feet, and cried in an outburst of rage, "You mustn't put your feet on my child." The child's imagination does not need a naturalistic

FIG. 176. GIRL WITH DOLL
Macout, Paris. About 1800

representation of reality; an indication of the most superficial kind is for it quite sufficient.

The more highly, then, did the professional pedagogues estimate the educational value of the toy doll, which not only provides a welcome soil for the thriving and blossoming of the childish imagination, but is also regarded as a concentration of all the functions making for serious thought and act. "Where all the thought and feeling of the child are directed toward the doll as an object of love," says Paul Hildebrandt, "the educationist has an easy job, for there is to be discovered already existent in embryo deep feeling, true inner culture, and sensibility for art." Unquestionably the development of the maternal

173

instinct in the little girl is deeply influenced by the interest she takes in her doll. George Sand and Victor Hugo provide us with examples—indeed, Konrad Lange goes so far as to assert

FIG. 177. NEW YEAR'S PRESENTS AT PARIS
Anonymous engraving. About 1800

that "Women who have not played much with dolls in their childhood are distinguished in their maturity by low taste in matters of art and especially by lack of feeling." It seems, however, that that is going too far. One must here keep well in view the precise nature of the doll. A doll representing a woman, dressed up like an adult, such as formerly were by far in the majority, cannot awaken maternal feelings in the little girl, for she cannot easily descry her child in the shape of a lady of fashion. The importance even of the dolls representing children is minimized by some writers; thus James Sully, G. Stanley Hall,

FIG. 178. COPTIC WOODEN DOLL
About 600 B.C.

and others are of the opinion that the "maternal feeling" aroused by playing with dolls may be grossly overestimated. The sheer joy taken in clothing dolls and in attending to them, which includes dressing and undressing, has at least a good deal to do with the child's love of the doll, and besides this there is the pleasure taken in imitating grown-ups and in exercising authority on one's own. For the development of the child's psychology the actual make-up of the doll is unimportant; the amount of life attributed to it by the child, as Robert Breuer rightly remarks, decreases in proportion to the elaboration of its form; the meanest shape and the simplest outlines release the

175

noblest ideas and energies. In view of this the Russian congress
which was held concurrently with the exhibition of dolls at St

FIG. 179. ABYSSINIAN CHILDREN'S DOLLS
Ethnographisches Rijksmuseum, Leiden

FIG. 180. SILESIAN BAST DOLLS
Spielzeug-Museum, Sonneberg

Petersburg condemned the large French dolls, and protested
against their power of walking, speaking, and singing. These do
not leave the smallest scope for the play of the child's imagination,

and demonstrate that the simpler object succeeds in its aims far better than the complex.

It was here that the reformers stepped in. The naturalistic doll was recognized as the phenomenon of our satiated, artistically unproductive, wholly unimaginative civilization, and it was felt that a remedy must be found. Not in vain do we live,

FIG. 181. MODERN SWEDISH DOLL MADE
ENTIRELY OF WOOD
Photo Kester and Co.

according to the unfortunate catchword of the charming Swedish woman in the *Century of the Child*; we make much of the life of the child; we take pains to educate it as little as possible, to make it prematurely vain and conceited, to awaken in it not the slightest feeling for duty; and consequently we are inevitably forced to bother our heads with its toys. The idea of reforming the doll arose from the desire of opposing mass production and of creating a characteristic, if possible individually conceived, toy doll. In the elegant fashion doll the children no longer were to get an unnatural object into their hands; the superabundance of the all too concrete details was to be opposed. The child itself was asked what it wanted, and then, when it was seen that it made no special demands, and when the insignificance of the

177

stimulus which it needed to arouse its imagination was realized, adults began to imitate children. Not only was simplicity aimed at, but even technical imperfection itself was pleaded for; it looked almost as if nothing could be too simple for the child.

The reforming movement in the doll trade originated in the artistic circles of Munich, and later was followed up by Berlin,

FIG. 182. ART DOLL
Else Kollmar-Hecht

Dresden, and Karlsruhe; it proceeded in the usual way to offer prizes and to arrange competitions and exhibitions. The astonishing discovery was then made that the pieces which gained the first prize were not favoured by the children. They were, indeed, made too childishly to be able to attract them—"super-toys," as Paul Hildebrandt calls them. They were freely stylized, always beautifully primitive and geometrical, and were considered to be as naïve as the child itself, because the child is in the habit of finding simple substitutes for dolls. But to become consciously naïve is to become affected; the purely literary idea of reform has turned out to be fruitless. Something notable has

FIG. 183. HUGO AND ADOLAR
Designed and executed by the sculptor Buchholz, Züllichau
Kunstgewerbehaus H. Schwerdtfeger, Berlin. Photo Delia

FIG. 184. PEASANT AND PEASANT WOMAN
Bonbonnière in *papier mâché.* Designs by Fritz Kleinhempel
Deutsche Werkstätten, Dresden, 1911

certainly been created in the doll line by these reformers, but such dolls make a greater appeal to the grown-ups than to children. Thus wooden dolls have been produced in Munich with the idea of endeavouring to secure the simplest possible forms; these fit like boxes into one another, one nest of boxes representing the royal family, another, the same shape only differently painted, showing little Snow-white and the Seven

FIG. 185. MR BANKER
Bonbonnière in *papier mâché*. Fritz
Kleinhempel
Werkstätte für den Hausrat, Theophil Müller,
Dresden

FIG. 186. ROCOCO LADY
Bonbonnière in *papier mâché*. Fritz
Kleinhempel
Werkstätte für den Hausrat, Theophil Müller
Dresden

Dwarfs or the peasant women of Dachau. It is the Dresdeners and the Viennese, however, who have gone to the greatest lengths in stylization. The character dolls of Fritz and Erich Kleinhempel in Dresden and the creations of the Viennese workshops are equally far removed from the actual world of the child. After sketches of Kolo Moser, Fanny Zakucka, Minka Podhabka, etc., wooden dolls have been turned and painted in which the principle of 'style at any price' seems driven to extremes. Even their cloth dolls were strictly geometricized. They may have introduced fresh *nuances* of feeling, may even have attained those "highest reaches of cultured taste" and that select composition of form which Adolf Braig asserts for them (no one will dispute that), but when this critic is able to find praise for "a

180

FIG. 187. ART DOLLS
C. Heinrich, Nürnberg

FIG. 188. CAR MASCOTS
Josephine Baker. Designed and executed by Brunhilde Einenkel
Kunstgewerbehaus-Schwerdtfeger, Berlin

decidedly languid beauty'' it becomes clear at once that these creations are certainly in their wrong place when considered as dolls. In the year 1903 the Bayerische Gerwerbemuseum, in Nürnberg, offered a prize for sketches of characteristic wooden toys designed to arouse and stimulate the taste and

FIG. 189. SPANISH COUPLE
Anna Bauknecht

the imagination of children. Among the works sent in those of August Geigenberger and Bernhard Halbreiter, of Wasserburg, were particularly felicitous, as were those of Marie von Uchatius, of Vienna. In the following year the Dresden handicraft workshops made an appeal for designs to express old familiar children's toys in new forms, and were answered by artists such as Riemerschmidt, Urban, Kirchner, Wenig, Eichrodt, who sent in sketches, the marked stylization of which the critics of the time praised or condemned according to their individual points of view. For a time the groping and the searching proceeded. The first real success was achieved by Munich artists, who in 1909 instituted an exhibition of toy dolls in the warehouse of Hermann Tietz;

FIG. 190. PEASANT WOMAN WITH BASKET OF EGGS
Anna Bauknecht

here they aimed at and reached simplicity, naturalness, and genuine childishness. The dolls exhibited were equally far removed from triviality and from coarseness; the golden mean between the rude naturalistic style and the sweetly unreal style in the formation of dolls was gained at last. Here for the first time was heard the name of Marion Kaulitz as a doll artist. Her dolls are full of individuality and character and yet always remain children, so true-hearted and bright, so charmingly pert and rakish. The heads, of *papier mâché*, were modelled by Paul Vogelsanger and painted by the artist, who also made the dresses.

183

The same heads, when given different wigs and dresses, provided a series of entirely different impressions. With her Lilian Frobenius, Alice Hegemann, and Marie Maré-Schur, won distinction with their dolls, made lovingly and with insight. While it could be believed, when looking at Kaulitz's dolls, that one was gazing at real boys and girls, the dolls of Josef Wackerle move in a clever, piquant realm which, it is true, gives them charm for grown-ups, but debars them from the sphere of toys.

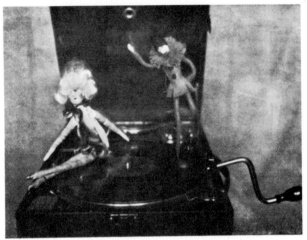

FIG. 191. AMUSING CLOTH DOLLS FOR THE GRAMOPHONE
Photo Delia

The example of Munich gave the Berliners no rest; they also had to have their exhibitions of dolls, with that flaring advertisement and that lack of taste which is so typical of all the Berlin institutions of that period. Because of that the whole thing fell flat, as such things always will in these circumstances. And yet it was in Berlin that at an exhibition of home-made toys held in 1912 was discovered an artist whose name, both in Germany and outside, is immediately called to mind whenever German dolls are spoken of—Käthe Kruse. Her maternal instinct has led her to the invention of new types of dolls. At first she made dolls only for her own children, making use then of raw potatoes as material for the heads. All her dolls arise from tender and intimate understanding of the child's mind—hence the great immediate and universal success which she yet enjoys. She has naturally replaced the potatoes with a more durable material, and now makes indestructible dolls. It is possible that the clever creations of other women artists arrest greater admiration in this sphere, but the dolls of Käthe Kruse compel love, and that is greater than admiration. The lively interest taken in her work has given the artist occasion for expressing her own views. Writing in 1923, she says:

> My dolls, particularly the little baby ones, arose from the desire to awaken a feeling that one was holding a real little baby in one's

FIG. 192. MUNICH ART DOLL
Designed and executed by Marion Kaulitz, Munich

arms. I must say, however, that this idea did not originate in my brain, but sprang from that of my sculptor father, who all his life long was concerned with the problem involved in the effect created by plastic form. Strange to say, the consideration of the emotional effect to be aroused and the recognition of the necessity of working on one's emotions is virgin soil for the doll. But it is always so; wherever there is creativeness a start must be made at the beginning in so far as there is a desire to solve the problem. And the problem of the doll, tantamount to education in maternal feeling, education in womanly act and in womanly bliss, perhaps even in a better understanding between mother and child, between mother and mother—this whole problem of the doll has certainly sufficient interest in itself.

DOLLS

At all exhibitions held since her discovery the dolls made by Käthe Kruse have been universal favourites, unrivalled by any competitor.

FIG. 193. DOLLS
Käthe Kruse

FIG. 194. MUNICH ART DOLLS
Designed and executed by Marion Kaulitz, Munich

As the German manufacturers were actuated by educational motives, French firms in 1902 offered a prize, principally with the object of finding ways and means of meeting the over-whelming German rivalry. Artists of renown, such as the sculptor Frémiet and the painters Détaille and Gérome, sent in

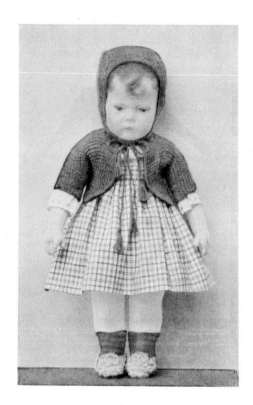

DOLL
Käthe Kruse

DUTCHMAN

GISELA

Made in the factory of Heinrich Zwanzger, Nürmberg

sketches, but this attempt resulted in nothing, for commercial circumstances do not allow themselves to be led by purely æsthetic considerations.

The attempts at reform have imparted new and powerful impulses to the interest taken in the toy doll; at a certain period

FIG. 195. DOLL: "DU MEIN SCHUFTERLE"
Käthe Kruse

the exhibitions came literally in crowds. At Brussels in 1892 the celebrated impresario Schürmann organized an exhibition of dolls which he believed required a charitable object as its excuse, but the doll-shows held in St Petersburg and in Vienna could renounce that pretext and were organized for their own sake. In 1905 at Leipzig six hundred dolls were collected together. Rich in types was the 'international' doll exhibition organized in October and November 1911 at Frankfort by the Frankfort Women's Club. Outside of Germany the Amis des Arts got up in 1926 at the once more alienated Strasbourg an

DOLLS

Exposition de Jouets Anciens, which showed much that was lovely, mainly from the collection of Robert Forrer. In the winter of 1927–28 the Märkische Museum in Berlin presented a cleverly and beautifully arranged exhibition of old dolls, mostly originating from the environs of the capital.

Formerly only the ethnographical museums had indulged in the collection of dolls, and these, as was natural, concentrated

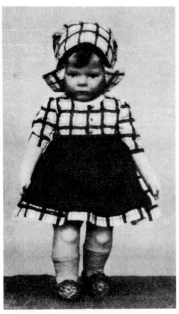

FIG. 196. DOLL: "MARINA"
Käthe Kruse

more on the exotic types, but now the other public collections freely indulge in the displaying of these objects. The Industrie-museum in Sonneberg, which must be given first place in this regard, possesses an important collection of toy dolls, including examples both of dolls and of dolls' heads dating from the year 1735. The museums of Berlin, Frankfort, Nürnberg, Prague, and Stuttgart have all directed their attention to this interesting object, and it seems to have a special fascination for the museums in the United States. The Metropolitan Museum in New York, the Children's Museum in Detroit, the Heye Foundation in New York, the Essex Institute in Salem, Massachusetts, the Fairchild Collection in Madison, Wisconsin, have permanent sections showing dolls arranged in complete series, following thus

FIGS. 197, 198. WASHABLE, UNBREAKABLE CLOTH DOLLS
Käthe Kruse

the example of the private collectors. Carmen Sylva possessed a splendid collection of dolls; that of Elisabeth Lemke passed into the hands of the Volkskunde Museum in Berlin; Rodman Wanamaker founded that of the Musée Carnavalet in Paris; while others, such as George Savile Seligmann in Paris and

FIG. 199. DOLLS
Dora Petzold
Photo Kester and Co.

Frau Wenz in Munich, carry on their collecting activities with love and ardour.

This ardour seems sometimes to overshoot the mark; the serial arrangement of dolls, such as was for a long time popular, has only a narrowly specialized value. The collection of dolls designed to provide a survey of local costumes arranged in 1893 by Dutch women in the Dutch East Indies as a present for the young Queen Wilhelmina was truly an undertaking of unquestionable value for the study of the customs of the Dutch colonies, of double value indeed, because the natives themselves joyously participated in it. The Sultan of Sambas commissioned one of

FIG. 200. DOLL: "THE GERMAN CHILD"
Käthe Kruse. After Julius Hübner's *Portrait of a Girl*

his relations, Pangeran Amar di Radja, to supervise the making of various figures painted by F. J. Duchâteau. These, in the opinion of experts, were excellently made, and the dolls are to be regarded as genuine miniature replicas of Malays and Dayaks.

FIG. 201. ITALIAN DOLLS (LENZI DOLLS) MADE OF FELT
Photo Kester and Co.

It is quite a different matter, however, when an historical object is on view. Thus in 1892 Mme Piogey at Paris exhibited sixteen dolls which were supposed to represent French feminine fashions from the year 1000 to the year 1890. At the world exhibition in Chicago in 1893 a similar collection of twenty-five dolls was on view, also designed to show the history of feminine dress in France. These attracted much attention then, but on looking at

FIG. 202. MALAYAN DOLLS

Left to right: Malay chief; Malay chieftainess; Malay in festive clothes; Malay woman in festive clothes
From the Padang Highlands of Sumatra

illustrations of the various figures now, we are compelled to describe them as merely toys, of absolutely no value from an historical point of view. Not only do the childish faces of the dolls fail to fit the *rôles* apportioned to them, a criticism which can generally be levelled at all the dolls supposed to represent women of older periods, but even the costumes themselves are

FIG. 203. BRIDEGROOM AND BRIDE FROM JAVA

only approximately correct, as is demonstrated by their measurements and by the lack of real old material. Fancy dress dolls they are, nothing more.

French women, however, have found great amusement in this game. Mme Charles Cosson in 1893 exhibited at Paris sixteen similar costume dolls, embarrassing the unfortunate Musée des Arts Décoratifs by presenting them to it. Mme Martet reproduced the figures of Balzac's *Comédie Humaine* in dolls; Mme Pulliche made six Venetian women of the eighteenth century

after the sketches of Georges Barbier, these later going to the
Metropolitan Museum in New York. This institute possesses
also a doll review showing seven centuries of fashion, which Miss

FIG. 204. COSTUME DOLL: WOMAN
PILGRIM (JAVA)

FIG. 205. COSTUME DOLL: HADJI
(JAVA)

Frances Morris executed from the paintings of old masters. The
Unions des Arts in Paris has established a collection of dolls
which represents the most celebrated actresses on the Parisian
stage—Sarah Bernhardt, Mme Réjane, Segond-Weber, Bartel,

Sorel, Granier, etc.—in their characteristic *rôles* and costumes. The wax heads were modelled by Mlle Lifraud and were painted

FIG. 206. PARISIAN COSTUME
DOLL: MARQUISE DE POMPADOUR

FIG. 207. PARISIAN COSTUME
DOLL: MERVEILLEUSE
(DIRECTORY)

FIG. 208. DOLLS IN PARISIAN POPULAR COSTUMES
Martin Guelliot
From the exhibition "L'Art pour l'Enfance" in the Musée Galliera

by Mme Claude Marlef. Mmes Lafitte and Désirat presented to the Musée National de la Guerre, in Vincennes, dolls designed to show women's fashions from 1914 to 1918; Mme Myrthas Dory

FIG. 209. FRENCH COSTUME DOLLS AT THE WORLD EXHIBITION AT
CHICAGO, 1893

in a similar set has traced the costumes of women war workers during the War years. "These will preserve for the future a memory of one of the most critical periods in French history,"

FIG. 210. DUTCH DOLLS FROM SEELAND
Nineteenth century. Presented to the Victoria and Albert Museum by
Miss Elize Frere

writes Mme Calmettes. During the War Mmes Paderewski, Lazarski, and Fiszerowni carried on propaganda by means of Polish dolls which they sent to Paris. American museums by means of dolls have exhibited all kinds of European local costumes and those of all the native Indian tribes. M. and Mme Martin Guelliot in Paris are said to possess more than six

FIG. 211. PARISIAN MODEL MANNEQUINS
Anne Lafitte Désirat
From the exhibition "L'Art pour l'Enfance" in the Musée Galliera

FIG. 213. SCHWABING PEASANT WOMAN
Bayerische Landesgewerbe-Anstalt, Nürnberg

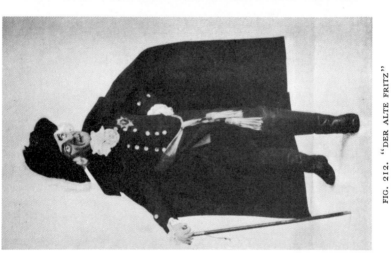

FIG. 212. "DER ALTE FRITZ"
Spielzeug-Museum, Sonneberg

hundred dolls, between 30 and 50 cm. high, representing all races of the world. Marie Koenig has been able to collect several hundred dolls from all countries for the ethnographical section of the Trocadéro. Such costume dolls have no more significance for scientific study of the folk or for the history of culture than a modern historical novel has for the study of history—that is to say, none at all. They remain embellished toys possessing value only in so far as they amuse the persons who make them and those who see them.

FIG. 214. DOLLS IN NATIONAL DRESS
Left to right: date, 1840; date, 1810; middle of the eighteenth century; beginning of the nineteenth century

XIII

DOLLS OF EXOTIC PEOPLES

IT is quite another matter with toy dolls of exotic peoples and of those classes among European nations which have not been influenced by town culture, and hence are inspired by their own imaginations. These possess a certain definite psychological interest.

> In them are reflected the talents and disposition of the various peoples. From these productions landscape and climate can be guessed at; from the manner of composition can be gauged the handicraft and the power of technical invention; from the forms the power of imagination and the artistic ability.

The elementary, or, as it may be called, the basic, doll consists of a stick, with a thickening at the end as a head; it has preserved the essentials of the human shape—the upright form. When another stick is introduced, placed cross-wise on the first, the line of the shoulders is indicated, and at once a great anatomical advance is attained. A second generation of dolls is represented in the soft bag, in which head and limbs are produced by tying up parts with string. Elisabeth Lemke found these rag dolls or 'patchwork dolls' (*Fleckerldocke*) from Sicily to Transylvania and beyond to the Ober Pfalz. In this style and manner the Hungarian children make their dolls; for the nose they use a grain of corn, with oats or pepper seeds for the eyes. At Plattensee the children pull down the petals of red poppies, wind round a blade of grass, and thus make the body and dress of a doll; the seeds form the head. The main principle remains always the vertical line, a principle which has influenced modern creative artists as well, so much so indeed that their dolls look more like wooden sticks than human figures. This primitive shape too appears in the oldest wooden dolls of Sonneberg, which reflect the human figure only in coarse outlines.

In all the five continents a survey of the toy doll will always lead us back to the three essential basic forms, and will always reveal anew the fact that toy dolls as well as magical dolls are prevailingly of the female sex. In Sanskrit the words for a doll all signify 'little daughter'; from these the words *putteli* and *puttalika* (Richard Pischel is quoted here) have survived in folk speech. The ancient Indian dolls consisted of wool, wood, buffalo-horn, or ivory, and seem to have attracted much attention among the young girls, for in the *Mahabharata* two of these ask some warriors to bring back pretty clothes for their

FIG. 215. INDIAN DOLLS
Spielzeug-Museum, Sonneberg

dolls as booty from the field of battle. The girls must have been devoted to this amusement up to the time they were marriageable, as Vatsyayana counsels boys and youths, when they desire to win the maidens' fancies, to join them in their playing with dolls. This lively interest in doll play has survived to our own times; in 1873 a doll's marriage was publicly celebrated with great festivities at Dacca, in Bengal.

Toy dolls in Siam are remarkable because they are exceptionally delicate, and the children there must either be improbably gentle or else these refined images are not intended to be played with at all. They are made of baked clay, the dresses being either represented by painting or made of real cloth; ear-rings and jewellery are rendered in silver wire. Their bearing follows the smooth elegance of the adults, although among them there are to be found some dolls representing children with the hair done up in tufts in the way characteristic of the young. The Siamese have also dolls of wood and paper.

In the Chinese and Korean languages the word 'doll' comes

FIG. 216. CLAY DOLLS FROM TIENTSIN, CHINA
Staatliches Museum für Völkerkunde, Munich

from the same root as the words for idol or fetish. This seems to confirm what Gustav Schlegel has observed; he says that little girls in China never play with dolls, these having always been regarded as endowed with magical power. Only in the last decades have come toy dolls, of puffed-out silk with heads of oiled paper and hands and feet of sepia (cuttle-fish); there are also others made of clay and *papier mâché* in the European style, but possibly these are intended only for export. In China the tumbling doll is a very popular toy; this is called in Chinese "Stand up, little priest."

According to Schlegel toy dolls were first introduced to Japan by the Dutch, nor do the great annual doll festivals of girls and boys disprove this statement, since the dolls used there could never be regarded as toys in the ordinary sense of the word.

FIG. 217. CLAY DOLLS FROM TIENTSIN, CHINA
Long Life, Wealth, and Good Fortune in Children
Staatliches Museum für Völkerkunde, Munich

DOLLS

The girls' doll festival takes place on the third day of the third month and lasts three days. Every better-class family in Japan possesses a series of dolls for this festival, these being handed down from generation to generation as treasured heirlooms. They are set on the steps of a platform, the highest always

FIG. 218. JAPANESE DOLL (TOKYO), NINETEENTH CENTURY
Victoria and Albert Museum

reserved for the Emperor and Empress. The whole is proceeded with according to certain ceremonial rites, and when the festival is over, the entire set is once more carefully packed away. The boys' doll festival takes place on May 5. The chief doll here is the Empress Jingo, a heroine of the olden days; indeed, all the dolls used in this festival are of an historical character. Japanese artists such as Hokusai delighted in depicting these festivals, which seem to have descended from an old Shinto purification feast originally held on March 3. On these occasions the whole family went to the river, and each member rubbed his body with

FIG. 219. CLAY DOLLS FROM TIENTSIN, CHINA
Staatliches Museum für Völkerkunde, Munich

a piece of paper cut by the priests in the semblance of human form, in the belief that his sins would thus be transferred to the dolls, which the boys then threw into the water. The girls' dolls

FIG. 220. ESKIMO DOLLS
Spielzeug-Museum, Sonneberg

belonged to a plastic tradition; they were the so-called 'sons of heaven'—that is to say, magical dolls which, according to popular belief, took voluntarily on themselves all possible misfortune a woman might encounter in her life. Originally the pair of dolls set highest on the platform was only a married couple, supposed to give the little girl some conception of marriage, but later the

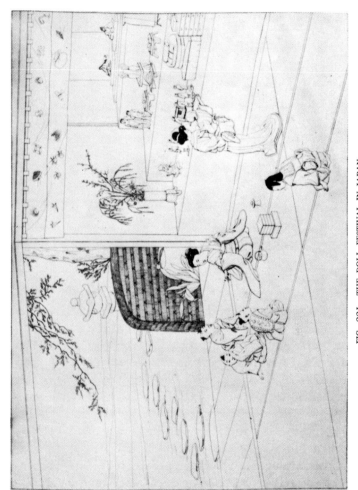

FIG. 221. THE DOLL FESTIVAL IN JAPAN

After Siebold's *Nippon*, 1840

royal couple was placed there. These Japanese dolls are diverse in kind; some, such as the *Ilinasama* figures from the Ryukyu Islands, are very roughly made of folded paper; others have heads of bamboo fibre. The ancient type consisted of a roll of paper with long threads instead of a head, but this material must originally have come from the province of Satsuma. To recog-

FIG. 222. MODERN RUSSIAN DOLL
Spielzeug Museum, Sonneberg

nize a doll in this shape one had to be told what it was. The Japanese doll festivals created a great sensation in the United States in 1927 when the Committee of World Friendship among Children, a branch of the Federal Council of the Churches of Christ in America, sent 11,000 representative dolls to the girls' festival on March 3. Thousands of these were previously exhibited at the Plaza Hotel in New York, and the finest were awarded prizes. In Tokyo the doll ship was ceremoniously received and befilmed, and there followed the usual exchange of cablegrams containing the most charming assurances of friendship. But will this "great social and educational mission" break down the difference between the United States and Japan in California and the Pacific?

In the Malay Archipelago toy dolls are made of lontava-leaves, of strips of palm-leaf plaited diagonally, or of a very roughly carved yellowish wood; they are also sewn together from cotton and palm-leaves and ornamented with glass beads. Rag dolls too, made out of a patterned cotton sacking, are to be found there. In spite of the prohibition of the Koran, the

FIG. 223. DOLL OF THE APACHE INDIANS
From the collection of A. L. Dickermann

Mohammedan children do not allow themselves to be deprived of their dolls. Mohammed himself was forced to recognize this, for his wife, Ayesha, at the time of her marriage only nine years old, brought her dolls with her to her husband's harem, and the prophet permitted her to play with them to her heart's content. The Turkish races inhabiting Russia give their children dolls made of bark, straw, and rags.

The Samoyedes make their toy dolls out of ducks' beaks, leather, or wood, and dress them in cloth; in spite of their primitive appearance they bear such resemblance to the civilized doll that we must regard the latter as their model. The Liberian dolls look like small furry creatures, somewhat similar to the Eskimo dolls, which also have connexions with the European dolls. In the Northern regions the fur doll predominates, for its dress, like that of the European dolls representing ladies, is based on the dress of the adults. Nordenskiöld met with many examples of these among the Tschuktchi, in Alaska, in East Greenland, and among the tribes of North-western America; similar toy dolls have been found in graves belonging to races long extinct.

The Indian tribes of the United States possess a great wealth of diverse kinds of toy dolls. Several scholars, such as C.

FIG. 224. DOLLS OF THE ZUÑI
Man and woman
From the collection of A. L. Dickermann

Steffens, support the view that the original discoverers of America must have found dolls already existent among these tribes, and that the Indians consequently had no need to learn from the settlers how to manufacture them. This theory, however, seems to be invalidated by the fact that the extant dolls are clearly copies of European models, using native technique and material certainly, but borrowing their shapes from abroad. Even now not all the tribes have toy dolls, and it is to be suspected that others make their dolls not so much for their own children as for foreign collectors. The Cheyennes, Iroquois, Sioux, and Apaches are said to be ignorant of the toy doll, but not so the Prairie Indians and those of the Dakota and Blackfoot tribes. These make their dolls of leather and embroider them with glass beads; the faces are grotesque, and the very carefully executed dresses seem based on models from the Old World. The Zuñi use a clay figure as a basis. The Katschina dolls of the Hopi Indians have already been referred to in another connexion; these are half cult dolls and half toy dolls, and remind us too of European types. The Pima, a Nearctic race in the south-west of the United States, have clay dolls which they paint

FIG. 225. TOY DOLL OF THE PIMA (SOUTH-WEST OF THE UNITED STATES)

and ornament with beads, with a bast apron and a girdle of wool.

In Mexico there have been discovered clay dolls, marked with the insignia of the sun, appertaining to the cults of the ancient Aztecs, supposed to belong to about the year 1000 B.C. The Indians of present-day Mexico in their exceedingly skilful way model little dolls of wax or put them together of rags and decorate them with flaxen ornaments. They also cut out of paper dolls which are very close to the prehistoric 'board idols.' The modern dolls of the natives in Guatemala, Bolivia, and Chile, which they are accustomed to crochet or knit from coloured wool over a wire frame and embellish with hair and glass beads, clearly betray Spanish influence. In Bolivia there are also primitive specimens in wax dressed in cloth or made of resin with a paper costume, and Columbia has its clay rattle dolls representing both men and women. Bone dolls with eyes of mother-of-pearl are to be found in the Rio Negro district, alongside others of plaited bark, painted and decorated with feathers in the likenesses of the local masked dancers. The Kadiueo, South American Indians, carve remarkably lifelike dolls out of wood;

FIG. 226. ANCIENT PERUVIAN DOLL, MADE OF GOLD-LEAF AND DRESSED IN CLOTH, FOUND NEAR LIMA

the Borero have male dolls made of narrow, rectangular strips of palm-leaf laid together and female dolls made of broader strips, neither the face nor the arms and legs being indicated. The dolls of the Karaya likewise dispense with head, arms, and legs; an indentation, however, marks the mouth, and the shape of the breasts is indicated in black wax. The most completely developed dolls of South America are those of Guatemala; these are small, but are most carefully dressed. The roughly carved wooden dolls of the Chaco Indians, in Paraguay, obviously derive from the sacred images which were introduced by the Jesuits, who were in power there in the eighteenth century.

FIG. 227. ANCIENT PERUVIAN CLAY DOLLS
Children's toys from the cemetery of Ancon

FIG. 228. ANCIENT PERUVIAN WOODEN DOLLS
Children's toys from the cemetery of Ancon

DOLLS

In ancient Peru, with the richly developed civilization it enjoyed before the entry of the Spaniards, there existed a doll-making art of a very high standard. Massive gold female dolls have been found there, dressed in cloth, as well as silver male dolls with three skirts and three wallets made of real cloth. When the Peruvian children died their toys were put in their graves, and the dry earth, for the most part permeated with saltpetre, has preserved them marvellously. These toy dolls were made of all conceivable materials; some, manufactured of clay pressed in moulds, had exceptionally large heads and stiffly extended

FIGS. 229, 230. ANCIENT PERUVIAN CLAY DOLLS
Children's toys from the cemetery of Ancon

limbs. They were intended to be dressed in cloth, while openings in the upper part of the head served for the securing of feathers, shells, or other ornaments. The ancient Peruvians seem to have set great store by durability. Some of the dolls which have been found there are so naïvely executed that they must have been made by the children themselves. Sometimes the faces were painted. Besides the clay dolls there were also toy dolls of carved wood, of wool, of Cabuya fibre, or of straw plaited into fairly rough shapes, in which eyes, mouth, and teeth were only indicated by indentations.

The modern toy dolls in the United States need hardly be differentiated from the European, but there are to be found among them some characteristic types. Leo Claretie bought in Kansas City a doll made out of iron wire and gutta-percha in the shape of a skeleton. This is typical, for we learn from Caswell Ellis, for example, that American children delight in playing at illness, death, and burial when they amuse themselves with their

216

dolls. During the Revolution French children, too, played with a dolls' guillotine, and even to-day Parisian shops offer for sale *chemin de fer à catastrophes* with plentiful dead and injured.

The toy dolls of African negro tribes, like those of the American Indian races, are undeniably influenced by the European. This is proved particularly by the examples originating in the Sudan, where the body is made of wood, the head and limbs of clay, and the hair of wool. The dress is of cloth, and ornaments of coins and glass beads are added. So far as the African doll has preserved its independence, generally it presents human forms only in rudest outlines. Thus the wooden dolls of the Ashanti, with bead hair, look more like shapeless chess-men than human beings; those of the Yoruba resemble blocks of wood even when they have heads attached. The dolls of the Basuto consist of bandages wound round a wooden base and provided with threads and strings of beads. These are cone-shaped, without any distinguishable head. The dolls of the Haussa are of wax, but, in spite of the nose ornaments of glass beads, they show little likeness to human form. The bone doll of the Somali has a cloth head, the hair is of wool, and the facial features are indicated by sewn-on glass beads. In Togo there are glass-eyed clay dolls which show clearly the male and female organs.

FIG. 231. ANCIENT PERUVIAN
CLAY DOLL

XIV

DOLLS USED FOR DECORATIVE PURPOSES

THE reform in the toy doll has created a strong reaction even among adults. It is not merely that the doll became a collector's object, making an appeal, after all, only to a small circle; it became fashionable, and that is a thing which always attracts the crowd. In America for a time grown-up women themselves took out dolls, and, when President Roosevelt was popular, teddy bears as well, for their daily walks. Among the follies emanating from Hollywood is the wearing of a doll as a pendant. This is attached to a silk cord and hung round the neck, a fashion truly so absurd that it deserves to be copied by female highbrows in other countries. German women are, however, content to play with their dolls indoors, taking rubber dolls with them to their baths. The tea-cosy dolls in particular, the fashion for which raged for several years, gave the greatest scope in this direction. These are common enough in the shape of a bulky balloon dress with a tiny porcelain upper part for the body, the one out of all proportion to the other. Their rapid popularity was due to the fact that they displayed fine workmanship; not being designed simply as toys, but serving a strictly practical purpose, they really depended entirely on the skill shown in making them. Apart from that they had the advantage of rapidly gathering dust and of so becoming unattractive, thus providing a welcome excuse for the preparation of a new *toilette*. While German women were still content with their tea-cosy dolls the Americans went much further, for they used the doll as a decoration for their rooms. Since a doll, from its resemblance to the human form, always retains something of a living being, when used as a piece of decoration it imparts to a room a kind of spiritual animation which no other small object of art can in any way equal. In the United States favour is given to burlesque puppets for adding an individual note to the drawing-room. These grotesque dolls are made out-of-joint; the limbs are too long, the faces repelling, the eyes squinting. In Germany Staudinger has made such dolls for the delectation of grown-ups. Emma von Sichart, of Munich,

DOLLS FOR DECORATIVE PURPOSES

using porcelain heads of Nymphenburg manufacture, has dressed very charmingly and tastefully clad figures in the tea-cosy style; Betty Krieger, of Frankfort, made series of costume dolls, in replicas of Bavarian, Hessian, and other peasant dresses, with love and accuracy; Hella Bibrawicz and Clarisse Spiegel at Nürnberg in 1921 held an exhibition of attractively attired drawing-room dolls. Clever fingers have composed all kinds of pretty things, but this type of doll first became art under the hands of Lotte Pritzel.

When this artist first introduced her work she came as a revelation; it was as if the curtain, hitherto concealing a completely unknown sphere of art, had been suddenly drawn. One hardly dares to use the term 'doll' for these creations, since this word so easily leads one astray. These figures possess a psychological strength, in marked contrast to their delicate butterfly-like forms. "They came to life," as H. Rupé says very beautifully, "like improvisations of the subconscious. Lotte Pritzel must herself feel surprised at her own fancies." Her methods are extraordinarily simple: a wire frame, a little slip of silk or *chiffon*, some glass beads or spangles, and at the top a wax head. And with these she creates works of art which, once seen, can never be forgotten. They recall Aubrey Beardsley and the canvases of Greco, yet they are inspired by a wholly individual note, a tremblingly

FIG. 232. THE SWORD-DANCER
Lotte Pritzel
Photo Delia

fervent rhythm. The artist has baptized her fantasies with the names of Simonetta, Ganymed, Bajadere, Chichette, the Unveiled, Hamlet, Adoration, and so on; these names originate from the difficulty of finding an expression for complexes of sentiment which are experienced, but cannot be defined. They are there so soon as the figure is seen; they have no binding motive, for Lotte Pritzel works freely, without any backward glance at artistic conventions. If one seeks the counterpart of these enigmatical figures in the world of the known, one might perhaps find it most fittingly in music. They shape themselves as harmonious tones, fleeting memories, half-forgotten dreams, ever threatening to vanish into the nothingness of which they were born. The faces are visionary, morbid; the figures are exaggeratedly slim; the attitudes are strained.

FIG. 233. DOLLS
Relly Mailander

Fascinating, bewildering, tormenting, if you like, is the sexlessness of these dolls; in their expression and in their indeterminate dress they possess something excitingly ambiguous. The secret they hold can never be reached. All the perversions of a soulless, hopeless species drowning in sensuousness are here carried to extremes, a ghostly existence in the world of reality. Lotte Pritzel's dolls have more of the essence of our age than a whole glass palace full of modern pictures. That word, then, so much misused is here in its proper place; every doll made by this artist is an experience for the person who looks at it, and an experience need not necessarily be merely one of pleasure; it can also sometimes arouse reflections. Before she discovered her own style Lotte Pritzel experimented in making

220

FIG. 234. ORPHEUS
Lotte Pritzel
Photo Delia

the heads of her dolls out of chestnuts; then she turned to toy
dolls with movable limbs, and, after developing her talents,

FIG. 235. DOLL
Relly Mailander

came at last to the wire skeleton, which granted her a flexibility
that does not belong to this world. The wax heads she models
and paints herself. She has found success from her very first

222

appearance (at Munich (?) in 1909 (?)) ; she has held exhibitions and received general recognition. The cultural section of the Universum-Film dedicated a whole film to her dolls. The sensitive, subtle art of Lotte Pritzel is, like everything genuinely

FIG. 236. DOLLS OF WOOL
Spielzeug-Museum, Sonneberg

original, incapable of imitation; maybe because of that so many have tried to imitate it.

The dolls made by Erna Pinner, to which she gives such titles as the Superior, the Elegant, the Distinguished, the Resolute, Woman of To-day, are made of cloth and have movable limbs; the head too is of cloth and painted. They are not fragile works of art like the dolls of Lotte Pritzel; on the contrary, they gain by being taken in the hand, although they remain creations of the drawing-room, far removed from the nursery. The

Pritzel dolls are unrivalled in their own sphere, just as the Käthe Kruse dolls in theirs; perhaps only the paper dolls of Erna Muth, of Dresden, can be considered artistic creations worthy of being compared with them. Erna Muth first exhibited her works in 1919, at a time when there was the greatest lack of

FIG. 237. PAPER DOLL
Erna Muth, Dresden
Photo Kester and Co.

materials, limiting herself to the cheapest substances, wire and silk paper. She succeeded both in surmounting the external difficulties inherent in the process of fashioning the materials at her command and in getting over the poverty of the stuff with which she worked, wresting effects from it which possibly costlier and more supple material would not have offered her. The flexible wire allowed the artist to give her dolls an attitude full of the suggestion of powerful movement; indeed, the further she went in that direction, the greater was the success of her figures.

DOLLS FOR DECORATIVE PURPOSES

Surprisingly simple in technique yet rich in appearance and worked out with sovereign skill, the dolls of Erna Muth make us regret nothing save their perishability.

The drawing-room doll of grown-ups is a fashion like all other fashions; it will vanish again from the vitrines as once it entered them. And that will not be the first occurrence of this phenomenon. It is to be remembered that eighteenth-century society likewise played with dolls, in point of fact even with the same sort of dolls, for the porcelain figures then in fashion could just as little be placed in the hands of children as could the dolls made by Pritzel and Erna Muth.

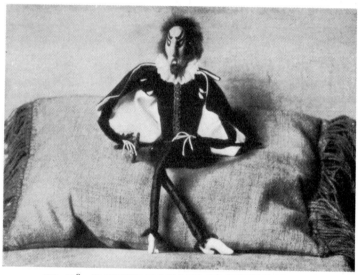

FIG. 238. GROTESQUE CLOTH DOLL REPRESENTING MEPHISTO
Photo Kester and Co.

XV

PORCELAIN FIGURES

THE art of porcelain had been introduced to Europe only a few years when modellers set to work on plastic objects as well as on crockery, and, indeed, reached immediately to a perfection

FIG. 239. CHINESE PRIEST
F. A. Bustelli
Staatliche Porzellan-Manufaktur,
Nymphenburg

in form through which the artists expressed by the means of porcelain the finest ideas of their period. Winckelmann, it is true, wrote disrespectfully at the time, declaring that "Porcelain is mostly used for making ridiculous dolls," but to-day we pass a different judgment. Indeed, this porcelain now appears to us, in the words of Max Sauerlandt, to be "the most perfect material for the self-portraiture of the eighteenth century." It became the real factor which, by settling style and giving direction, influenced rococo art; to-day it would be difficult to form

226

a mental picture of that epoch without the help of its china, just as it would be difficult to picture the *Biedermeier* age without its lithography or the Second Empire without its photography. From the very beginning porcelain, on account of its delicacy, was fit for the use of a pampered society, and this delicacy has been assumed by the shapes into which it was formed, being,

FIG. 240. DOLL WITH PASSAU CHINA HEAD
Emma von Sichart

indeed, imposed upon them by the fragility of the material. The shaping of the models was by no means a simple affair; even the smallest figure had often to be divided into numerous little pieces, later set together. The seams were then plastered; little details were touched up by hand; the whole was worked over with the modelling stick; and even then the firing could bring completely unexpected surprises, for the figures shrank by a third in the oven. This circumstance influenced the attitudes taken by the figures, and compelled little arms and legs to assume twists not always intended, but certainly through these means was produced a contour, the arbitrary nature of which

227

attained to what the rococo art desired and strove after. The gleaming lights which play so constantly over the reflecting glazed surface, and often change the emphasis so marvellously, produce that capricious modulation of expression, that constantly shimmering ebb and flow of light, that precious coquetry, which was so peculiar to the whole society of the time—a society whose elders rouged and whose young powdered themselves white.

FIG. 241. CAVALIER AT A PEDESTAL
F. A. Bustelli
Staatliche Porzellan-Manufaktur,
Nymphenburg

FIG. 242. LEDA
F. A. Bustelli
Staatliche Porzellan-Manufaktur,
Nymphenburg

The material itself, thus newly bestowed on European art, possessed great advantages—the pure white of its substance, the animating shimmer of its glaze, and the permanence of its colours. Happy chance, too, brought it immediately into the right hands. The first modeller of Meissen ware, Johann Joachim Kändler, was a commanding artistic personality, to whom it was granted to conjure up elegance and grace, the ideals of the life of his time, into porcelain plastic form. He found worthy followers in the rival factories which sprang up so rapidly during the period. Dominik Auliczek and Franz Anton Bustelli in Nymphenburg, Johann Peter Melchior in Höchst, Karl Gottlieb Lück in Frankenthal, Wilhelm Beyer in

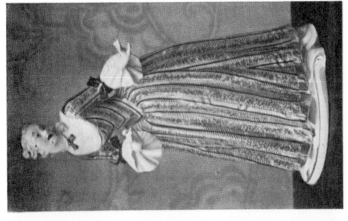

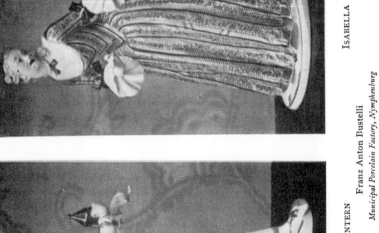

PIERROT WITH LANTERN

ISABELLA

Franz Anton Bustelli

Municipal Porcelain Factory, Nymphenburg

FIGURE OF A HORSEMAN, AFTER LEONHARDI
Theodor Kerner
Staatliche Porzellan-Manufaktur, Nymphenburg

PORCELAIN FIGURES

Ludwigsburg, Simon Feilner in Fürstenberg, besides many others who might be named, brought a great deal of talent to their work. To them all belongs a surprising power in invention and in the shaping of forms and a truly inexhaustible imagination. The models of china dolls emanating from German factories may be counted in their thousands, and perhaps as many more have

FIG. 243. SCARAMOUCHE, FROM THE ITALIAN COMEDY
F. A. Bustelli
Staatliche Porzellan-Manufaktur, Nymphenburg

perished. In their multiplicity these plastic motives comprehend the whole world of rococo life—cavaliers and their ladies, gods and goddesses, figures of the Italian comedy, dancers, singers, soldiers, Turks, and Chinese. Whatever names they were given, whether they were taken from real life or had only a mythological significance, whether they took their conception from the higher spheres or descended to the lower orders of hand-workers, peasants, fishermen, huntsmen, shepherds, gardeners, is of no import; they all belong to the Court circles, an exclusively aristocratic style being reflected in their deportment and dress.

Spirit, taste, temperament, *joie de vivre*, and amiability seem to have united to produce in these china dolls a smiling reflection of eighteenth-century society. The interest in the rococo period, still so vital in our own time and still exercising such a powerful charm on cultured people, is mainly inspired by this porcelain plastic art which gives to the epoch such a high importance. No other period and no artists so gifted as these had such

FIG. 244. LADY IN A HOOPED DRESS
F. A. Bustelli
Staatliche Porzellan-Manufaktur, Nymphenburg

material at their disposal. We grant to the ladies and gentlemen of that long-vanished age a pre-eminent charm; we like to dream of their superior grace and their playful mastery of all that concerns social intercourse. But who knows whether these beloved dolls do not deceive us and lead us astray? Do we not attribute to their models merits which perhaps spring only from the artists' imaginations? Were the Upper Bavarians whom Auliczek and Bustelli saw before them about the middle of the eighteenth century really so utterly different a type of people from what their descendants are to-day? Were they indeed so slim and agile, so bewitching in every movement, so expressive in every gesture? Was it not really but the spirit of the creative artist which incidentally granted to these dolls that charm through which they yet exercise their fascination? Have they not perhaps borrowed charms which assuredly could not have been justified by sober reality? Kändler, Melchior, Bustelli, and others are those from whom rococo art borrows the transfiguring glitter which shines around it; from them the little gentlemen take their bold gallantry, the little ladies their

FIG. 245. CHINAMAN WITH A LUTE
F. A. Bustelli

coquettish reticence; from them come the artlessness of the little affectations of the figures and the grace of their artificiality.

The modellers, too, were those who found in these porcelain dolls an expression for the entire temper and culture of the period, who, with their modelling sticks in their hands, traced all *nuances* of feeling, and accompanied their contemporaries from the wantonness of courtly gallantry to the bliss of sentimental *bourgeois* tears, starting with polite inuendoes and finishing with little funereal monuments. But seldom has such a sovereign skill been applied to objects of so narrow a range and of so playful a tendency, and Georg Hirth is unquestionably right when, in his enthusiastic praise of this German art, he wishes to compare it with the Tanagra figures of classical Greece alone. In

231

their bold conception they resemble these; in the care with which they are executed they surpass the classical dolls. This truly is

FIG. 246. WOMAN FROM TEGERNSEE
J. Wackerle
Staatliche Porzellan-Manufaktur, Nymphenburg

a precious province of rococo art through which Germany has enriched the whole art of the eighteenth century.

When rococo art had died away in a riot of colour and movement, and the antique style gained predominance, this porcelain plastic art lost its charm. The white, unglazed, and unpainted biscuit china was given preference by those who raved about the

FIG. 247. LADY WITH A MUFF
J. Wackerle
Staatliche Porzellan-Manufaktur, Nymphenburg

marble whiteness of Greek sculpture. The precious rococo plastic was accused of tastelessness, and, as of old the images of gods, the ancestor images, and the idols had ended as toy dolls, about the beginning of the nineteenth century these irreplaceable porcelain figures were put into the hands of ignorant youth and destroyed. Marie von Ebner-Eschenbach relates that in her father's palace the old Meissen crockery was handed over to the domestics; the family ate only from pressed English earthenware, this being considered more modern and elegant. In the *Biedermeier* period the Viennese manufacturers produced a new sort of very charming china doll, but the dolls of Thüringer ware brought the porcelain of the time into disrepute. Very beautiful costume figures, the subjects of which came mostly from the old town of Ulm, were made by the potter and embosser J. J. Rommel and his sons Septimus and Nonus in Ulm during the first half of the nineteenth century. These were made of clay, baked and painted.

XVI

UTENSILS IN DOLL FORM

THE china plastic ware of the eighteenth century, in addition
to its uncommon richness in ornamental figures, took up another
style which had been popular from ancient times as an element

FIG. 248. EGYPTIAN
IVORY PAINT-BOX IN
HUMAN SHAPE

FIG. 249. EGYPTIAN WOODEN
PAINT-BOX IN HUMAN
SHAPE

in decoration; this was the making of various utensils in doll form.
It is generally assumed that the old Egyptian 'stick figures'
show the first beginnings of the introduction of the human shape
into various utensils. However that may be, it is certainly met
with at an early date in all parts of the world and at all stages of
culture. For the classical period there is sufficient evidence to
show that dolls were used in diverse ways as supports and

235

handles for vessels and lamps. Large Greek vases are extant which are decorated with small clay dolls.

How closely the ideas harmonize is shown by a comparative glance at remnants of ancient art in this kind. The Romans, for example, loved to make their bronze weights in the form of little figures, a custom which is also to be found among the Ashanti negroes in Africa. For the weighing of gold-dust the

FIG. 250. KOKA-EATER—CLAY VESSEL
Chan Chan Chimu civilization, Peru

latter make brass weights in the shape of little men and women, between 3 and 5 cm. high. The natives of New Guinea give human form to the hooks they make for hanging up their food in order to protect it from being devoured by wild beasts; and in the shape of vessels the human form is to be discovered in all latitudes. The Bakuba, in the Belgian Congo, carve wooden goblets in the form of dolls, but the most extraordinary testimony of this style, carried out absolutely systematically, is provided by the New World. The Chimu civilization of ancient Peru had hardly any vessels except those made in human shape; they even introduced cripples and blind men in this way. Similar pots and other utensils were made by the Tzapoteks in prehistoric Mexico.

The Middle Ages inherited this taste from the ancients. While the art of sculpture on this side of the Alps was making its earliest,

236

FIG. 251. CLAY VESSELS IN HUMAN SHAPE FOUND IN COLUMBIA

tentative experiments the Germani were already engaged in making their utensils in plastic rounded human forms. They thus loved to give human appearance to cast vessels, reliquaries, candlesticks, and other similar objects of daily utility. The Renaissance, baroque, and rococo periods adopted and transformed this

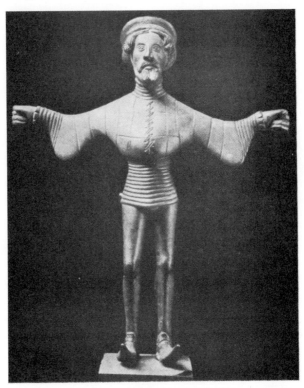

FIG. 252. CANDLESTICK, ABOUT 1400
Louvre, Paris

motif in their art work. During the sixteenth century the virgin goblet provided a popular pastime. This represents in precious metal a full-length figure of a woman dressed in the fashion characteristic of the time, with large hoop dress. With both its hands this figure holds aloft a little cup, which is on a swivel. When the goblet was in use the large vessel was first filled and then the smaller. The gallant endeavoured to empty the large one to the dregs, and if he succeeded the lady drained the smaller. In a drink-loving age such pastimes formed a pleasant spice for the stupid carousals to which it did homage. In the Castle of

Rosenborg is preserved a silver goblet representing King Christian IV racing on horseback. The horse's head forms the cover, the forelegs the handle, and the body the goblet. The whole thing was made at Brunswick in 1596. Similar drinking toys (Diana on a stag, for example), sometimes fitted with clockwork, are to be found to-day in almost all collections concerned with the history of culture.

FIGS. 253, 254. SKETCHES FOR GOBLETS
Water-colours by Jakob Mores, of Hamburg. About 1570

The cheapest earthenware proceeded on the same path. In this ware were produced tankards fitted with lids, intended to be emptied before being set down. Karl Simm refers to a goblet made in this shape by a Cologne tile-baker of 1550, as well as to others representing monks, nuns, and other figures of the time transformed into drinking vessels. The Tirol clay-modeller Christoph Gandtner, of Innsbruck, who worked about 1585, was particularly skilful in inventing such things. He has foot-soldiers, girls, Franciscan monks, women innkeepers, and so on, all glazed in variegated colours and all made to be used as tankards. In the seventeenth century the glass-works too made goblets in human form out of bottle glass; in this blown-glass style monks formed a favourite subject. There are also lady

239

tankards intended to be emptied without being set down; sometimes their dresses were decorated with glass threads. During the seventeenth and eighteenth centuries the pockets of elegant ladies and gentlemen were filled with all kinds of little useless trinkets which commonly assumed human form. There were,

FIG. 255. LARGE VIRGIN GOBLET OF
FRIEDRICH HILLEBRAND
Nürnberg. 1580

for instance, tobacco-grinders, by means of which one could grind one's own snuff. These were made of ivory, box-wood, or bronze, and represented shepherds, shepherdesses, drinkers. Italian comedians, and so on. The smoking tobacco too required its little trinkets: pipe-cleaners of silver in the shape of chimney sweeps or harlequins, pipe-fillers of amber in the shape of ,beautiful girls or crouching little men. As was natural, the greater proportion of these pretty treasures was intended for the ladies. The chief place was taken by the perfume bottle,

240

which it was difficult to do without at a time when no one bathed and no one washed save in exceptional cases. There are peculiar and pretty examples of these in plenty: King David in amber, young girls in ivory, squatting men, often in not very decent postures, in box-wood, but the greater proportion are in porcelain. The manufacturers in Meissen, Höchst, Veilsdorf,

FIG: 256. AQUAMANILE, AFTER 1300
National Museum, Copenhagen

and Vienna produced in every conceivable shape little dolls designed to be used as flagons—babies in swaddling clothes, gentlemen, ladies, Moors, Savoyards, pierrots—painted in various colours and mounted in gold and silver. Even Shakespeare was made use of as a flask in Chelsea ware.

Another object utilized by women was the needle-box, which in the hands of the peasants, during all periodical changes in style, preserved its original shape of a child in swaddling clothes. This object is closely connected with the nutcracker and the smoking mannequin, which too have been preserved in the houses of the peasantry. The latter is made to resemble a

241

Rübezahl (a fabulous mountain spirit). In its empty stomach is placed a fumigating pastille, the vapour of which comes through the open mouth, giving the illusion that the little man is smoking.

FIG. 257. AQUAMANILE, FOURTEENTH CENTURY
Bargello, Florence

The nineteenth century discovered the daily use of water and soap and thus made the perfume bottle superfluous, but in its place it provided good society (before the invention of the electric bell) with the table-bell. The Musée Rétrospectif of

NUTCRACKERS, EIGHTEENTH CENTURY
Bayerisches National-Museum, Munich

the Paris exhibition in 1900 succeeded in bringing together a multitudinous array of these handbells, the most popular shapes among which were those of ladies in hooped dresses of all styles, from the sixteenth century down to the period of Louis-Philippe of France, although there were also dozens of figures representing, in the greatest possible variety, characters as different as charwomen, Jeanne d'Arc, and Napoleon I in his cloak. To a certain extent this exhibition drew attention to their value as collectors' objects. Candle-extinguishers well deserved to be placed alongside of these. Such extinguishers, indispensable at a time when one dared not blow out a tallow candle for fear of the unpleasant smell it caused, represented monks, nuns, hermits, *curés*, and ladies, making us admire the inventive spirit which had been expended so fruitfully on this trivial object. We ought, however, to consider ourselves lucky that we can now collect without having to make use of them.

FIG. 258
NUTCRACKER
Erzgebirge

The doll gave its form to some objects; it gave its name to others. In heraldry the common representation of a human body with mutilated arms is called a *Docke*, and in several parts of Germany, in Thuringia and Saxony for example, a bundle of yarn, since it looks like a doll, is called a *Döckchen* of yarn, in spite of the fact that that word otherwise has long disappeared from both colloquial and written language. The proverbial expression in Berlin for something far distant is 'as far off as the dolls.' This is explained by the fact that in the eighteenth century the Grosser Stern in the Tiergarten was embellished with statues, and when the citizens wanted to take a long Sunday walk they went 'as far as the dolls.'

The peasant, of course, knows the doll as well as the townsman. In Silesia, Bohemia, and Slovakia the beehives are often made to assume human shape by the use of branches of poplar- or lime-trees, and scarecrows are obviously made to resemble human beings. In Bavaria the latter are called *Tadema*, which, according to Schmeller, derives from *tattern*, which is synonymous with *zittern* ('to tremble'). Grimm, however, thinks that a derivation from *Tatar* (wild, dissolute fellows) is more probable. These

243

figures always retain the original shape of the doll—the stick with a cross-piece attached, completely covered with clothes. At harvest time too one speaks of 'dolls,' although in this connexion the word is used only by students concerned with matters appertaining to folk-life, and not by the peasants themselves.

FIG. 259. BEEHIVE FROM HÖFEL

In some districts, as, for instance, Lippe, both for the sake of drying the corn and for its easy handling, the sheaves are bound into a bundle by the reaper, such a bundle being referred to as a 'doll' because of its doll-like appearance. One of these sheaves is then set up perpendicularly with its stump on the ground; usually eight other sheaves are arranged round about it in a circle, and the whole is covered with a large sheaf, the ears of corn hanging down like thatch over the others. In the shadow these 'dolls' of corn ripen, and the grain is protected from heavy rains.

XVII

THE DOLL AND THE STAGE

THE theatre has not been able to do without the doll. The medieval stage made use of the doll in its production of mystery plays; at that period the representation of martyrdoms and other horrors was popular, and, as such scenes could not well be interpreted by living actors, for these particular episodes the actors were replaced by dolls, described in French texts as *feinctes*. The stage directions for the *Mystère des Trois Doms*, which was produced at Romans in 1509, devoted special attention to the costume of the dolls utilized for this purpose. The materials for the dresses on that occasion cost thirty-seven florins, a sum equivalent to about forty pounds pre-War.

Dolls were essential, too, for the rich entries and pageants of that time. When, for example, Duke Borso of Milan entered Reggio in 1453, a pretty little girl, dressed as Fides, greeted him and allegorically destroyed Heathen Idolatry, which was represented by a doll on a pedestal.

Even to-day the stage cannot get on without dolls; many dumb parts fall to these, in particular those of very little children. Up to the closing years of last century the *rôles* of little children at the Hoftheater in Weimar were taken by the great toy doll Frieda, which belonged to a family which lived at Frauenplan. One of Frieda's loveliest memories was of the time when Privy Councillor Goethe once found her in the park and sent her back to those who had lost her.

The doll is indispensable at many folk pastimes and festivals, such as have survived up to at least a short time ago. To the Christmas ceremonies in Mexico was attached the *pinata*, a clay-headed doll which blindfolded children sought to seize and break. At the New Year there was a certain sport practised in the factories of Basle, when a doll, the 'Silvester bag,' was given to the workwoman who was the last to arrive. On Twelfth Night in the Sarntal of Switzerland *Glöckelsinger* ('bell-singers') used to go in procession through the village carrying with them a female straw doll and asking for gratuities. At the conclusion the figure was beaten into shreds. Most common were the so-called *Winteraustragen* at the close of the carnival. This particular custom has survived longest in Italy, Spain, and Portugal. There the doll in the shape of an old woman used to be carried over the boundaries and then burned or thrown into the water. In Oporto a straw doll in female dress used to be carried through the streets to the door of the oldest woman inhabitant and then burned in the market square.

On this side of the Alps too there were to be found, not so very long ago, traces of this ancient custom. In Baden Sauerland and in Lower Austria a hideous straw doll was carried out of the village and buried in snow or dung. In the region of Glogau, in Silesia, on Mid-Lent Sunday a doll made of straw or wood was borne in procession and then was beaten, burned, or thrown into the water. The *Sechseläuten* ('Six Strokes of the Bell') in Zürich was, or is, a very similar custom. On one of the last Mondays in April there used to be a great procession of the guilds there with carts and horses. At the conclusion the *Bögg* was burned at the lake on a pile of wood, this *Bögg* being a grotesque doll, representing winter. The festival was called *Sechseläuten* because of the big bell rung then and not again until September. Among the Saxons in Transylvania the girls dress up a pretty doll in festival clothes and carry it through the village to a girl who represents life. To her they present the dress and throw the doll itself into a brook. In Mexico during Passion Week life-size dolls, often beautifully dressed and sometimes representing negroes, were until recently burned publicly under the name of Judas. This custom is to be found also in some Catholic districts of Germany. On Whit Sunday the peasants in Prignitz used to organize a dolls' riding match; in the Altmark the doll used to be placed on a cow. On Whit Sunday in Steiermark a life-size doll clad in rags, the so-called *Pfingslötter*, is placed before the window of any girl who sleeps in past sunrise.

About 1850 Harry Phelps, an eleven-year-old lad in Stratford, Ontario, Canada, amused himself by making dolls stuffed with old clothes so that they resembled human beings and might be transformed into 'spirits.' The thing created such a sensation that Andrew Jackson Davis was dispatched to investigate the matter. In such harmless way was born the American spiritualism of to-day. In 1873 a 'spirit photographer,' famous in his own time, Buguet by name, made use of dolls, enveloped in sheets, for his pictures. He was certainly condemned for his rude fraud, but that did not make much impression on those who believed in him.

XVIII
EDIBLE DOLLS

THAT dolls—that is to say, objects resembling human form—can be made of all possible materials was shown at the exhibition at Frankfort in 1911. Here there were not only imitation bottles and work-bags made in doll shape, not to speak of the inevitable tea-cosy, but also little cork dolls which had originated from a competition organized by the wine stores of Matheus Müller in Eltville. This exhibition showed many similarly clever toys, such as dolls made of balls of cotton, short sticks, fish bladders, and fir-cones. Whether they had edible dolls there we do not know, although these might well have had a place, for they are at least as old as the toy doll. Technically this kind of bakery is called 'picture bread.' The articles baked generally represented domestic animals and were used as substitutes for these when sacrifices were to be made. Human figures of this kind were, of course, by no means rare, these being mainly connected with annual and family festivals. Herodotus heard of them in Egypt, and they were popular too in Greece. When Christianity succeeded in quelling idolatry the idol figures continued to be copied in bakery at least. This superstitious custom, connected with the New Year, was reproved by St Eligius (588–659), while the Synod of Liptinæ, in 743, prohibited the making of idols of sanctified flour.

The *Indiculus Superstitionum*, of the eighth or ninth century, speaks of "simulacra de consparsa farina," which perhaps refers to gingerbread. *Frithjof's Saga* tells how the heathens baked idols at the *dîsa blôt* and smeared them with oil; through Frithjof's error or misfortune a baked *baldur* dropped into the fire, the flames fell on the fat, and the house was burned down.

Perhaps it was on this account that Norwegian laws of the thirteenth century prohibited the ceremonial baking of bread in human shape. The severest punishments were meted out to those in whose houses dough offerings in the shape of the human form were found concealed. Such an one was declared an outlaw and was exiled after being deprived of his possessions.

In ancient Mexico the edible doll was utilized at certain high feasts in connexion with divine service. For the main feast of Huitzilopochtli, in the fifteenth month of the year, a large image of that god was made by the temple virgins out of seeds and the blood of children, and on touching it men were supposed to receive absolution from their sins. After the offering of human

sacrifice a priest in the dress of the war-god shot an arrow at this image and divided the separate pieces among the people, the king receiving the heart. He who ate of it pledged himself to Huitzilopochtli in regard to certain services, sacrificial presents, and acts of penitence.

The gingerbread doll had a tenacious life, perhaps because it appealed to the stomach and not to the spirit. The shapes which it assumed remained the same for centuries. Thus, the three holy virgins St Einbede, St Warbede, and St Willebede have long survived the worship once devoted to them; genera-tions ago that became

FIGS. 260, 261. GINGERBREAD FIGURES
Dresden. About 1810

merely mythical, but in the shape of cakes, which are still to be found to-day, they continue to give delight both to children and to grown-ups. On his eleventh birthday Schreiber received a gingerbread man which was as large as himself. In the Middle Ages sweets in the form of small figures used to be offered for sale in the streets of Paris. Vasari records that Jacopo Sansovino made sugar figures for artists' feasts, and legend declares that the genius of Thorwaldsen was discovered by this means when he modelled a dough-cake figure for a dinner. At the great feasts of the courts little figures made of sugar or marzipan continued popular for long; porcelain took the place of these substances for the first time in the eighteenth century. In his description of the "spectacular dishes" which were provided at Munich in November 1613 for the nuptials of the Duchess Magdalene and the Count Palatine Wolfgang, Philipp Hainhofer tells us that several of the figures were made to move, in spite of the fact that they were eatable. The devil, always thought of as connected with St Nicholas, is still made, under the name of *Kletzenmännlein*, *Krampus*, or *Klaubauf*, out of chocolate, gingerbread, baked fruit, or raisins. These once used to be sold at the Fair of St Nicholas in Vienna, held on December 6, some of them being even life-size. The *Zwetschgen*, or *Kletzenkrampus*, consists only of two sticks put together in the shape of a cross and ornamented with dried plums, dates, figs, etc. August Geigenberger, of Munich, used to make these up very cleverly, dressing them in costumes of tissue paper.

At Warmbrunn, in the Riesengebirge, there is a *Tallsacken* fair held on Palm Sunday. The *Tallsack* is a human-shaped figure made of dough with eyes of currants, holding an egg at the breast. Both sexes are represented in this type of baking, the male sex being distinguished by a little beard of thread.

THE DOLL IN LITERATURE

It is, indeed, only natural that play and play dolls—two such important elements in the life of the child—could not remain without an echo in fine literature. One need but refer to Andersen's charming fairy-tales to see how great a part is taken there by little dolls representing girls and by tin soldiers. The much more powerful poetic genius of Clemens Brentano, in whose *Gockel, Hinkel, und Gackeleia,* too, "a beautiful figure of art" is the chief centre of interest, has been completely eclipsed by the great success of the Danish writer.

In his tales Hoffmann often makes dolls and nutcrackers the main characters of his stories, and by their means the whole romantic spirit of his riotous imagination is thrown into relief. These, however, were not written for children. For the latter Cosmar's *Puppe Wunderhold,* written in the *Biedermeier* period, with illustrations by Luise Thalheim, was much more suitable. This is a German forerunner of Lewis Carroll's *Alice's Adventures in Wonderland,* and was not less dear to little German girls than Alice was to English childhood.

Dickens's humorous and warm-hearted genius delighted in dolls and in their makers, but the *Fitzebutze* of Richard Dehmel, who regards "the childish toy in the higher, philosophical perspective of eternity," made only a slight appeal to children.

Playing with the doll, which, although it is a lifeless being, may yet exercise so strongly suggestive a power, has led to playing the doll. In the ancient Indian *Kamasutra* a game is referred to which is named there the "imitation of the doll," and this indeed consists of naught else than the imitation on the part of the players of doll-like actions and movements. In the eighties E. Rathgeber wrote a ballet, *Spielwarenzauber* (*The Magic of Toys*), the subject of which was based on a fairy-tale from *Fantaska,* where the dolls in a shop come to life and discuss the purchasers each of them would desire.

The greatest and most lasting success, however, was gained by the ballet of Josef Bayer, *Puppenfee* (*The Doll Fairy*), which

THE DOLL IN LITERATURE

appeared on the stage about 1890 and is still being played after the passing of so many years. At New York in 1914 Anna Pavlova danced as a doll, dressed in a costume which Albert Rutherston had designed for her.

FIG. 262. FIRST LESSONS IN RIDING
After the lithograph by Francis, 1832

BIBLIOGRAPHY

WHILE this bibliography of books and articles is not intended to be exhaustive, I have considerably expanded the list of such works given in the original German edition of this book. The present bibliography provides, I think, a fuller list of available material on the theme than is elsewhere to be found.—*Translator.*

ADAMS, M.: *Toy-making at Home* (1915).

ALLEMAGNE, H. R. D': *Histoire des Jouets* (Paris, 1903).

ANDREE, R.: *Ethnographische Parallelen und Vergleiche* (Leipzig, 1889).

—— "Rachepuppen" (*Globus*, lxxvii, 1900).

—— *Votive und Weihegaben des katholischen Volkes in Süddeutschland* (Brunswick, 1904).

ANTONIELLI, U.: "Una statuetta femminile di Savignano sul Panaro e il problema delle figure dette Steatopigi" (*Bulletino di Paletnologia italiana*, 1925).

BAESSLER, —: *Altperuanische Kunst* (Leipzig, 1902–3).

BANGE, E. T.: *Die Kleinplastik der deutschen Renaissance in Holz und Stein* (Munich, 1928).

BARTRAM, N. D.: Игрушка. Ея исторія и значеніе (Moscow, 1912).

BASTIAN, A.: *Der Fetisch an der Westküste Guineas* (Berlin, 1884).

BAUMEISTER, A.: *Denkmäler des klassischen Altertums* (Munich, 1885).

BAUR, E. E. VOM: "Insurgents in Toyland: Frau Kruse" (*Good House-keeping*, December 1911).

BAYER, J.: "Die eiszeitlichen Venusstatuetten" (*Die Eiszeit*, I, ii, 1924).

BECQ DE FOUQUIÈRES, L.: *Les Jeux des anciens* (Paris, 1873).

BENKARD, E.: *Das ewige Antlitz* (Berlin, 1927).

BENNDORF, —: *Antike Gesichtshelme und Sepulcralmasken* (Vienna, 1878).

BISCARI, PRINCIPE: *Sopra gli ornamenti e trastulli de' bambini* (Florence, 1781).

BLANCHET, A.: *Étude sur les figurines en terre cuite de la Gaule* (Paris, 1891).

BLÜMMER, H.: *Technologie und Terminologie der Gewerbe bei Griechen und Römern* (1897).

BOAS, K.: "Über Warenhausdiebinnen mit besonderer Berücksichtung sexueller Motive" (*Archiv für Kriminal-Anthropologie und Kriminalistik*, lxv, Leipzig, 1916).

—— "Weitere Beiträge zur forensischen Bedeutung des Puppenfetischismus" (*Archiv für Kriminal-Anthropologie und Kriminalistik*, lxviii, 1918).

BOESCH, —: *Kinderleben in der deutschen Vergangenheit* (Leipzig, 1900).

—— "Die Puppe als Spielzeug für das Kind" (*Kind und Kunst*, i, 1904–5).

253

DOLLS

Böttiger, —: *Hainhofersche Kunstschrank Gustav Adolfs in Upsala* (Stockholm, 1910).

Breuer, R.: "Puppen" (*Neue Revue*, Berlin, 1908).

Bronner, I.: "Puppenmodelle in der Festtracht polnisch-jüdischer Bürgerfrauen aus dem 17. bis 19. Jahrh." (*Jahrbuch für jüdische Volkskunde*, 1923).

Brook, D.: *Terra-cottas* (1921).

Brücker-Embden, O.: *Chinesische Frühkeramik* (Leipzig, 1922).

Brüning, A.: "Schauessen und Porzellanplastik" (*Kunst und Kunsthandwerk*, vii, Vienna, 1904).

Bulle, H.: "Eine altgriechische Gliederpuppe" (*Zeitschrift des Münchner Alterthums-Vereins*, N. F. x, 1899).

Buren, E. D. van: *Foundation Figurines and Offerings* (Berlin, 1931).

Buschan, G.: *Illustrierte Völkerkunde* (Berlin, 1924).

Buss, G.: "Die Puppe in der Kulturgeschichte" (*Velhagen und Klasings Monatshefte*, December 1907).

Calmettes, P.: *Les Joujoux: leur histoire, leur technique* (Paris, 1924).

Canning-Wright, H. W.: *Peeps at the World's Dolls* (New York, 1923).

Cartault, A.: *Terres cuites grecques* (Paris, 1890).

Claretie, L.: *Les Jouets: histoire-fabrication* (Paris, 1894).

Cöster, R.: "Lotte Pritzel" (*Deutsche Kunst und Dekoration*, xlv, 1919–20).

Crämer, K.: "Spielzeug und Volkswirtschaft" (*Leipziger Illustrierte Zeitung*, 1920).

Cremeans, L. M.: "Eskimo Toys" (*Journal of Home Economics*, April 1931).

Cruickshank, M.: *Dolls' Clothes and how to make them* (1923).

Culin, S.: "The Story of the Japanese Doll" (*Asia*, October 1922).

Déchélette, J.: *Manuel d'Archéologie* (Paris, 1908).

Deonna, W.: *Les Statues de terre cuite en Grèce* (Athens, 1906).

Doin, J.: "La Renaissance de la poupée française" (*Gazette des Beaux Arts*, 1914–16).

Döring, W. H.: "Papierpuppen von Erna Muth-Dresden" (*Deutsche Kunst und Dekoration*, xlv, 1919–20).

Ebert, M.: "Die Anfänge des europäischen Totenkultus" (*Prähistorische Zeitschrift*, xiii, 1922).

—— *Reallexikon der Vorgeschichte* (Berlin, 1924).

Ehlotzky, F.: *Die Herstellen von Holzspielzeug mit einfachen Mitteln* (Ravensburg, 1929).

Elderkin, K. M.: "Jointed Dolls in Antiquity" (*American Journal of Archeology*, October 1930).

Ellis, A. C., and Hall, G. S.: "A Study of Dolls" (*Pedagogical Seminary*, iv, Worcester, Massachusetts, 1896–97).

Enderlin, M.: *Das Spielzeug in seiner Bedeutung für die Entwicklung des Kindes* (Langensalza, 1907).

Erman, A.: *Ägypten und ägyptisches Leben im Alterthum* (Tübingen, 1923).

Fechheimer, H.: *Kleinplastik des Ägypter* (Berlin, 1923).

Feldhaus, F. M.: *Die Technik der Vorzeit* (Leipzig, 1914).

Fewkes, J. W.: "Dolls of the Tusayan Indians" (*Internat. Archiv für Ethnogr.* vii, 1894).

BIBLIOGRAPHY

FEWKES, J. W.: "Clay Figurines made by Navaho Children" (*American Anthropologist*, October 1923).

FISHBURN, T.: "Spool Dolls" (*School Arts Magazine*, November 1929).

FORRER, R.: *Reallexikon der prähist. etc. Altertümer* (Stuttgart, 1907).

FOY, W.: "Südafrikan. Zauberpuppen" (*Ethnologica*, Leipzig, 1909).

FRAZER, SIR JAMES: *The Golden Bough* (third edition, 1911).

FUCHS, E.: *Tang-Plastik. Chinesische Grabkeramik des 6. bis 10. Jahrh.* (Munich, 1924).

—— *Selbstzuarbeitendes Spielzeug für Knaben und Mädchen* (Leipzig, 1930).

FURTWÄNGLER, A.: *Die Sammlung Sabouroff* (Berlin, 1883–87).

GABNAY, F. VON: "Rachepuppen aus Ungarn" (*Globus*, lxxx, 1901).

GOODWIN, B. M.: *How to make a Doll and Other Toys in the Classroom* (1919).

GORDON-STABLES, MRS: "The Vogue of Figurines revives" (*The International Studio*, May 1923).

GRATZ, P.: *Püppchens Kleidung* (Leipzig, 1930).

GRIMM, J.: *Deutsche Mythologie* (fourth edition, Berlin, 1875).

GRISSEMAN, O.: *Bastelbuch für Väter* (contains "Mädchenspielzeug," Berlin, 1929).

GRÖBER, J.: *Kinderspielzeug aus alter Zeit* (Berlin, 1928; translated by P. Hereford as *Children's Toys of Bygone Days*, 1928).

GROSS, A.: "Ritterlich Spielzeug" (*Festschrift für Julius Schlosser*, Vienna, 1927).

GROSSE, E.: *Anfänge der Kunst* (Leipzig, 1893).

GRUDZINSKA, A.: "The Study of Dolls among Polish Children" (*The Pedagogical Seminary*, September 1907).

GRÜHL, M.: "Die Bedeutung der Puppen beim letzten grossen Gräberfunde von Theben" (*Cosmos, Handweiser für Naturfreunde*, xix, 1922).

HADDON, J.: *Magic and Fetishism* (1906).

HALL, A. N.: *Home-made Toys for Girls and Boys* (1915).

HAMPE, T.: *Der Zinnsoldat* (Berlin, 1924).

HARRIS, M.: *The "Truth" History of Dolls* (1913).

HARTL-MITIUS, —: "Münchener Künstlerpuppen" (*Leipziger Illustrierte Zeitung*, cxxxiii, 1909).

HAVARD, —: *Dictionnaire de l'Ameublement* (Paris, n.d.).

HENRY, V.: *La Magie dans l'Inde antique* (Paris, 1909).

HENSCHEL VOM HAIN: "Künstlerpuppen als Zimmerschmuck" (*Das Echo*, xl, No. 1971, 1921).

HENTZE, K.: *Les Figurines de la céramique funéraire* (Hellerau, 1928).

HERSKOVITS, M. J., and F. S.: "Bush Negro Art" (*Arts Monthly*, October 1930).

HETZER, H.: *Richtiges Spielzeug für jedes Alter* (Dresden, 1931).

HILDEBRAND, H.: "Beiträge zur Kenntnis der Kunst der niederen Naturvölker" (in Nordenskiöld, *Studien und Forschungen*, Leipzig, 1885).

HILDEBRANDT, P.: *Das Spielzeug im Leben des Kindes* (Berlin, 1904).

HILLMAN, R.: "Kinderspielzeug in Siam" (*Globus*, lxxviii, 1900).

HÖBER, F.: "Alte Puppen" (*Kunst und Kunsthandwerk*, xv, 1912).

HÖFLER, M.: *Gebildbrote* (Leipzig, 1908–11).

DOLLS

HOPFGARTEN, E. VON: "Die neuesten Käthe-Kruse-Puppen" (*Das Echo*, xlii, No. 2080, 1923).

HOPKINS, U. N.: "Christmas Dolls from Russia" (*The Ladies' Home Journal*, December 1913).

HÖRNES, M.: *Urgeschichte der bildenden Kunst in Europa* (third edition, Vienna, 1925).

HOUGH, W.: "The Story of Dolls tells the Story of Mankind" (*The World Review*, December 1927).

HUISH, M. B.: *Greek Terra-cotta Statuettes* (1900).

JACKSON, F. N.: *Toys of Other Days* (1908).

—— "Some Old Dolls" (*The Connoisseur*, December 1927).

JENKINS, R. L.: "Industrial Art in Toyland" (*Arts Monthly*, June 1923).

JOHNSON, DOROTHY; "Theban Toys" (*The Fortnightly Review*, July 1932).

JOHNSON, G. F.: *Toys and Toy-making* (1912).

JOSTEN, H. H.: *Fulder Porzellanfiguren* (Berlin, 1929).

KARUTZ, R.: "Eine schottische Rachepuppe" (*Globus*, xlix, 1901).

KATE, H. TEN: "Eine japanische Rachepuppe" (*Globus*, xlix, 1901).

KESTER, P.: "On Dolls" (*The International Studio*, 1923).

KITTREDGE, G. L.: *Witchcraft in Old and New England* (Cambridge, U.S.A., 1929).

KRONFELD, M.: *Zauberpflanzen und Amulette* (Vienna, 1898).

KRUSE, KÄTHE: "Playing with the Christmas Doll" (*The Ladies' Home Journal*, January 1914).

—— "Meine Puppen" (*Deutsche Kunst und Dekoration*, liii, 1923–24).

—— "Aus den Kinderjahren meiner Puppenwerkstatt: eine Weihnachtsplauderei" (*Westermanns Monatshefte*, December 1924).

—— "Meine Puppen" (*Velhagen und Klasings Monatshefte*, xl, 1925).

KÜHN, H.: *Die Kunst der Primitiven* (Munich, 1923).

KUNZE, F.: "Die Puppe in der Kulturgeschichte" (*Leipziger Illustrierte Zeitung*, cxxi, 1903).

LABORDE, L. DE: *Glossaire français du moyen âge* (Paris, 1872).

LANGE, K.: *Die künstlerische Erziehung der deutschen Jugend* (Darmstadt, 1893).

LEHMANN, A.: *Aberglaube und Zauberei* (second edition, Stuttgart, 1908).

LEMKE, E.: "Spiel-, Zauber-, und andere Puppen" (*Zeitschrift des Vereins für Volkskunde*, xxv, 1915).

LEOPOLD, A.: "Alte und neue Puppen" (*Leipziger Illustrierte Zeitung*, cxxxv, 1910).

LIE, I.: "Spielzeug aus dem Erzgebirge" (*Westermanns Monatshefte*, December 1930).

LOOSCHEN, H.: "Primitive Kunst aus der Kindheit der Völker" (*Kind und Kunst*, i, 1904–5).

LOVETT, E.: *The Child's Doll: its Origin, Legend, and Folk-lore* (1915).

LOW, F. H.: *Queen Victoria's Dolls* (1894).

LOWE, M. A.: *The Use of Dolls in Child-training* (New York, 1921).

LUKIN, J.: *Toys and Toy-making* (1881).

MAKINSON, J. T.: *Toy-manufacture* (1921).

BIBLIOGRAPHY

MARTIN, F. R.: *Sibirica. Beitrag zur Kenntnis der Vorgeschichte und Kultur sibirischer Völker* (Stockholm, 1897).

MATTHEI, A.: *Werke der Holzplastik in Schleswig-Holstein bis zum Jahre* 1530 (Leipzig, 1928).

MATZDORFF, A.: "Old Dolls of the Orient" (*The International Studio*, September 1923).

MERRIAM, E.: "Toy-making in Germany" (*Harper's Bazaar*, January 1911).

MEYER, C.: *Die Aberglaube des Mittelalters* (Munich, 1884).

MICHEL, É.: "Deux Mannequins en bois du 16ᵉ siècle" (*Gazette des Beaux Arts*, I, 1904).

MILLS, W.: "Sacred Dolls of the Italian Christmas" (*House and Garden*, December 1929).

MOLLE, S.: "Elogio della bambola" (*Nuova Antologia*, April 1929).

MONKHOUSE, W. C.: *History of Chinese Porcelain* (1901).

MOSS, A.: "A Cubist Doll-maker of Montparnasse" (*Arts and Decoration*, May 1923).

MOUNT, M. W.: "Character Dolls" (*Harper's Bazaar*, November 1911).

MÜLLER, E.: *Die Wiedergeburt des Porzellans* (Munich, 1930).

MÜLLER, M.: "Wie stehts um die bayerische Spielwarenindustrie?" (*Industrie und Gewerbeblätter*, 1927).

MÜLLER, S., and VOGELSANG, W.: *Hollandische Patrizierhäuser* (Utrecht, 1909).

MUNN, M.: "Christmas Dolls" (*The Ladies' Home Journal*, December 1929).

NASSAU, R. H.: *Fetishism in West Africa* (1904).

NOËL, A.: *Les Jeux de la poupée* (Paris, 1806).

PARSONS, E. C.: "The Toy Soldier" (*The Educational Review*, June 1915).

PARTHUM, R.: "Erzgebirg. Spielzeug aus Kinderhand" (*Die Arbeitsschule*, xliii, pp. 577–581).

PEARSON, C. S.: "Idols in Hopi Worship" (*The Mentor*, September 1928).

PERDRIZET, P.: *Les Terres cuites grecques d'Égypte de la collection Fouquet* (Nancy, 1921).

PERGER, —: "Über den Alraun" (*Mitteilungen des Wiener Altertumsvereins*, v).

PHILLIPS, A. M.: "Mme Paderewski's Dolls: designed and made by Polish Young People to help their Native Land" (*The Craftsman*, October 1915).

PICARD, M.: *Mittelalterliche Holzfiguren* (Erlenbach, Zürich, 1920).

POLKINGHORNE, R. K., and M. I. R.: *Toy-making in School and Home* (1916).

POTTIER, E.: *Les Statuettes de terre cuite dans l'antiquité* (Paris, 1890).

PUCKETT, —: *Folk Beliefs of the Southern Negro* (New York, 1926).

RATHGEBER, E.: "Die Heimat der Puppenfee" (*Signale für die musikalische Welt*, lii, 1894).

REISS, —, and STÜBEL, —: *Das Todtenfeld von Ancon in Peru* (Berlin, 1880–87).

RILKE, R. M.: *Lotte-Pritzel-Puppen* (Munich, 1921).

ROBERT, L.: *Zerlegbares Puppenhaus. Anleitung zum Bau eines modernen Puppenhauses mit Autogarage, Terasse u.a. Komfort* (Ravensburg, 1930).

ROBINSON, —: "Funeral Effigies of the Kings and Queens of England" (*Archæologia*, lx, 1907).

ROBINSON, M.: "Some Eighteenth-century Toys" (*The Connoisseur*, October 1926).

RUMPF, F.: *Spielzeug der Völker* (Berlin, 1922).

DOLLS

Rupé, H.: "Neue Vitrinenpuppen von Lotte Pritzel" (*Deutsche Kunst und Dekoration*, xlviii, 1921).

Sauerlandt, M.: *Deutsche Porzellanfiguren* (Berlin, 1923).

Schefold, M.: "Das Kind und das Spielzeug" (*Westermanns Monatshefte*, December 1927).

Schiebelhuth, H.: "Puppen als Zimmerschmuck" (*Deutsche Kunst und Dekoration*, xlviii, 1921).

Schliemann, H.: *Ilios* (Leipzig, 1881).

Schlosser, J. von: "Geschichte der Porträtbildnerei in Wachs" (*Jahrbuch der Kunstsammlungen des Allerh. Kaiserhauses*, xxix, 1910–11).

—— "Aus der Bildnerwerkstatt der Renaissance" (*Jahrbuch der Kunstsammlungen des Allerh. Kaiserhauses*, xxxi, 1913–14).

Schmitz, G.: "Weihnachtliches Kunstgewerbe" (*Westermanns Monatshefte*, December 1925).

Schultz, F. T.: "Kulturgeschichte des Spielzeugs" (*Leipziger Illustrierte Zeitung*, clv, 1920).

Schumacher, F.: *Wie ich zu meiner Puppensammlung kam. Erinnerungen einer Achtzigjährigen* (Stuttgart, 1929).

Schur, E.: "Neue Puppen" (*Dekorative Kunst*, xvii, 1909).

Seaby, A. W.: "Toys at the Whitechapel Art Gallery" (*The International Studio*, September 1916).

Serrurier, L.: *Kleiderdrachten in Nederlandsch. Indie vorgesteld door Poppen. Geschenk van de Dames in Nederl. Indie aan H.M. de Koningin* (The Hague, 1894).

Seyffert, O., and Trier, W.: *Spielzeug* (Berlin, 1922).

Sherbon, F. B.: "The Educational Value of Doll Play" (*American Childhood*, February 1927).

Shetelig, H.: "Statuetter fra istidens stenalder" (*Konst og Kultur*, ii, 1924).

Silber, M.: *Die Tonfiguren vom römischen Gräberfeld am Bürglstein in Salzburg* (*Anthropologigische Gesellschaft in Wien*, Mittheilungen, 1926).

Simon, K.: *Figürliches Kunstgerät aus deutscher Vergangenheit* (Berlin, 1926).

Singleton, E.: *Dolls* (New York, 1927).

Smith, C.: "Merry Figures from Vegetables" (*Better Homes and Gardens*, January 1931).

Starr, F.: "Japanese Toys and Toy-collectors" (*Transactions of the Asiatic Society of Japan*, December 1926).

Starr, L. B.: "The Educational Value of Dolls" (*The Pedagogical Seminary*, December 1909).

Steffens, C.: "Die Indianerpuppensammlung von Frau A. L. Dickermann" (*Globus*, lxxv, 1899).

Strele, R.: "Der Palmesel" (*Zeitschrift des deutschen u. österreichischen Alpenvereins*, xxviii, 1897).

Sully, J.: *Studies of Childhood* (new edition, 1903).

—— "Dollatry" (*The Contemporary Review*, lxxv, 1899).

Sy, M.: *Die Thüringer Spielwarenindustrie im Kampf um ihre Existenz* (Jena, 1929).

Sydow, E. von: *Die Kunst der Naturvölker und der Vorzeit* ((Berlin, 1923).

—— *Ahnenkult und Ahnenbild der Naturvölker* (Berlin, 1924).

—— *Kunst und Religion der Naturvölker* (Oldenburg, 1926).

Talbot, P.: "Some New Chelsea" (*The House Beautiful*, May 1924).

BIBLIOGRAPHY

TALMAN, C. F.: "Little Ladies from Tanagra" (*The Mentor*, October 1923).

TAUBE, E.: *Allerlei Puppen und ihre Bekleidung* (Leipzig, 1929).

THATCHER, E.: "Doll Furniture that is a Joy to make" (*The Ladies' Home Journal*, November 1925).

TRAWNICZEK, M.: "Eingeschaffenes Spielzeug für Weihnachten" (*Die Arbeitsschule*, xliii, p. 604).

UHLE, M.: *Kultur und Industrie südamerikanischer Völker* (Berlin, 1889).

VATTER, E.: *Religiöse Plastik der Naturvölker* (Frankfort-on-the-Main, 1926).

VERSTI, V.: *Puppen und Spielzeug aus Bast und Holz* (Vienna, 1930).

VETH, —: "De Mandragora" (*Internat. Archiv für Ethnogr.*, vii, 1894).

VILLIERS, —, and PACHINGER, —: *Amulette und Talismane* (Munich, 1928).

VINCHON, —: "Le Fétichisme de la poupée et le vol aux étalages" (*Journal de Médécine de Paris*, 1914).

VOLKER, A. E.: "Puppenkunst" (*Leipziger Illustrierte Zeitung*, cxxxi, 1908).

WADE, M. H.: *Dolls of Many Lands* (New York, 1913).

WADSWORTH, B. M.: "Inspiration from German Toys" (*The School Arts Magazine*, April 1929).

WARBURG, E.: "Revolution im Kösener Puppenstaat" (*Westermanns Monatshefte*, December 1923).

—— "Kinderspielzeug in alter und neuer Zeit" (*Westermanns Monatshefte*, December 1928).

WEEKS, J.: *Among the Primitive Batongo* (1914).

WEIGLIN, P.: "Der standhafte Zinnsoldat" (*Velhagen und Klasings Monatshefte*, December 1914).

WEIXLGÄRTNER, A.: *Dürer und die Gliederpuppe. Beiträge zur Kunstgeschichte Franz Wickhoff gewidmet* (Vienna, 1903).

WHITE, G.: *A Picture-book of Ancient and Modern Dolls* (1928).

WILKINSON, J. G.: *Manners and Customs of the Ancient Egyptians* (1837).

WINKLER, H.: *Wertvolles Spielzeug* (Munich, 1931).

WINTER, F.: *Die Typen der figürlichen Terrakotten* (Berlin, 1903).

WITH, K.: *Chinesische Kleinbildnerei in Steatit* (Oldenburg, 1926).

WLISLOCKI, H. VON: *Volksglaube und religiöser Brauch der Zigeuner* (1891).

—— "Amulette und Zauberapparate der ungarischen Zeltzigeuner" (*Globus*, lix, 1891).

WOLDT, H.: "Kultusgegenstände der Golden und Giljaken (am Amur)" (*Internat. Archiv für Ethnogr.*, i, 1888).

WRIGHT, H. W. C.: *Peeps at the World's Dolls* (1923).

WÜNSCH, R.: "Eine antike Rachepuppe" (*Philologus*, lxi, 1902).

ZINGERLE, I. V.: *Das deutsche Kinderspiel* (second edition, Innsbruck, 1873).

MISCELLANEOUS

"The Origin and Uses of Dolls" (*Harper's Weekly*, December 1910).

"Dolls in Old Silesian Costume" (*The International Studio*, December 1911).

"New German Dollies with Personality" (*The Craftsman*, December 1911).

"Käthe Kruse Dolls" (*The International Studio*, January 1912).

"Doll-making in Germany" (*American Homes*, July 1912).

"The Doll-head Industry" (*The Literary Digest*, January 1915).

DOLLS

"Toys by a Russian Artist" (*The International Studio*, July 1915).

"The New Era in Dolls" (*The World's Work*, December 1916).

"Art in Toys" (*The International Studio*, December 1917).

"The Child and the Toy" (*The Spectator*, December 1919).

"Some French Toys of To-day" (*The International Studio*, April 1921).

"Dolls of All Nations" (*The Mentor*, December 1921).

Das Puppenbuch (Berlin, 1921).

"Toys of American Indians" (*Science*, January 1923).

"Indian Dolls" (*Science*, October 1923).

Everybody's Book of the Queen's Doll's House (1924).

The Book of the Queen's Doll's House (1924).

"Famous Dollies and their Home" (*Arts and Decoration*, December 1926).

"La Féerie des jouets" (*L'Illustration*, January 1927).

"Inventors turn to Toys" (*The Scientific American*, December 1928).

"Czechoslovakian Toys" (*The School Arts Magazine*, January 1930).

Die deutsche Porzellan- und Steingut-Industrie (Berlin, 1931).

"Toy Soldiers and Real Wars" (*The World To-morrow*, February 1931).

INDEX

*AE*gean Sea, 'island figures' of, 33
Africa, ancestor images in, 41, 42, used as marionettes, 43; dolls in, of negro tribes, 217; fetish cult in, 51 *sqq.*; funeral sacrifices in, 77; image magic in, 57, 63—64; obese female figurines of, 28—29; 'stake figures' in, 34; utensils in doll form in, 236
Alaska, ancestor images in, 43—44; dolls in, 212
Algarotti, ————, 146
Allermannskraut (mandrake), the, 65
Amakatsu or *otagiboko*, Japanese doll-amulets, 54
Amber figures, Prussian, 26
Amulets, 44, 51, 53, 54, 55; the idea involved in, 56; transition into, of the idol, 49
Amur region, amulets in, 55; ancestor images in, 38, 48
Ancestor images, 37 *sqq.*; change of, into idols, 46; development of, 39—41; magic associated with, 38 *sqq.*, 103
Ancestor-worship, images associated with, 37 *sqq.*
Andersen, Hans, dolls in the stories of, 250
Andree, Richard, 64, 73, 74, 75
Animism, and early sculptures, 36; in North American Indian 'dolls of misfortune,' 7, 64
Annam, image magic in, 58
Anthologia Palatina, the, 108
Argei, the, legend on, 70
Armenino, G.B., 96
Art and the child's child doll, 173, 174
Ashanti, the, dolls of, 217; weights in doll form of, 236
Aulnoy, Baronne d', 127
Australia, native use in, of fertility image magic, 57
Australian islands, idol-worship on, 47
Austria, character dolls of, 180; doll-burning in, 246; dolls in folk-doings in, 246; French fashion dolls sent to, 145; image magic in, 66, 67; lay figures and other figures in, 99, 100, 101; waxworks in, 95. *See also* Vienna

Baby dolls, 150, 156, 185
Baghdad, dolls regarded as spirits at, 36
Bakuba goblets, in doll form, 236
Balkan lands, figurines of, 29, 31, 39; idol statuary of the Stone Age in, 31—32; image magic in, 61, 62; Ballets in imitation of dolls, 250—251
Bange, E.F., 99—100
Baphomet, the, images of, 67
Barbier, ————, 131
Barbier, Georges, dolls from sketches by, 195
Basuto dolls, 217
Bébés porte-bonheur, 55
Beehives in human form, 243
Benoist, Antoine, waxworks of, 94
Bertin, Rose, and the fashion doll, 144—145, 146
Bertuch, —, and the paper fashion doll, 153
Bibrawicz, Hella, dolls by, 219
Biedermeier period, the, art of, 227; dolls in stories during, 250; porcelain dolls of, 234
Birds—*see* Animals
'Board idols,' 26, 28
Bögg, the, burning of, 246
Bolivia, dolls of, 213-214
Book of the Dead, The, 80
Boos, Roman Anton, crib-figures by, 282
Borero dolls, 214
Borneo, luck images in, 63
Boti, life-size, 72
Boys, attitude of, to dolls and toys, 287; Japanese, dolls of, 206—208
Braig, Adolf, 180
Bran dolls, 128
Brentano, Clemens, 250
Bresciano, Prospero, anatomical figure by, 100
Breuer, Robert, 175

Calmettes, Mme, 198
Campi, Bernardino, 96
'Captives of St Leonard,' or 'Leonard's louts,' 75
Carmen Sylva, and her dolls, 172—173, 191

DOLLS

Carnival season, close of, dolls burned at, 246
Catacombs, the, dolls found in, 109
Catlin, —, 64
Caucasus, the, ancestor images in, 38; rain-making image magic in, 62—63
Chaldea, image magic of, 59
Chambre de parade, the, 90, 92
Character dolls, 180
Chemins de fer à catastrophes, sold in Paris, 217
Child, the, and its doll, 170 *sqq.*
Children, Christian, of antiquity, dolls of, 109; votive figures of, 73
Chile, dolls of, 213
China, dolls not played with in, 204; house idols in, 49; human sacrifice in, at burials, 77—78, grave figures substituted for, 83—84, those made of clay, 85—87; image magic in, 61, 64
Christian peoples, idol beliefs among, 49—50; use by, of *ex voto* figures, 71—75, of grave figures, 80
Christmas season, ceremonies of, dolls in, 245—246
Claretie, Leo, 216
Classical writers, on funeral images of wax, 89—90; on the Greek doll, 107; on image magic, 59, 87; on the mandrake, 65; on the origin of the *lares*, 38; on the *pantin*, 132; on 'picture bread,' 247; on slaughter at funerals, 77; on votive images, 69; on wizardry by means of wax figures, 59
Clay idols in Cyprus, 26—27
Clay rattle dolls, 106—106, 112, 214
Cloth dolls, 170
Clothing of statuettes, evolution of, 30
Columbia, clay rattle dolls of, 214
Cone shape of early idols and dolls, 26, 30, 130, 217
Cork dolls, 247
Corp creadh, the, 61
Cosmar, —, 250
Cosson, Mme Charles, costume dolls exhibited by, 194
Costume dolls, French, 194 *sqq.* (see also Fashion dolls); modern German, 219
Crete, female votive images found in, 68—69
Creutz, Johann C., waxworks of, 94
Crib—see Christmas cribs
Crib-figures, 125
Cristo de Burgos, the, 100—101
Crucifixes, animated, 36
Cyprus, clay idols in, 26—27
Czech images (*dziady*), 50

Dagynon, the, 106
Dagys, the, 106
Dalem Kamenuh, Malay goddess, 47
'Dead men' of Hungarian gipsies, 65
Death, as influencing early sculpture, 37
Death-masks, 89
Dehmel, Richard, 250
Delille, —, 146
Demonic element, the, in sculpture, 36, 45—46
Demons, favour of, images to secure, 65
Devil, the, in edible form, 249
Dickens, Charles, 250
Docke, the, in heraldry, 243
Dog in Punch-and-Judy show—see Toby
Doin, Jeanne, 164-165
'Doll' in Chinese and Korean, connotation of, 204; in English, when first so called, 150, etymology of the word, 151; in German—see *Tocha* or *Docke*
Doll, the, definition of, 23; evolution of, 23—24, 26, 33, 76; in literature, 250—251; and the stage, 245—246
Doll ballets, 250—251
Doll festivals in Japan, 204—211
Doll fetishism, 55—56
Doll, playing the, 250—251
Doll-dressing, by manufacturers, 160 *sqq.*; by owners, 158—160
Doll-making, details of, 157 *sqq. See also* Nurnberg *and* Sonneberg
Dolls, adult, generally female, 106, 150, 152, 156, 170, 175, 204, sixteenth-century, 113—115; of African negroes, 217; animation of, decreasing with realism, 175—176 (*see also* Image magic); associated with harvest, 64, 65, 244; attire of, 104—105, 108, 112, 113, 114, 116—117, 123, 124—125, 126, 156, 160—161, 175 (*see also* Costume dolls *and* Fashion dolls); baby, English, 150—152, 156, German, 184—185; basic form of, 202; bran-stuffed, 128; character, German, 180; child, 170 *sqq.*, 204; clay, magical, of the Akikuyu, 64; clockwork, 262; cloth, 170; collectors of, 191—192, 198—201; cone-shaped, 26, 30, 130, 217; considered as spirits, 36; cork, 247; costume, 190 *sqq.*; dedication of, to divinities, 107—108, 109; drawing-room, 218 *sqq.*; dress-, used by tailors, 95—96; dressed, French, 160—162, German, 162 *sqq.*; edible, 247—249; educational value of, 171 *sqq.*, 185;

INDEX

exhibitions of, 178, 183, 184, 187—190, 192, 194, 198, 219, 223, 247; of exotic peoples, 202—217, psychological interest of, 202; fashion, 143 *sqq.*, French, of 1914—18, 196—198; female, 105—106, 114 *sqq.*, 123, 125, 134 *sqq.*, 160, 175, 192 *sqq.*, 218 *sqq.*, predominance of, 106, 202; gingerbread, 248; Greek, earliest known, mostly female, 105—108; grotesque, of U.S.A., 217, 218; heads of, 127, 128, 155—156, 164, 183—184; of Hopi Indians, 48—49, 213; illustrating costumes of women war-workers, 196—198; indestructible German, 184; love of adults for, 55—56; male, 114, 125—126, 160, 214; materials used for, in the nineteenth century, 247; of misfortune, 64; with movable heads and eyes, 127; museum collections of, 188; paper, 208, 210, 224; *papier mâche,* 154, 155; prehistoric, 35 *sqq.*; in propaganda work, 198; rag, 110, 202, 211, 213; rattle, 105—106, 112, 214; sawdust-stuffed, 128; Siberian Tschuktchi, 45, 212; sin-bearing Japanese, 208; of South American nations and tribes, 213 *sqq.*; speaking and walking, 156; and spiritualism, 246; substitution of, for human victims, 70; *tapa,* of the Santa Cruz islands, 65; tea-cozy, 218, 247; teddy-bear, 218; toy, 24, in ancient times, 103, early, in Europe, 110, German, 105, 110, in the nineteenth century, 154 *sqq.*, in the modern period, 171 *sqq.*, American, modern, 216 (*see also* Nürnberg *and* Sonneberg); tumbling, Chinese, 204 *sqq.*; used for decorative purposes, 218—225; used in magic and magical rites, 57 *sqq.*, 204, 208; utensils in the form of, 235—244; of various lands and peoples—*see under names;* warrior, of the Winnebagos, 49 (*see also* Tin soldiers *and* Warriors); wax, English, 155, German, 115, Greek, 106, Haussa, 217, Mexican Indian, 213, wooden, 128, 180; worn as pendants, 218

Dolls' guillotine, a, 217

Dolls' houses, seventeenth-century, 118 *sqq.*

Dolls' marriage, a, in India, 203

Dolls' riding match, Prignitz, 246

Dolls' utensils in Swiss lake-dwellings, 103

Dory, Mme Myrthas, war-worker, dolls by, 196—198

Drawing-room dolls, 218 *sqq.*

Dresden artists, dolls designed by, 182—183

Dress-figures, or -dolls, 95-96. *See also* Mannequin

Dressmakers, dolls used by, 134 *sqq.*

Dürer, Albrecht, lay figures ascribed to, 96, 98—99

Dutch East Indies (Sumatra, etc.) ancestor images of, 42; dolls illustrating native costumes of, 190; image magic in, 64—65

Dziady, the, 50

Ebner-Eschenbach, Marie Von, 234

Edgeworth, Canon Roger, 103—104

Edible dolls, 247—249

Education, the doll as medium of, 171, 173

Effigies, burning of, 87—88. *See also* 'Ragged regiment' *and* Waxworks

Egypt, dolls of, 104—105; dress figures in, 96; edible figures in, 247; funeral images in, 78 *sqq.*; image magic of, 59; obese female idols in, 29; portrait-masks of mummies in, 89; prehistoric 'stake figures' in, 34; 'stick figures' of, 235; talismans and amulets in, 53—54; toy figures in, 104

Ellis, Caswell, 216

Éloffe, Mme, dolls or mannequins of, 144, 145

England, baby dolls first made in, 156; flat paper mannequins of, 153; French fashion dolls in, 140, 144; funeral images in, 90—91; image burned in scorn in, 88; image magic in, 60; the paper fashion doll in, 150 *sqq.*

English dolls, 150—152, of wax, 155; heads of, 128

English lay figures, 100

Eschenbach, Wolfram von, and his daughter's doll, 111

Eskimo, doll-amulets of, 54; statuettes, 26; toy dolls, 211

Ethnographical dolls, 191, 192, 198

Etruscan figurines of soldiers, 34

Europe, centres of idol statuary in, in the Stone Age, 30—33; early toy dolls in, 110 *sqq.*; image magic in, 60

Ex voto, the, 68 *sqq.*

Fakse, the, 49

Falschkind, ex voto figures, 73

Farmyards with dolls, German, 117—118

Fashion dolls, 134 *sqq.*; exhibitions of, 192 *sqq.*; names for, 138, 144; of 1914—18, 196—198

Fashion journals, fashion dolls superseded by, 150
Feinctes, on the medieval stage, 245
Female dolls and figures, predominance of, 28—29, 33, 106, 202
Female obesity in prehistoric and early negro art, with accentuation of sexual attributes, 28—29, 33
Féré, —, 55
Fetishes, 51 *sqq.*; the idea involved in, 56
Feuerbach, —, 37
Fewkes, J.W., 49
Filarete, —, 96
Fillon, Mlle, mannequin doll ordered from, 140—141
Finland, ancestor images of the Cheremis in, 44
Fiszerowni, Mme, 198
Fitzebutze, the (Dehmel), 250
Flat paper mannequins, English, 153
Forbes, —, 104
Forrer, Robert, 33, 105, 290; doll collection of, 188
Foy, W., 57
France, dolls of, edible, 248—249; fashion dolls of, 134 *sqq.*, 192 *sqq.*, 196—198, renaissance of, 166—168; dolls' dressmakers of, 160—161; image magic in, 60; prehistoric figurines in, 28; wax *ex voto* figures in, 71—72
French actresses, doll collection representing, 195—196
French artists, dolls designed by, 186—187, 194—195
'French doll,' 124—125
French doll industry, the, 164, 165, 166—170
French dolls with movable heads and eyes, 127
French fashion dolls, of 1914—18, 196—198. See also Fashion dolls
Frieda, the theatre doll of Weimar, 245
Frithjof's Saga, 247
Frobenius, Lilian, dolls by, 184
Fur dolls, 211—212
Furetière, —, 138
Furtwängler, Adolf, 69, 81, 82

Gandtner, Christoph, tankards in doll form by, 239
Geigenberger, August, dolls designed by, 182
Gelenktäufling, the, 156
Gentleman's Magazine, The, 146
German artist doll-makers, 218 *sqq.*
German artists, dolls depicted by, 113 dolls designed by, 182 *sqq.*

German writers, fifteenth century onward, on the doll, 110—111
Germany, doll in, types of, character, 180, costume, 219 *sqq.*, decorative, 218 *sqq.*, dressed, 162 *sqq.*, edible, 248, 249, toy, 105, 110 *sqq.*, 128; doll industry of, 112—113, 121—122, 128, 162 *sqq.*, present-day centres of, 165—166, reforms in, 178 *sqq.*; doll-destroying in, after Carnival, 246; doll-form utensils in, 238 *sqq.*; dolls' heads of china in, 164; dress figures in, 96; *ex voto* wax figures in, 70, 72, 73 *sqq.*; French fashion dolls in, 138—139; funeral figures in, 83; funeral sacrifice in, 76—77; Hopi *ti'hus* in, 49; house images in, 74; image magic in, 58; the lay figure in, 96, 98 *sqq.*; marionettes in, porcelain figures made in, 228 *sqq.*, prehistoric figures in, 28; processional images in, 101, 102; Shamanistic figurines in, 48; silhouette fashion sheets of, 152—153; wax figures in, 101—102; wax-image offerings in, 70, 72, 73; waxworks in, 93, 94, itinerant, 93
Gingerbread doll, the, 248
Gipsies, Hungarian, image magic of, 65; Transylvanian, image love-magic of, 60
Girardi, —, songs of, 338
Girolamo, 341
Glass utensils in doll form, German, 239
Goblets in human form, 236, 238—239
Gockel, Hinkel, und Gackeleia (Brentano), doll in, 250
Goethe, J. W. von, and the Weimar theatre doll, 245
Goncourt, Edmond de, 96
Grands courriers de la mode, the, 144
Grave images—see Funeral images *under* Images
Greece, clay sculpture of, 81; dolls of, 105 *sqq.*, the oldest known, 105; edible figures in, 247; *ex voto* figures in, 69; funeral sacrifice in and funeral images in, 77, 80 *sqq.*; image magic of, 59, 64; processional figure in, 87; warrior dolls found in, 34
Greek islands, idol statuary of, 32
Greek vases, etc., decorated with clay dolls, 236
Greenland, East, dolls in, 212
Grimm, Melchior, 145—146
Guatemala, modern dolls of, 213, 214
Guelliot, M. and Mme, doll collection of, 198—201

INDEX

Hagemann, Carl, 34
Hainhofer, Philipp, dolls by, 116—118
Hairdressers, dolls used by, 145—146
Haiti, idol-makers of, 47
Halbreiter, Bernhard, dolls designed by, 182
Hall, G. Stanley, 175
Hallstatt period, bronzes of, 27, 34, 'board idols' among, 27; votive images of, 68; warrior figurines of, 34
Hammer-Purgstall, Joseph von, 67
Hampelmann, the, 132
Harm-doing, images used for, 56
Harvest, dolls associated with, 64, 65, 244
Haussa wax dolls, 217
Hefner-Alteneck, 112
Hennsla buben, a, 114
Hentze, —, 59
Hernos, the, 49—50
Hildebrand, —, 26
Hildebrandt, Paul, 178
Hissarlik, 'board idols' of, 28
Hoffmann, E. T. A., dolls in stories of, 250
Homer, on funeral sacrifices, 77
Hopi Indians, dolls of, 48—49, 213
Hörnes, —, 25, 27, 33, 68
Hortus Sanitatis, the, illustrations in, of dolls, 113
Hough, Walter, 103
House idols, 47 *sqq.*; German, 74; Norwegian, 49—50; Siberian, 47—48; stone, of the Tusayan Indians, 49. *See also* Ancestor images
Huc, É, and Gabet, J., 77
Hugo, Victor, 174
Huitzilopochtli, edible image of, 248
Hungary, children's dolls in, 202

Idol figures in bakery, condemned by the Church, 247
Idol statuary, centres of, 30—33
Idols, ancestor images changed into, 46; female, obesity emphasized in, 28—29, predominance of, 33; magic associated with, 45—46, 103; materials of which made, 39 *sqq.*; prehistoric, 23—36
Ilinasama figures, Japanese, 210
Image magic, 56, 57—67; Balkan, 61—62; dolls in, 57 *sqq.*; Greek, 59, 64; Indian, 62, 65; Italian, 60; Japanese, 61; North American Indian, 57, 60, 62, 64; in Oceania, 57; Oriental origin of, 59; Russian, 58; South American Indian, 62; used to procure injury, 56, 58—59, 60—62
Images, of earth spirits, made by Hungarian gipsies, 65; funeral, or grave,

76 *sqq.*, Chinese, 83—87, Christian use of, 80, Egyptian, 78—80, Greek, 78, 80—83, Japanese, 87, Roman, 83, of clay, 88, of wax, 88 *sqq.* (*see also* Votive images); iron *ex voto*, 73—75; luck, Borneo, 63; miracle-working, 50, 58; movable, 252 *sqq.* (*see also* Automata); processional, 87, 102, 252 *sqq.*; in religious cults, 87; substituted for human sacrifice, 65, 70, 78 *sqq.*, 81, 83 *sqq.*; symbolic of scorn or of revenge, 87—88; votive —see Ex voto, the; wax *ex voto*, 69 *sqq.*, funeral, 88—89
Imagines of the Romans, 39
Imagines de vestir in Spanish churches, 100
India, Brahmin ancestor figures in, 42; image magic in, 62, 65
Indian dolls, 203
Indian game of 'imitation of the doll,' 250
Indiculus Superstitionum, 110, 247
Ipsullices, the, 59
Iron, votive figures of, 73—75
Iron Age, 'board idols' of metal in, 27
Iron man of Buttenwiesen, the, 74
'Island figures,' centres of, 32—33
Italian painters, lay figures used by, 96 *sqq.*
Italy, doll-burning in, after Carnival, 246; dress figures in, 96 *sqq.*; edible dolls in, 248; funeral images in, 92; image magic in, 60; *schardana* figures in, 34; wax *ex voto* figures in, 72; wax figures in, 101

Japan, doll festivals in, 204—211; doll-making in, 166; funeral sacrifices in, images substituted for, 87; image magic for revenge in, 61; rag-doll amulets of, 54
Journal des Luxus und der Moden, the, 153
Judas dolls, 246
Jumeau and Son, movable necks for dolls invented by, 155

Kadiueo dolls, 214
Käferlin, Anna, doll's house of, 120
Kager, Mathias, 117
Kaiserberg, Geiler von, 110, 111
Kamasutra, the, 250
Kändler, Johann, modeller of Meissen figures, and his followers, 228—229
Karaya dolls, 214
Kaulitz, Marion, doll artist, 183-184
Kekule, —, 88
Kings and notables in waxwork shows, 93—94

DOLLS

Klaatsch, H., 27
Klaubauf, the, 249
Kleinhempel, Fritz and Erich, character dolls of, 180
Kletzenkrampus, the, 249
Kletzenmännlein, the, 249
Knights Templars, the, and the alleged idol Baphomet, 67
Koenig, Marie, ethnographical dolls collected by, 201
Koran, the, on idol-making, 36, 211
Koroplastoi, the, 106
Korwars, Papuan, 41—42
Krampus, the, 249
Krieger, Betty, costume dolls by, 219
Kruse, Käthe, dolls by, 184—186, 224

La Tène period, metal warrior figurines of, 34; votive images of, 68
Lange, Konrad, 174, 397
Lares and *penates*, the, 38—39, 109
Lay figures, 96 *sqq.*
Lazarski, Mme, 198
Lazarus, tin grave figures of, 80
Lectisternium, the, images entertained at, 87
Legros, —, the 'hair artist,' 145—146
Lemke, Elisabeth, 202; doll collection of, 191
Liberian dolls, 211
Lifraud, Mlle, modeller of dolls' heads, 196
Literature, the doll in, 250—251
Lithuania, funeral sacrifice in, 76—77
Lösskindel, 24—25
Love magic, images in, 59—60, 61—62
Luck images, 63
'Lucky mannequins' (mandrakes), 67
Luschan, —, 67
Luther, Martin, 68

Magic, association of, with dolls and images, 24, 46, 55, 57 *sqq.*
Mahabharata, the, 203
Malay Archipelago, dolls of, 211; idols of, 47
Malays and Dayaks, dolls representing, 192
Male dolls, 125—126, 160. *See also* Tin soldiers *and* Warrior doll
Male figurines, accessories of, 33—34
Malekula, ancestor images of, 44
Mälzel, —, and the first speaking doll, 155
Mandrake, the, as a talisman, 65—67
Mannequin, the, 95—96; English flat paper, 153; evolution of, 95; French fashion dolls as mannequins, 144, 145, 147—149; smoking, 241—242
Manush mulengré, the, 65

Maré-Schur, Marie, dolls by, 184
Marionettes, African, 43
Marlef, Mme Claude, doll-artist, 196
Martet, Mme, 'Balzac' dolls by, 194
Martin, F. R., 47—48
Maschurdalo, image, the, 65
Maternal feeling, said to be aroused by playing with dolls, 173—174
Mediterranean islands, obese female figurines in, 29
Meissen ware, the first modeller of, and his followers, 228—229
Mercier, S., 144
Mesopotamia, nail-goddesses of, 46
Mess, H., doll-maker, 113
Metal idols, Iron Age, 27
Mexico, dolls of, 213, in Christmas festivities, 245, edible, 247—248, Judas, 246; Tzapotek utensils of, in doll form, 236; wax figures in, 95
Michel, Emil, 99
Michel's March Acquisitions, Toys of Right and Left for Old and Young, 132-133
Middle Ages, image magic in, 59—60, 62
Miracle-working images of the Catholic Church, 50
Mohammedan children, dolls of, 36, 211
Mongolia, ancestor images in, 38; funeral sacrifices in, 77—78
Monk doll, a, 126
Montanari, Napoleon, English wax dolls of, 155
Morris, Frances, doll review executed by, 195
Moscherosch, —, 138
Moser, Kolo, dolls after, 180
Mother-right, in relation to predominance of female idols, 33
Motor-car talismans, 55
Müller, the Hofstatuarius, waxworks by, 95
Müller, Matheus, 247
Munich artists, dolls designed by, 183—184; exhibition by, of toy dolls, 183—184
Mycenae, figures and dolls at, 30, 105—106; funeral gold ornaments at, 78
Mycenaean period, votive images of, 69
Myrina, terra-cottas from, 82
Mystery plays, dolls in, 245

Nail fetishes, 53
Nail-goddesses, Mesopotamian, 46
Needle-boxes in human form, 241
Neolithic Age, 'board idols' of, 26

266

INDEX

Nests of boxes, dolls made as, 180
Neuberger, Daniel, wax dolls made by, 115
New England Weekly Journal, The, a fashion doll advertised in, 147
New Guinea, hooks in, in human form, 236; Papuan *korwars* of, 41—42
New World, the, idolatry in, 46—47
New York, Metropolitan Museum in, dolls and doll review of, 195
New Zealand, Maori ancestor images of, 41, 42; Maori use in, of image magic, 57; *tiki* images of the Maori in, 44
Nivaschi image, the, 65
Nomori, the, of Sierra Leone, 63
Nordenskiöld, —, 212
North America, the fashion doll in, 147—148; Indians of, dolls of, 48—49, 212—213, words used for dolls of, 104, dolls representing costumes of, 198, house idols of, 49, image magic of, 57, 60, 64, *Ti' hus* of, 48—49
Norway, 'picture bread' banned in, 247
Nürnberg, doll industry of, 112-113, 121, 122, 128, 162 *sqq.*
Nutcracker in human form, 241

Obesity, emphasized in early and African female idols, 28—29
Oceania, ancestor images in, 39 *sqq.*; image magic in, 57
Ornament, on idols, preceding clothing, 30
Ott, —, doll-maker, 113

Pacheco, —, 98
Paderewski, Mme, 198
Pageants, dolls in, 245
'Palm ass,' the, 101, 102
Pandoras, 138, 144
Pangwe tribe, ancestor images of, used as marionettes, 42—43
Panja, the, 38
Pantin, the, 130—132
Paper dolls, of Erna Muth, 224; Japanese, 208, 210
Paper figures, burned at Chinese funerals, 83—84
Papier mâché, dolls made of, 154, 156; dolls' heads of, 183; *ex voto* figures of, 72
Paraguay, Chaco Indian dolls of, 214
Pasos, in Spain, 100
Pastoral doll forms, 128—130
Pavlova, Anna, dance of, as a doll, 251
Pechuel-Loesche, —, 51-52
Penck, —, 28

Perfume bottles in human form, 240—241, 242
Perger, —, 66—67
Perminak, the, of the Bataks, 54
Peru, Chimu civilization of, utensils of, in doll form, 236; funeral sacrifice in, 77; idolatry, presumable, in, 47; pre-Conquest dolls of, 216
Pfingslötter, the, 246
Phelps, Harry, dolls of, and American spiritualism, 246
Philistines, the, votive images of, 68
Phuwusch image, the, 65
'Picture bread,' 247
Pinata, the, in Mexico, 245
Pinner, Erna, dolls by, 223
Piogey, Mme, and her exhibition of dolls, 192
Pischel, Richard, 203
Plaggon, the, 106
Play doll, evolution of, 103—104
Playing the doll, 250—251
Podhabka, Minka, dolls made after, 180
Poets, references by, to fashion dolls, 146
Polish dolls, propaganda by, 198
Polish images (*dziady*), 50
Polo, Marco, 84
Pompeii, clay funeral images at, 83, 88
Porcelain figures, eighteenth-century, 225, 226—234
Precious metals, *ex voto* figures of, 73
Prévost, Abbé, 140
Pritzel, Lotte, fantastic dolls by, 219—223, 224, 225
Prussia, funeral images in, 92
Pulliche, Mme, Venetian dolls by, 194—195
Puppe, derivation and derivatives of, 108; early used for 'doll,' 110
Puppe Wunderhold (Cosmar), 250
Puppenfee ballet (Bayer), 250
Putteli or *puttalika* (dolls), 203

Rag dolls, 128, 202, 211, 213
'Ragged regiment,' the, at Westminster Abbey, 90—91
Rain, image magic to bring, 62—63
Rattle dolls, 105—106, 109, 112
Reinach, —, 32
'Rhakmany idols' of Thessaly, 30
Rio Negro district, dolls of, 214
Roman Catholic Church, the miracle-working images of, 50; movable images of, 36
Romans, ancestor images of, 38—39; dolls among, 108—109; funeral figures of, 83, 87, 88—90; image magic among, 59, 87; *lares* and *penates*

of, 38—39, 109; Saturnalia of, *sigilla* exchanged at, 69; tin soldiers of, 291; weights in human form among, 236

Rommel family, the, porcelain figures by, 234

Rondot, Natalis, 160—161

Rübezahl, the, smoking mannequin resembling, 242

Russia, centre of idol statuary westward from Southern, 31; fashion dolls in, 146—147; image magic in, 58; image shown in scorn in, 88

Sacrifice, human, 76 *sqq.*; images substituted for, 47, 63, 65, 70, 78 *sqq.,* 81, 83 *sqq.*

Saint-Genois, A. and C. de—*see* Hewelt

Saint-worship, Catholic, heathen affinities of, 71

Sakti Kumulan, Malay god, 47

Samoyede dolls, 211

Sand, George, 174

Santa Cruz islands, image magic of, 65

Sardinia, soldier figurines of, 33—34

Sardis, dolls made at, 106

Satanism, image magic in, 60—61

Sauerlandt, Max, 227

Savary, —, 142

Scarecrows, German, 243—244

Schardana figures, 33—34

Schlegel, Gustav, 204

Schliemann, —, 26, 35, 78, 105

Schlosser, I. von, 71, 93, 99

Schmidt, Robert, 81

Schomburgk, Richard, 104

Schreiber, —, 248

Schuchhardt, —, 35

Schwegler, J., animals modelled by, 117

Schweinfurth, 29

Scottish Highlanders, image magic of, 61

Scythians, the, funeral sacrifice among, 77

Sechseläuten festival, the, 246

Seligmann, George S., doll-collector, 191

Semitic belief in the demonic in sculpture, 36

Sexual features, exaggeration of, in idols, etc., 28, 33 *et al.*

Shamanist idols or ancestor images, 48

Siam, the shadow-play in, 351—352

Siberia, house idols in, 47—48; Tschuktschi tribe of, amulet dolls of, 54—55, ancestor images of, 44

Sichart, Emma von, dolls by, 218—219

Sidi viranna, the, used in Indian magic, 65

Sierra Leone, the *nomori* of, 63

Sigilla, gifts of, in ancient Rome, 69

Silhouettes, as fashion-plates, 152—153

Singleton, Esther, 127

Skeleton dolls, modern American, 216

Soldier toys—*see* Tin soldiers, Warrior doll, *and* Warriors

Somali dolls, 217

Sonneberg, doll and toy industry of, 130, 154, 164, 202; doll collection at, 189

South America, dolls of, 213—216; Indians of, image magic of, 62

Spain, doll-burning in, after carnival, 246; lay figures in, 98; wax figures in, 100—101

Spiegel, Clarisse, costume dolls by, 219

Spielwarenzauber, doll ballet (Rathgeber), 250

Spirits, idols reproducing, 46—47

Spiritualism, American, origin of, 246

'Stake figures,' 34

Steatopygy in idols, 28—29

Steffens, C., 212

Steiff, Margarethe, and her cloth dolls, 170

Stick figures and dolls, 29, 34, 235, 244, 249

Stone Age centres of idol statuary, 30—33

Sudan, the, dolls in, 29, 217

Sully, James, 175

Sumatra, ancestor images of, 42; guardian dolls of, 63; the Perminak in, 54

Switzerland, folk pastimes of, dolls in 245—246; image magic in, 58, 88; lake dwellings of, dolls' utensils in, 103; prehistoric figurines in, 28

Sydow, Eckart von, 39, *sqq.*, 46, 52—53

Tadema (scarecrows), derivation of the term, 243

Talismans, 43, 53 *sqq.*; the idea involved in, 56

Tallsack, the, and its fair, 249

Tanagra figures, 81 *sqq.*; considered as grave images, 81 *sqq.*; German figures compared with, 231—232

Tangarva, image of, 47

Tankards, trick, in doll form, 238—239

Tapa doll, the, 65

Tea-cosy dolls, 218, 247

Teddy-bear dolls, 218

INDEX

Theatres, use of dolls in, 245
Thorwaldsen, B., and his dough-cake figure, 248
Thüringer ware, dolls of, 234
Tietz, Hermann, 183
Tiki images, Maori, 44
Tin soldiers, ancestry and evolution of, 27; in Andersen's fairy-tales, 250
Tocha, Tocke, or *Docke,* early German for 'doll,' 110—111
Togo, clay dolls in, 217
Toy dolls, ancient Egyptian, 104-105; English, 128, 155, 156, 158—160; exhibitions and collections of, 187—201; French, 122—127, 130—132, 155, 160—162, 166—170, 176; German, 105, 110 *sqq.*, 128, 132—133, 154, 162—166, 178, 180, 182—186; Greek and Trojan, 105, 106—108; historical development of, 24; of Hopi Indians, 103; Indian, 104; modern American, 216; Roman, 108—109
Toy soldiers—*see* Tin soldiers
Toys, wooden, designers of, 180, 182
Transylvania, the doll in festivals of, 246
Trinkets, in human form, 240—242
Troy, dolls, idols, and figurines found at, 26, 30, 33, 39, 105, 112
Tumbling doll, Chinese, 204
Tussaud, Mme, and her waxworks, 94—95
Tut-ench-Amun, death image of, 96; dress figure of, *ibid.*

United States of America, cult in, for dolls as decorations, 218; modern toy dolls of, 216
Ushabti figures, 80
Utensils in doll form, 235—243

Vasari, —, 96, 248
Vatter, Ernst, 24, 45
Venice, French fashion doll in, 139

Victoria, Queen, and her dolls, 158—160
Vikings, the, funeral sacrifices of, 77
Vinchon, —, 55
Violin-shaped idols, 29—30; dissemination of, 30
Virgin goblet, the, 238
Virgin saints, commemorated in cakes, 248
Volkmann, Johann Jacob, 91
Votive images, 68—75, life-size, 71—73

Wackerle, Josef, dolls by, 184
Walpole, Horace, 148
Wanamaker, Rodman, doll collection founded by, 191
Warrior doll of the Winnebagos, 49
Warriors, metal figurines of, 34. See *also* Tin soldiers
Wax dolls, English, 155; German, 115; Greek, 106; Haussa, 217; Mexican Indian, 213
Wax *ex voto* figures, 72—73
Wax figures, Spanish, 100—101
Waxworks, 93—95
Weber, E. von, 57
Weights in human form, Roman and Ashanti, 236
Weimar, the theatre doll of, 245
Wenz, Frau, doll-collector, 191
West Indies, the, idolatry in, 46—47
Wilkinson, —, 105
'Willendorf Venus,' the, 28
Winckelmann, J. J., 226
Winteraustragen, the, the doll in, 246

Yoruba dolls, 217

Zakucka, Fanny, dolls designed by, 180
Zappelmann, the, 132
Zwetschgen, the, 249

A CATALOGUE OF
SELECTED DOVER BOOKS
IN ALL FIELDS OF INTEREST

A CATALOGUE OF SELECTED DOVER
BOOKS IN ALL FIELDS OF INTEREST

CELESTIAL OBJECTS FOR COMMON TELESCOPES, T. W. Webb. The most used book in amateur astronomy: inestimable aid for locating and identifying nearly 4,000 celestial objects. Edited, updated by Margaret W. Mayall. 77 illustrations. Total of 645pp. 5⅜ x 8½.
20917-2, 20918-0 Pa., Two-vol. set $10.00

HISTORICAL STUDIES IN THE LANGUAGE OF CHEMISTRY, M. P. Crosland. The important part language has played in the development of chemistry from the symbolism of alchemy to the adoption of systematic nomenclature in 1892. ". . . wholeheartedly recommended,"—Science. 15 illustrations. 416pp. of text. 5⅝ x 8¼.   63702-6 Pa. $7.50

BURNHAM'S CELESTIAL HANDBOOK, Robert Burnham, Jr. Thorough, readable guide to the stars beyond our solar system. Exhaustive treatment, fully illustrated. Breakdown is alphabetical by constellation: Andromeda to Cetus in Vol. 1; Chamaeleon to Orion in Vol. 2; and Pavo to Vulpecula in Vol. 3. Hundreds of illustrations. Total of about 2000pp. 6⅛ x 9¼.
23567-X, 23568-8, 23673-0 Pa., Three-vol. set $32.85

THEORY OF WING SECTIONS: INCLUDING A SUMMARY OF AIRFOIL DATA, Ira H. Abbott and A. E. von Doenhoff. Concise compilation of subatomic aerodynamic characteristics of modern NASA wing sections, plus description of theory. 350pp. of tables. 693pp. 5⅜ x 8½.
60586-8 Pa. $9.95

DE RE METALLICA, Georgius Agricola. Translated by Herbert C. Hoover and Lou H. Hoover. The famous Hoover translation of greatest treatise on technological chemistry, engineering, geology, mining of early modern times (1556). All 289 original woodcuts. 638pp. 6¾ x 11.
60006-8 Clothbd. $19.95

THE ORIGIN OF CONTINENTS AND OCEANS, Alfred Wegener. One of the most influential, most controversial books in science, the classic statement for continental drift. Full 1966 translation of Wegener's final (1929) version. 64 illustrations. 246pp. 5⅜ x 8½.(EBE)61708-4 Pa. $5.00

THE PRINCIPLES OF PSYCHOLOGY, William James. Famous long course complete, unabridged. Stream of thought, time perception, memory, experimental methods; great work decades ahead of its time. Still valid, useful; read in many classes. 94 figures. Total of 1391pp. 5⅜ x 8½.
20381-6, 20382-4 Pa., Two-vol. set $17.90

YUCATAN BEFORE AND AFTER THE CONQUEST, Diego de Landa. First English translation of basic book in Maya studies, the only significant account of Yucatan written in the early post-Conquest era. Translated by distinguished Maya scholar William Gates. Appendices, introduction, 4 maps and over 120 illustrations added by translator. 162pp. 5⅜ x 8½.

23622-6 Pa. $3.00

THE MALAY ARCHIPELAGO, Alfred R. Wallace. Spirited travel account by one of founders of modern biology. Touches on zoology, botany, ethnography, geography, and geology. 62 illustrations, maps. 515pp. 5⅜ x 8½.

20187-2 Pa. $6.95

THE DISCOVERY OF THE TOMB OF TUTANKHAMEN, Howard Carter, A. C. Mace. Accompany Carter in the thrill of discovery, as ruined passage suddenly reveals unique, untouched, fabulously rich tomb. Fascinating account, with 106 illustrations. New introduction by J. M. White. Total of 382pp. 5⅜ x 8½. (Available in U.S. only) 23500-9 Pa. $5.50

THE WORLD'S GREATEST SPEECHES, edited by Lewis Copeland and Lawrence W. Lamm. Vast collection of 278 speeches from Greeks up to present. Powerful and effective models; unique look at history. Revised to 1970. Indices. 842pp. 5⅜ x 8½. 20468-5 Pa. $9.95

THE 100 GREATEST ADVERTISEMENTS, Julian Watkins. The priceless ingredient; His master's voice; 99 44/100% pure; over 100 others. How they were written, their impact, etc. Remarkable record. 130 illustrations. 233pp. 7⅞ x 10 3/5. 20540-1 Pa. $6.95

CRUICKSHANK PRINTS FOR HAND COLORING, George Cruickshank. 18 illustrations, one side of a page, on fine-quality paper suitable for watercolors. Caricatures of people in society (c. 1820) full of trenchant wit. Very large format. 32pp. 11 x 16. 23684-6 Pa. $6.00

THIRTY-TWO COLOR POSTCARDS OF TWENTIETH-CENTURY AMERICAN ART, Whitney Museum of American Art. Reproduced in full color in postcard form are 31 art works and one shot of the museum. Calder, Hopper, Rauschenberg, others. Detachable. 16pp. 8¼ x 11.

23629-3 Pa. $3.50

MUSIC OF THE SPHERES: THE MATERIAL UNIVERSE FROM ATOM TO QUASAR SIMPLY EXPLAINED, Guy Murchie. Planets, stars, geology, atoms, radiation, relativity, quantum theory, light, antimatter, similar topics. 319 figures. 664pp. 5⅜ x 8½.

21809-0, 21810-4 Pa., Two-vol. set $11.00

EINSTEIN'S THEORY OF RELATIVITY, Max Born. Finest semi-technical account; covers Einstein, Lorentz, Minkowski, and others, with much detail, much explanation of ideas and math not readily available elsewhere on this level. For student, non-specialist. 376pp. 5⅜ x 8½.

60769-0 Pa. $5.00

CATALOGUE OF DOVER BOOKS

THE SENSE OF BEAUTY, George Santayana. Masterfully written discussion of nature of beauty, materials of beauty, form, expression; art, literature, social sciences all involved. 168pp. 5⅜ x 8½.   20238-0 Pa. $3.50

ON THE IMPROVEMENT OF THE UNDERSTANDING, Benedict Spinoza. Also contains *Ethics, Correspondence,* all in excellent R. Elwes translation. Basic works on entry to philosophy, pantheism, exchange of ideas with great contemporaries. 402pp. 5⅜ x 8½.   20250-X Pa. $5.95

THE TRAGIC SENSE OF LIFE, Miguel de Unamuno. Acknowledged masterpiece of existential literature, one of most important books of 20th century. Introduction by Madariaga. 367pp. 5⅜ x 8½.
20257-7 Pa. $6.00

THE GUIDE FOR THE PERPLEXED, Moses Maimonides. Great classic of medieval Judaism attempts to reconcile revealed religion (Pentateuch, commentaries) with Aristotelian philosophy. Important historically, still relevant in problems. Unabridged Friedlander translation. Total of 473pp. 5⅜ x 8½.   20351-4 Pa. $6.95

THE I CHING (THE BOOK OF CHANGES), translated by James Legge. Complete translation of basic text plus appendices by Confucius, and Chinese commentary of most penetrating divination manual ever prepared. Indispensable to study of early Oriental civilizations, to modern inquiring reader. 448pp. 5⅜ x 8½.   21062-6 Pa. $6.00

THE EGYPTIAN BOOK OF THE DEAD, E. A. Wallis Budge. Complete reproduction of Ani's papyrus, finest ever found. Full hieroglyphic text, interlinear transliteration, word for word translation, smooth translation. Basic work, for Egyptology, for modern study of psychic matters. Total of 533pp. 6½ x 9¼. (USCO)   21866-X Pa. $8.50

THE GODS OF THE EGYPTIANS, E. A. Wallis Budge. Never excelled for richness, fullness: all gods, goddesses, demons, mythical figures of Ancient Egypt; their legends, rites, incarnations, variations, powers, etc. Many hieroglyphic texts cited. Over 225 illustrations, plus 6 color plates. Total of 988pp. 6⅛ x 9¼. (EBE)
22055-9, 22056-7 Pa., Two-vol. set $20.00

THE STANDARD BOOK OF QUILT MAKING AND COLLECTING, Marguerite Ickis. Full information, full-sized patterns for making 46 traditional quilts, also 150 other patterns. Quilted cloths, lame, satin quilts, etc. 483 illustrations. 273pp. 6⅞ x 9⅝.   20582-7 Pa. $5.95

CORAL GARDENS AND THEIR MAGIC, Bronslaw Malinowski. Classic study of the methods of tilling the soil and of agricultural rites in the Trobriand Islands of Melanesia. Author is one of the most important figures in the field of modern social anthropology. 143 illustrations. Indexes. Total of 911pp. of text. 5⅝ x 8¼. (Available in U.S. only)
23597-1 Pa. $12.95

CATALOGUE OF DOVER BOOKS

THE PHILOSOPHY OF HISTORY, Georg W. Hegel. Great classic of Western thought develops concept that history is not chance but a rational process, the evolution of freedom. 457pp. 5⅜ x 8½. 20112-0 Pa. $6.00

LANGUAGE, TRUTH AND LOGIC, Alfred J. Ayer. Famous, clear introduction to Vienna, Cambridge schools of Logical Positivism. Role of philosophy, elimination of metaphysics, nature of analysis, etc. 160pp. 5⅜ x 8½. (USCO) 20010-8 Pa. $2.50

A PREFACE TO LOGIC, Morris R. Cohen. Great City College teacher in renowned, easily followed exposition of formal logic, probability, values, logic and world order and similar topics; no previous background needed. 209pp. 5⅜ x 8½. 23517-3 Pa. $4.95

REASON AND NATURE, Morris R. Cohen. Brilliant analysis of reason and its multitudinous ramifications by charismatic teacher. Interdisciplinary, synthesizing work widely praised when it first appeared in 1931. Second (1953) edition. Indexes. 496pp. 5⅜ x 8½. 23633-1 Pa. $7.50

AN ESSAY CONCERNING HUMAN UNDERSTANDING, John Locke. The only complete edition of enormously important classic, with authoritative editorial material by A. C. Fraser. Total of 1176pp. 5⅜ x 8½.
20530-4, 20531-2 Pa., Two-vol. set $16.00

HANDBOOK OF MATHEMATICAL FUNCTIONS WITH FORMULAS, GRAPHS, AND MATHEMATICAL TABLES, edited by Milton Abramowitz and Irene A. Stegun. Vast compendium: 29 sets of tables, some to as high as 20 places. 1,046pp. 8 x 10½. 61272-4 Pa. $17.95

MATHEMATICS FOR THE PHYSICAL SCIENCES, Herbert S. Wilf. Highly acclaimed work offers clear presentations of vector spaces and matrices, orthogonal functions, roots of polynomial equations, conformal mapping, calculus of variations, etc. Knowledge of theory of. functions of real and complex variables is assumed. Exercises and solutions. Index. 284pp. 5⅝ x 8¼. 63635-6 Pa. $5.00

THE PRINCIPLE OF RELATIVITY, Albert Einstein et al. Eleven most important original papers on special and general theories. Seven by Einstein, two by Lorentz, one each by Minkowski and Weyl. All translated, unabridged. 216pp. 5⅜ x 8½. 60081-5 Pa. $3.50

THERMODYNAMICS, Enrico Fermi. A classic of modern science. Clear, organized treatment of systems, first and second laws, entropy, thermodynamic potentials, gaseous reactions, dilute solutions, entropy constant. No math beyond calculus required. Problems. 160pp. 5⅜ x 8½.
60361-X Pa. $4.00

ELEMENTARY MECHANICS OF FLUIDS, Hunter Rouse. Classic undergraduate text widely considered to be far better than many later books. Ranges from fluid velocity and acceleration to role of compressibility in fluid motion. Numerous examples, questions, problems. 224 illustrations. 376pp. 5⅝ x 8¼. 63699-2 Pa. $7.00

THE AMERICAN SENATOR, Anthony Trollope. Little known, long unavailable Trollope novel on a grand scale. Here are humorous comment on American vs. English culture, and stunning portrayal of a heroine/villainess. Superb evocation of Victorian village life. 561pp. 5⅜ x 8½.
23801-6 Pa. $7.95

WAS IT MURDER? James Hilton. The author of *Lost Horizon* and *Goodbye, Mr. Chips* wrote one detective novel (under a pen-name) which was quickly forgotten and virtually lost, even at the height of Hilton's fame. This edition brings it back—a finely crafted public school puzzle resplendent with Hilton's stylish atmosphere. A thoroughly English thriller by the creator of Shangri-la. 252pp. 5⅜ x 8. (Available in U.S. only)
23774-5 Pa. $3.00

CENTRAL PARK: A PHOTOGRAPHIC GUIDE, Victor Laredo and Henry Hope Reed. 121 superb photographs show dramatic views of Central Park: Bethesda Fountain, Cleopatra's Needle, Sheep Meadow, the Blockhouse, plus people engaged in many park activities: ice skating, bike riding, etc. Captions by former Curator of Central Park, Henry Hope Reed, provide historical view, changes, etc. Also photos of N.Y. landmarks on park's periphery. 96pp. 8½ x 11. 23750-8 Pa. $4.50

NANTUCKET IN THE NINETEENTH CENTURY, Clay Lancaster. 180 rare photographs, stereographs, maps, drawings and floor plans recreate unique American island society. Authentic scenes of shipwreck, lighthouses, streets, homes are arranged in geographic sequence to provide walking-tour guide to old Nantucket existing today. Introduction, captions. 160pp. 8⅞ x 11¾. 23747-8 Pa. $7.95

STONE AND MAN: A PHOTOGRAPHIC EXPLORATION, Andreas Feininger. 106 photographs by *Life* photographer Feininger portray man's deep passion for stone through the ages. Stonehenge-like megaliths, fortified towns, sculpted marble and crumbling tenements show textures, beauties, fascination. 128pp. 9¼ x 10¾. 23756-7 Pa. $5.95

CIRCLES, A MATHEMATICAL VIEW, D. Pedoe. Fundamental aspects of college geometry, non-Euclidean geometry, and other branches of mathematics: representing circle by point. Poincare model, isoperimetric property, etc. Stimulating recreational reading. 66 figures. 96pp. 5⅝ x 8¼.
63698-4 Pa. $3.50

THE DISCOVERY OF NEPTUNE, Morton Grosser. Dramatic scientific history of the investigations leading up to the actual discovery of the eighth planet of our solar system. Lucid, well-researched book by well-known historian of science. 172pp. 5⅜ x 8½. 23726-5 Pa. $3.50

THE DEVIL'S DICTIONARY. Ambrose Bierce. Barbed, bitter, brilliant witticisms in the form of a dictionary. Best, most ferocious satire America has produced. 145pp. 5⅜ x 8½. 20487-1 Pa. $2.50

HISTORY OF BACTERIOLOGY, William Bulloch. The only comprehensive history of bacteriology from the beginnings through the 19th century. Special emphasis is given to biography-Leeuwenhoek, etc. Brief accounts of 350 bacteriologists form a separate section. No clearer, fuller study, suitable to scientists and general readers, has yet been written. 52 illustrations. 448pp. 5⅝ x 8¼. 23761-3 Pa. $6.50

THE COMPLETE NONSENSE OF EDWARD LEAR, Edward Lear. All nonsense limericks, zany alphabets, Owl and Pussycat, songs, nonsense botany, etc., illustrated by Lear. Total of 321pp. 5⅜ x 8½. (Available in U.S. only) 20167-8 Pa. $4.50

INGENIOUS MATHEMATICAL PROBLEMS AND METHODS, Louis A. Graham. Sophisticated material from Graham *Dial*, applied and pure; stresses solution methods. Logic, number theory, networks, inversions, etc. 237pp. 5⅜ x 8½. 20545-2 Pa. $4.50

BEST MATHEMATICAL PUZZLES OF SAM LOYD, edited by Martin Gardner. Bizarre, original, whimsical puzzles by America's greatest puzzler. From fabulously rare *Cyclopedia*, including famous 14-15 puzzles, the Horse of a Different Color, 115 more. Elementary math. 150 illustrations. 167pp. 5⅜ x 8½. 20498-7 Pa. $3.50

THE BASIS OF COMBINATION IN CHESS, J. du Mont. Easy-to-follow, instructive book on elements of combination play, with chapters on each piece and every powerful combination team—two knights, bishop and knight, rook and bishop, etc. 250 diagrams. 218pp. 5⅜ x 8½. (Available in U.S. only) 23644-7 Pa. $4.50

MODERN CHESS STRATEGY, Ludek Pachman. The use of the queen, the active king, exchanges, pawn play, the center, weak squares, etc. Section on rook alone worth price of the book. Stress on the moderns. Often considered the most important book on strategy. 314pp. 5⅜ x 8½. 20290-9 Pa. $5.00

LASKER'S MANUAL OF CHESS, Dr. Emanuel Lasker. Great world champion offers very thorough coverage of all aspects of chess. Combinations, position play, openings, end game, aesthetics of chess, philosophy of struggle, much more. Filled with analyzed games. 390pp. 5⅜ x 8½. 20640-8 Pa. $5.95

500 MASTER GAMES OF CHESS, S. Tartakower, J. du Mont. Vast collection of great chess games from 1798-1938, with much material nowhere else readily available. Fully annotated, arranged by opening for easier study. 664pp. 5⅜ x 8½. 23208-5 Pa. $8.50

A GUIDE TO CHESS ENDINGS, Dr. Max Euwe, David Hooper. One of the finest modern works on chess endings. Thorough analysis of the most frequently encountered endings by former world champion. 331 examples, each with diagram. 248pp. 5⅜ x 8½. 23332-4 Pa. $3.95

THE COMPLETE BOOK OF DOLL MAKING AND COLLECTING, Catherine Christopher. Instructions, patterns for dozens of dolls, from rag doll on up to elaborate, historically accurate figures. Mould faces, sew clothing, make doll houses, etc. Also collecting information. Many illustrations. 288pp. 6 x 9. 22066-4 Pa. $4.95

THE DAGUERREOTYPE IN AMERICA, Beaumont Newhall. Wonderful portraits, 1850's townscapes, landscapes; full text plus 104 photographs. The basic book. Enlarged 1976 edition. 272pp. 8¼ x 11¼. 23322-7 Pa. $7.95

CRAFTSMAN HOMES, Gustav Stickley. 296 architectural drawings, floor plans, and photographs illustrate 40 different kinds of "Mission-style" homes from *The Craftsman* (1901-16), voice of American style of simplicity and organic harmony. Thorough coverage of Craftsman idea in text and picture, now collector's item. 224pp. 8⅛ x 11. 23791-5 Pa. $6.50

PEWTER-WORKING: INSTRUCTIONS AND PROJECTS, Burl N. Osborn. & Gordon O. Wilber. Introduction to pewter-working for amateur craftsman. History and characteristics of pewter; tools, materials, step-by-step instructions. Photos, line drawings, diagrams. Total of 160pp. 7⅞ x 10¾. 23786-9 Pa. $3.50

THE GREAT CHICAGO FIRE, edited by David Lowe. 10 dramatic, eyewitness accounts of the 1871 disaster, including one of the aftermath and rebuilding, plus 70 contemporary photographs and illustrations of the ruins—courthouse, Palmer House, Great Central Depot, etc. Introduction by David Lowe. 87pp. 8¼ x 11. 23771-0 Pa. $4.00

SILHOUETTES: A PICTORIAL ARCHIVE OF VARIED ILLUSTRATIONS, edited by Carol Belanger Grafton. Over 600 silhouettes from the 18th to 20th centuries include profiles and full figures of men and women, children, birds and animals, groups and scenes, nature, ships, an alphabet. Dozens of uses for commercial artists and craftspeople. 144pp. 8⅜ x 11¼. 23781-8 Pa. $4.50

ANIMALS: 1,419 COPYRIGHT-FREE ILLUSTRATIONS OF MAMMALS, BIRDS, FISH, INSECTS, ETC., edited by Jim Harter. Clear wood engravings present, in extremely lifelike poses, over 1,000 species of animals. One of the most extensive copyright-free pictorial sourcebooks of its kind. Captions. Index. 284pp. 9 x 12. 23766-4 Pa. $8.95

INDIAN DESIGNS FROM ANCIENT ECUADOR, Frederick W. Shaffer. 282 original designs by pre-Columbian Indians of Ecuador (500-1500 A.D.). Designs include people, mammals, birds, reptiles, fish, plants, heads, geometric designs. Use as is or alter for advertising, textiles, leathercraft, etc. Introduction. 95pp. 8¾ x 11¼. 23764-8 Pa. $4.50

SZIGETI ON THE VIOLIN, Joseph Szigeti. Genial, loosely structured tour by premier violinist, featuring a pleasant mixture of reminiscenes, insights into great music and musicians, innumerable tips for practicing violinists. 385 musical passages. 256pp. 5⅝ x 8¼. 23763-X Pa. $4.00

CATALOGUE OF DOVER BOOKS

TONE POEMS, SERIES II: TILL EULENSPIEGELS LUSTIGE STREICHE, ALSO SPRACH ZARATHUSTRA, AND EIN HELDEN-LEBEN, Richard Strauss. Three important orchestral works, including very popular *Till Eulenspiegel's Marry Pranks,* reproduced in full score from original editions. Study score. 315pp. 9⅜ x 12¼. (Available in U.S. only)
23755-9 Pa. $8.95

TONE POEMS, SERIES I: DON JUAN, TOD UND VERKLARUNG AND DON QUIXOTE, Richard Strauss. Three of the most often performed and recorded works in entire orchestral repertoire, reproduced in full score from original editions. Study score. 286pp. 9⅜ x 12¼. (Available in U.S. only)
23754-0 Pa. $8.95

11 LATE STRING QUARTETS, Franz Joseph Haydn. The form which Haydn defined and "brought to perfection." (*Grove's*). 11 string quartets in complete score, his last and his best. The first in a projected series of the complete Haydn string quartets. Reliable modern Eulenberg edition, otherwise difficult to obtain. 320pp. 8⅜ x 11¼. (Available in U.S. only)
23753-2 Pa. $8.95

FOURTH, FIFTH AND SIXTH SYMPHONIES IN FULL SCORE, Peter Ilyitch Tchaikovsky. Complete orchestral scores of Symphony No. 4 in F Minor, Op. 36; Symphony No. 5 in E Minor, Op. 64; Symphony No. 6 in B Minor, "Pathetique," Op. 74. Bretikopf & Hartel eds. Study score. 480pp. 9⅜ x 12¼. 23861-X Pa. $10.95

THE MARRIAGE OF FIGARO: COMPLETE SCORE, Wolfgang A. Mozart. Finest comic opera ever written. Full score, not to be confused with piano renderings. Peters edition. Study score. 448pp. 9⅜ x 12¼. (Available in U.S. only)
23751-6 Pa. $12.95

"IMAGE" ON THE ART AND EVOLUTION OF THE FILM, edited by Marshall Deutelbaum. Pioneering book brings together for first time 38 groundbreaking articles on early silent films from *Image* and 263 illustrations newly shot from rare prints in the collection of the International Museum of Photography. A landmark work. Index. 256pp. 8¼ x 11.
23777-X Pa. $8.95

AROUND-THE-WORLD COOKY BOOK, Lois Lintner Sumption and Marguerite Lintner Ashbrook. 373 cooky and frosting recipes from 28 countries (America, Austria, China, Russia, Italy, etc.) include Viennese kisses, rice wafers, London strips, lady fingers, hony, sugar spice, maple cookies, etc. Clear instructions. All tested. 38 drawings. 182pp. 5⅜ x 8.
23802-4 Pa. $2.75

THE ART NOUVEAU STYLE, edited by Roberta Waddell. 579 rare photographs, not available elsewhere, of works in jewelry, metalwork, glass, ceramics, textiles, architecture and furniture by 175 artists—Mucha, Seguy, Lalique, Tiffany, Gaudin, Hohlwein, Saarinen, and many others. 288pp. 8⅜ x 11¼. 23515-7 Pa. $8.95

CATALOGUE OF DOVER BOOKS

THE CURVES OF LIFE, Theodore A. Cook. Examination of shells, leaves, horns, human body, art, etc., in *"the* classic reference on how the golden ratio applies to spirals and helices in nature . . . . "—Martin Gardner. 426 illustrations. Total of 512pp. 5⅜ x 8½. 23701-X Pa. $6.95

AN ILLUSTRATED FLORA OF THE NORTHERN UNITED STATES AND CANADA, Nathaniel L. Britton, Addison Brown. Encyclopedic work covers 4666 species, ferns on up. Everything. Full botanical information, illustration for each. This earlier edition is preferred by many to more recent revisions. 1913 edition. Over 4000 illustrations, total of 2087pp. 6⅛ x 9¼. 22642-5, 22643-3, 22644-1 Pa., Three-vol. set $28.50

MANUAL OF THE GRASSES OF THE UNITED STATES, A. S. Hitchcock, U.S. Dept. of Agriculture. The basic study of American grasses, both indigenous and escapes, cultivated and wild. Over 1400 species. Full descriptions, information. Over 1100 maps, illustrations. Total of 1051pp. 5⅜ x 8½. 22717-0, 22718-9 Pa., Two-vol. set $17.00

THE CACTACEAE,, Nathaniel L. Britton, John N. Rose. Exhaustive, definitive. Every cactus in the world. Full botanical descriptions. Thorough statement of nomenclatures, habitat, detailed finding keys. The one book needed by every cactus enthusiast. Over 1275 illustrations. Total of 1080pp. 8 x 10¼. 21191-6, 21192-4 Clothbd., Two-vol. set $50.00

AMERICAN MEDICINAL PLANTS, Charles F. Millspaugh. Full descriptions, 180 plants covered: history; physical description; methods of preparation with all chemical constituents extracted; all claimed curative or adverse effects. 180 full-page plates. Classification table. 804pp. 6½ x 9¼. 23034-1 Pa. $13.95

A MODERN HERBAL, Margaret Grieve. Much the fullest, most exact, most useful compilation of herbal material. Gigantic alphabetical encyclopedia, from aconite to zedoary, gives botanical information, medical properties, folklore, economic uses, and much else. Indispensable to serious reader. 161 illustrations. 888pp. 6½ x 9¼. (Available in U.S. only) 22798-7, 22799-5 Pa., Two-vol. set $15.00

THE HERBAL or GENERAL HISTORY OF PLANTS, John Gerard. The 1633 edition revised and enlarged by Thomas Johnson. Containing almost 2850 plant descriptions and 2705 superb illustrations, Gerard's *Herbal* is a monumental work, the book all modern English herbals are derived from, the one herbal every serious enthusiast should have in its entirety. Original editions are worth perhaps $750. 1678pp. 8½ x 12¼. 23147-X Clothbd. $75.00

MANUAL OF THE TREES OF NORTH AMERICA, Charles S. Sargent. The basic survey of every native tree and tree-like shrub, 717 species in all. Extremely full descriptions, information on habitat, growth, locales, economics, etc. Necessary to every serious tree lover. Over 100 finding keys. 783 illustrations. Total of 986pp. 5⅜ x 8½. 20277-1, 20278-X Pa., Two-vol. set $12.00

GREAT NEWS PHOTOS AND THE STORIES BEHIND THEM, John Faber. Dramatic volume of 140 great news photos, 1855 through 1976, and revealing stories behind them, with both historical and technical information. Hindenburg disaster, shooting of Oswald, nomination of Jimmy Carter, etc. 160pp. 8¼ x 11. 23667-6 Pa. $6.00

CRUICKSHANK'S PHOTOGRAPHS OF BIRDS OF AMERICA, Allan D. Cruickshank. Great ornithologist, photographer presents 177 closeups, groupings, panoramas, flightings, etc., of about 150 different birds. Expanded Wings in the Wilderness. Introduction by Helen G. Cruickshank. 191pp. 8¼ x 11. 23497-5 Pa. $7.95

AMERICAN WILDLIFE AND PLANTS, A. C. Martin, et al. Describes food habits of more than 1000 species of mammals, birds, fish. Special treatment of important food plants. Over 300 illustrations. 500pp. 5⅜ x 8½. 20793-5 Pa. $6.50

THE PEOPLE CALLED SHAKERS, Edward D. Andrews. Lifetime of research, definitive study of Shakers: origins, beliefs, practices, dances, social organization, furniture and crafts, impact on 19th-century USA, present heritage. Indispensable to student of American history, collector. 33 illustrations. 351pp. 5⅜ x 8½. 21081-2 Pa. $4.50

OLD NEW YORK IN EARLY PHOTOGRAPHS, Mary Black. New York City as it was in 1853-1901, through 196 wonderful photographs from N.-Y. Historical Society. Great Blizzard, Lincoln's funeral procession, great buildings. 228pp. 9 x 12. 22907-6 Pa. $8.95

MR. LINCOLN'S CAMERA MAN: MATHEW BRADY, Roy Meredith. Over 300 Brady photos reproduced directly from original negatives, photos. Jackson, Webster, Grant, Lee, Carnegie, Barnum; Lincoln; Battle Smoke, Death of Rebel Sniper, Atlanta Just After Capture. Lively commentary. 368pp. 8⅜ x 11¼. 23021-X Pa. $11.95

TRAVELS OF WILLIAM BARTRAM, William Bartram. From 1773-8, Bartram explored Northern Florida, Georgia, Carolinas, and reported on wild life, plants, Indians, early settlers. Basic account for period, entertaining reading. Edited by Mark Van Doren. 13 illustrations. 141pp. 5⅜ x 8½. 20013-2 Pa. $6.00

THE GENTLEMAN AND CABINET MAKER'S DIRECTOR, Thomas Chippendale. Full reprint, 1762 style book, most influential of all time; chairs, tables, sofas, mirrors, cabinets, etc. 200 plates, plus 24 photographs of surviving pieces. 249pp. 9⅞ x 12¾. 21601-2 Pa. $8.95

AMERICAN CARRIAGES, SLEIGHS, SULKIES AND CARTS, edited by Don H. Berkebile. 168 Victorian illustrations from catalogues, trade journals, fully captioned. Useful for artists. Author is Assoc. Curator, Div. of Transportation of Smithsonian Institution. 168pp. 8½ x 9½. 23328-6 Pa. $5.00

SECOND PIATIGORSKY CUP, edited by Isaac Kashdan. One of the greatest tournament books ever produced in the English language. All 90 games of the 1966 tournament, annotated by players, most annotated by both players. Features Petrosian, Spassky, Fischer, Larsen, six others. 228pp. 5⅜ x 8½.   23572-6 Pa. $3.50

ENCYCLOPEDIA OF CARD TRICKS, revised and edited by Jean Hugard. How to perform over 600 card tricks, devised by the world's greatest magicians: impromptus, spelling tricks, key cards, using special packs, much, much more. Additional chapter on card technique. 66 illustrations. 402pp. 5⅜ x 8½. (Available in U.S. only)   21252-1 Pa. $5.95

MAGIC: STAGE ILLUSIONS, SPECIAL EFFECTS AND TRICK PHO-TOGRAPHY, Albert A. Hopkins, Henry R. Evans. One of the great classics; fullest, most authorative explanation of vanishing lady, levitations, scores of other great stage effects. Also small magic, automata, stunts. 446 illus-trations. 556pp. 5⅜ x 8½.   23344-8 Pa. $6.95

THE SECRETS OF HOUDINI, J. C. Cannell. Classic study of Houdini's incredible magic, exposing closely-kept professional secrets and revealing, in general terms, the whole art of stage magic. 67 illustrations. 279pp. 5⅜ x 8½.   22913-0 Pa. $4.00

HOFFMANN'S MODERN MAGIC, Professor Hoffmann. One of the best, and best-known, magicians' manuals of the past century. Hundreds of tricks from card tricks and simple sleight of hand to elaborate illusions involving construction of complicated machinery. 332 illustrations. 563pp. 5⅜ x 8½.   23623-4 Pa. $6.95

THOMAS NAST'S CHRISTMAS DRAWINGS, Thomas Nast. Almost all Christmas drawings by creator of image of Santa Claus as we know it, and one of America's foremost illustrators and political cartoonists. 66 illustrations. 3 illustrations in color on covers. 96pp. 8⅜ x 11¼.
23660-9 Pa. $3.50

FRENCH COUNTRY COOKING FOR AMERICANS, Louis Diat. 500 easy-to-make, authentic provincial recipes compiled by former head chef at New York's Fitz-Carlton Hotel: onion soup, lamb stew, potato pie, more. 309pp. 5⅜ x 8½.   23665-X Pa. $3.95

SAUCES, FRENCH AND FAMOUS, Louis Diat. Complete book gives over 200 specific recipes: bechamel, Bordelaise, hollandaise, Cumberland, apri-cot, etc. Author was one of this century's finest chefs, originator of vichyssoise and many other dishes. Index. 156pp. 5⅜ x 8.
23663-3 Pa. $2.75

TOLL HOUSE TRIED AND TRUE RECIPES, Ruth Graves Wakefield. Authentic recipes from the famous Mass. restaurant: popovers, veal and ham loaf, Toll House baked beans, chocolate cake crumb pudding, much more. Many helpful hints. Nearly 700 recipes. Index. 376pp. 5⅜ x 8½.
23560-2 Pa. $4.95

ILLUSTRATED GUIDE TO SHAKER FURNITURE, Robert Meader. Director, Shaker Museum, Old Chatham, presents up-to-date coverage of all furniture and appurtenances, with much on local styles not available elsewhere. 235 photos. 146pp. 9 x 12.   22819-3 Pa. $6.95

COOKING WITH BEER, Carole Fahy. Beer has as superb an effect on food as wine, and at fraction of cost. Over 250 recipes for appetizers, soups, main dishes, desserts, breads, etc. Index. 144pp. 5⅜ x 8½. (Available in U.S. only)   23661-7 Pa. $3.00

STEWS AND RAGOUTS, Kay Shaw Nelson. This international cookbook offers wide range of 108 recipes perfect for everyday, special occasions, meals-in-themselves, main dishes. Economical, nutritious, easy-to-prepare: goulash, Irish stew, boeuf bourguignon, etc. Index. 134pp. 5⅜ x 8½.
23662-5 Pa. $3.95

DELICIOUS MAIN COURSE DISHES, Marian Tracy. Main courses are the most important part of any meal. These 200 nutritious, economical recipes from around the world make every meal a delight. "I . . . have found it so useful in my own household,"—N.Y. Times. Index. 219pp. 5⅜ x 8½.   23664-1 Pa. $3.95

FIVE ACRES AND INDEPENDENCE, Maurice G. Kains. Great back-to-the-land classic explains basics of self-sufficient farming: economics, plants, crops, animals, orchards, soils, land selection, host of other necessary things. Do not confuse with skimpy faddist literature; Kains was one of America's greatest agriculturalists. 95 illustrations. 397pp. 5⅜ x 8½.
20974-1 Pa. $4.95

A PRACTICAL GUIDE FOR THE BEGINNING FARMER, Herbert Jacobs. Basic, extremely useful first book for anyone thinking about moving to the country and starting a farm. Simpler than Kains, with greater emphasis on country living in general. 246pp. 5⅜ x 8½.
23675-7 Pa. $3.95

PAPERMAKING, Dard Hunter. Definitive book on the subject by the foremost authority in the field. Chapters dealing with every aspect of history of craft in every part of the world. Over 320 illustrations. 2nd, revised and enlarged (1947) edition. 672pp. 5⅜ x 8½.   23619-6 Pa. $8.95

THE ART DECO STYLE, edited by Theodore Menten. Furniture, jewelry, metalwork, ceramics, fabrics, lighting fixtures, interior decors, exteriors, graphics from pure French sources. Best sampling around. Over 400 photographs. 183pp. 8⅜ x 11¼.   22824-X Pa. $6.95

ACKERMANN'S COSTUME PLATES, Rudolph Ackermann. Selection of 96 plates from the Repository of Arts, best published source of costume for English fashion during the early 19th century. 12 plates also in color. Captions, glossary and introduction by editor Stella Blum. Total of 120pp. 8⅜ x 11¼.   23690-0 Pa. $5.00

THE ANATOMY OF THE HORSE, George Stubbs. Often considered the great masterpiece of animal anatomy. Full reproduction of 1766 edition, plus prospectus; original text and modernized text. 36 plates. Introduction by Eleanor Garvey. 121pp. 11 x 14¾.   23402-9 Pa. $8.95

BRIDGMAN'S LIFE DRAWING, George B. Bridgman. More than 500 illustrative drawings and text teach you to abstract the body into its major masses, use light and shade, proportion; as well as specific areas of anatomy, of which Bridgman is master. 192pp. 6½ x 9¼. (Available in U.S. only)
22710-3 Pa. $4.50

ART NOUVEAU DESIGNS IN COLOR, Alphonse Mucha, Maurice Verneuil, Georges Auriol. Full-color reproduction of Combinaisons ornementales (c. 1900) by Art Nouveau masters. Floral, animal, geometric, interlacings, swashes—borders, frames, spots—all incredibly beautiful. 60 plates, hundreds of designs. 9⅜ x 8-1/16.   22885-1 Pa. $4.50

FULL-COLOR FLORAL DESIGNS IN THE ART NOUVEAU STYLE, E. A. Seguy. 166 motifs, on 40 plates, from Les fleurs et leurs applications decoratives (1902): borders, circular designs, repeats, allovers, "spots." All in authentic Art Nouveau colors. 48pp. 9⅜ x 12¼.
23439-8 Pa. $6.00

A DIDEROT PICTORIAL ENCYCLOPEDIA OF TRADES AND INDUSTRY, edited by Charles C. Gillispie. 485 most interesting plates from the great French Encyclopedia of the 18th century show hundreds of working figures, artifacts, process, land and cityscapes; glassmaking, papermaking, metal extraction, construction, weaving, making furniture, clothing, wigs, dozens. of other activities. Plates fully explained. 920pp. 9 x 12.
22284-5, 22285-3 Clothbd., Two-vol. set $50.00

HANDBOOK OF EARLY ADVERTISING ART, Clarence P. Hornung. Largest collection of copyright-free early and antique advertising art ever compiled. Over 6,000 illustrations, from Franklin's time to the 1890's for special effects, novelty. Valuable source, almost inexhaustible.
Pictorial Volume. Agriculture, the zodiac, animals, autos, birds, Christmas, fire engines, flowers, trees, musical instruments, ships, games and sports, much more. Arranged by subject matter and use. 237 plates. 288pp. 9 x 12.
20122-8 Clothbd. $15.00

Typographical Volume. Roman and Gothic faces ranging from 10 point to 300 point, "Barnum," German and Old English faces, script, logotypes, scrolls and flourishes, 1115 ornamental initials, 67 complete alphabets, more. 310 plates. 320pp. 9 x 12.   20123-6 Clothbd. $15.00

CALLIGRAPHY (CALLIGRAPHIA LATINA), J. G. Schwandner. High point of 18th-century ornamental calligraphy. Very ornate initials, scrolls, borders, cherubs, birds, lettered examples. 172pp. 9 x 13.
20475-8 Pa. $7.95

GEOMETRY, RELATIVITY AND THE FOURTH DIMENSION, Rudolf Rucker. Exposition of fourth dimension, means of visualization, concepts of relativity as Flatland characters continue adventures. Popular, easily followed yet accurate, profound. 141 illustrations. 133pp. 5⅜ x 8½.
23400-2 Pa. $2.75

THE ORIGIN OF LIFE, A. I. Oparin. Modern classic in biochemistry, the first rigorous examination of possible evolution of life from nitrocarbon compounds. Non-technical, easily followed. Total of 295pp. 5⅜ x 8½.
60213-3 Pa. $5.95

PLANETS, STARS AND GALAXIES, A. E. Fanning. Comprehensive introductory survey: the sun, solar system, stars, galaxies, universe, cosmology; quasars, radio stars, etc. 24pp. of photographs. 189pp. 5⅜ x 8½. (Available in U.S. only)
21680-2 Pa. $3.75

THE THIRTEEN BOOKS OF EUCLID'S ELEMENTS, translated with introduction and commentary by Sir Thomas L. Heath. Definitive edition. Textual and linguistic. notes, mathematical analysis, 2500 years of critical commentary. Do not confuse with abridged school editions. Total of 1414pp. 5⅜ x 8½. 60088-2, 60089-0, 60090-4 Pa., Three-vol. set $19.50

Prices subject to change without notice.

Available at your book dealer or write for free catalogue to Dept. GI, Dover Publications, Inc.,31 East 2nd St.Mineola., N.Y. 11501.Dover publishes more than 175 books each year on science, elementary and advanced mathematics, biology, music, art, literary history, social sciences and other areas.